First World War
and Army of Occupation
War Diary
France, Belgium and Germany

61 DIVISION
Headquarters, Branches and Services
Commander Royal Artillery
1 July 1918 - 30 May 1919

WO95/3038/1

The Naval & Military Press Ltd
www.nmarchive.com
Published in association with The National Archives

Published by

The Naval & Military Press Ltd

Unit 10 Ridgewood Industrial Park,

Uckfield, East Sussex,

TN22 5QE England

Tel: +44 (0) 1825 749494

www.naval-military-press.com

www.nmarchive.com

This diary has been reprinted in facsimile from the original. Any imperfections are inevitably reproduced and the quality may fall short of modern type and cartographic standards.

© **Crown Copyright**

Images reproduced by permission of The National Archives, London, England, 2015.

Contents

Document type	Place/Title	Date From	Date To
Heading	WO95/3038/1		
Heading	61st Division C.R.A July 1918 1919 May		
Heading	61st Div. Artillery War Diary For July 1918 Vol 27		
War Diary	Molinghem	01/07/1918	14/07/1918
War Diary	Estree-Blanche	15/07/1918	22/07/1918
War Diary	Pont Asquin	23/07/1918	26/07/1918
Operation(al) Order(s)	61st Divisional Artillery Order No:131	10/07/1918	10/07/1918
Operation(al) Order(s)	61st. Divisional Artillery Order No:.132	22/07/1918	22/07/1918
Miscellaneous	March Table		
Operation(al) Order(s)	61st. Divisional Artillery Order No. 133.	26/07/1918	26/07/1918
Miscellaneous	March Table	26/07/1918	26/07/1918
Operation(al) Order(s)	61st Divisional Artillery Order No:134.	30/07/1918	30/07/1918
Miscellaneous	March Table	30/07/1918	30/07/1918
Miscellaneous	Administrative Instructions Issued with 61 Div. Art Order 134.	30/07/1918	30/07/1918
Heading	War Diary 61 Div Artillery 1st To 31st August 1918 Vol XXVIII		
Miscellaneous	Guns requiring Calibration 307		
War Diary	Estree-Blanche	01/08/1918	07/08/1918
War Diary	I 20A 3-4 (Map Sheet 36a 1/40,000) About 1 Mile Due W Of Thiennes	08/08/1918	31/08/1918
Miscellaneous	61st Divisional Artillery	01/08/1918	01/08/1918
Miscellaneous	Table A		
Miscellaneous	61st Division Locations Of Units.		
Miscellaneous	Amendment No.1 To 61st Divisional Artillery Instructions No.1	02/08/1918	02/08/1918
Miscellaneous	Amendment No.2 To 61st.Divisional Artillery Instructions No 1	03/08/1918	03/08/1918
Miscellaneous	To all recipients Of 61 Div. Artillery Defence Instructions No.1	04/08/1918	04/08/1918
Operation(al) Order(s)	61st. Divisional Artillery Order No: 135.	05/08/1918	05/08/1918
Miscellaneous	Movement Table To Accompany 61st Div. Artillery Order No. 135	05/08/1918	05/08/1918
Miscellaneous	Administrative Instructions with reference To 61 Div. Art Order No. 135.	05/08/1918	05/08/1918
Miscellaneous	Amendment No:1 To 61st Divisional Artillery Order No:135.	06/08/1918	06/08/1918
Miscellaneous	Amendment No:2 To 61st Divisional Artillery Order No:135.	07/08/1918	07/08/1918
Operation(al) Order(s)	61st. Divisional Artillery Order No:136.	09/08/1918	09/08/1918
Miscellaneous	61st.D.A. No. R.G.1.	09/08/1918	09/08/1918
Miscellaneous	61st. Divisional Artillery Location Statement Of 9 Aug 1918		
Miscellaneous	Amendment No:1 To 61st. Divisional Artillery Order No:137	10/08/1918	10/08/1918
Miscellaneous	61st. Divisional Artillery Order No:137	10/08/1918	10/08/1918
Diagram etc	Red Opening Barrage Brown Protective Green Infantry Objective.		
Diagram etc	Red Opening Barrage Greens Special Targets Brown Protective Barrage		

Diagram etc	Barrage arranged by 5th D.a. To Cover Advance Of 182 L.b. Troops On Evening 07/08/18		
Operation(al) Order(s)	61st.Divisional Artillery Order No:138	13/08/1918	13/08/1918
Miscellaneous	Amendment No:2 To 61st. Divisional Artillery Order No:137	14/08/1918	14/08/1918
Operation(al) Order(s)	61st Divisional Artillery Order No:139	13/08/1918	13/08/1918
Diagram etc	Diagram		
Miscellaneous	61st. Divisional Artillery Instructions No:1.		
Miscellaneous	A Form. Messages And Signals.		
Operation(al) Order(s)	61st. Divisional Artillery Order No:140.	14/08/1918	14/08/1918
Miscellaneous	61st.Divisional Artillery Instructions No.2	14/08/1918	14/08/1918
Miscellaneous	61st. Divisional Artillery Instructions No:3	15/08/1918	15/08/1918
Miscellaneous	61st Divisional Artillery Instructions No:4	16/08/1918	16/08/1918
Diagram etc	Sheet No 36 A.N.E 120000		
Miscellaneous	61st. Divisional Artillery Instructions No:5	16/08/1918	16/08/1918
Diagram etc	Diagram		
Miscellaneous	Amendment No:1 To 61st. Divisional Artillery Instructions No:5	17/08/1918	17/08/1918
Miscellaneous	To all recipients Of 61 D.A.Instructions No.6	18/08/1918	18/08/1918
Miscellaneous	61st. Divisional Artillery Instructions No:6	18/08/1918	18/08/1918
Diagram etc			
Miscellaneous	61st Divisional Artillery Instructions No:7		
Operation(al) Order(s)	61st Divisional Artillery Order No:141.	20/08/1918	20/08/1918
Operation(al) Order(s)	61st. Divisional Artillery Order No:142.	22/08/1918	22/08/1918
Miscellaneous	61st.D.A. No.R.G.1.	22/08/1918	22/08/1918
Operation(al) Order(s)	61st. Divisional Artillery Order No:143.	23/08/1918	23/08/1918
Operation(al) Order(s)	61st Divisional Artillery Order No: 144.	23/08/1918	23/08/1918
Miscellaneous	61st. Divisional Artillery Instructions No:8.	23/08/1918	23/08/1918
Operation(al) Order(s)	61st. Divisional Artillery Order No:145.	25/08/1918	25/08/1918
Miscellaneous	Table Issued with 61st Divisional Artillery Order No. 145		
Miscellaneous	61st Div Art. R.A.Q.539/2	25/08/1918	25/08/1918
Operation(al) Order(s)	61st. Divisional Artillery Order No:146.	26/08/1918	26/08/1918
Operation(al) Order(s)	61st Divisional Artillery Order No:147.	26/08/1918	26/08/1918
Diagram etc	18 Pdr. Barrage For Batteries Adv. Guard		
Diagram etc	Barrage Line		
Operation(al) Order(s)	61st Divisional Artillery Order No. 157	26/08/1918	26/08/1918
Miscellaneous	61st Divisional Artillery Instructions No. 9	29/08/1918	29/08/1918
Miscellaneous	61st Divisional Artillery Instructions No:10.	30/08/1918	30/08/1918
Operation(al) Order(s)	61st. Divisional Artillery Order No. 148.	30/08/1918	30/08/1918
Heading	61st Divisional Artillery War Diary For September 1918 Vol:29		
War Diary	Croix Marraisse	01/09/1918	08/09/1918
War Diary	Rill Works (L33b W Of La Gorgue)	09/09/1918	30/10/1918
Operation(al) Order(s)	61st. Divisional Artillery Order No. 148	30/08/1918	30/08/1918
Miscellaneous	Amendment No.2 To 61st. Divisional Artillery location Statement	31/08/1918	31/08/1918
Miscellaneous	Amendment No.1 To 61st. Divisional Artillery location Statement	31/08/1918	31/08/1918
Operation(al) Order(s)	61st Divisional Artillery Order No:149.	01/09/1918	01/09/1918
Miscellaneous	Amendment No.3 To 61st. Divisional Artillery Location Statement	31/08/1918	31/08/1918
Operation(al) Order(s)	61st Divisional Artillery Order No. 150.	02/09/1918	02/09/1918
Miscellaneous	61st Divisional Artillery Order No:151.	03/09/1918	03/09/1918
Miscellaneous	61st. Divisional Artillery Instructions No:11	04/09/1918	04/09/1918
Miscellaneous	61st. Divisional Artillery Location Statement	05/09/1918	05/09/1918

Miscellaneous	61st Divisional Artillery Instructions No:13.		
Miscellaneous	61st. Divisional Artillery Order No. 152.	10/09/1918	10/09/1918
Miscellaneous	Amendment No.1 To 61st D.A. Instructions No.11	10/09/1918	10/09/1918
Miscellaneous	61st Divisional Artillery Instruction No.14	12/09/1918	12/09/1918
Operation(al) Order(s)	61st Divisional Artillery Order No. 153.	13/09/1918	13/09/1918
Miscellaneous	61st. Divisional Artillery Instructions No. 16.	14/09/1918	14/09/1918
Miscellaneous	61st. Divisional Artillery Instructions No: 17.	16/09/1918	16/09/1918
Miscellaneous	A Form. Messages And Signals.		
Miscellaneous	To All Recipients Of 61 D.A. Order No. 153.	17/09/1918	17/09/1918
Miscellaneous	61st Divisional General Artillery		
Miscellaneous	61st. Divisional Artillery Defence Instructions No:1.		
Miscellaneous	61st. Divisional Artillery	19/09/1918	19/09/1918
Miscellaneous	61st. Divisional Artillery Instructions No:1		
Miscellaneous	61st. Divisional Artillery Defence Instructions No:1		
Diagram etc	Appendix "C" S.O.S. Lines for 1 Brigade R.F.A.		
Diagram etc	Appendix "C" S.OS. Lines for 2 Brigade R.F.A.		
Miscellaneous	61st. Divisional Artillery Defence Instructions No:1.	21/09/1918	21/09/1918
Miscellaneous	Amendment No:1 To 61st. Divisional Artillery Order No. 154.	22/09/1918	22/09/1918
Miscellaneous	61st. Divisional Artillery Order No:154	22/09/1918	22/09/1918
Operation(al) Order(s)	61st Divisional Artillery Order No. 155	22/09/1918	22/09/1918
Miscellaneous	61st. Divisional Artillery Order No:154	23/09/1918	23/09/1918
Miscellaneous	Amendment No :1 To 61st Divisional Artillery Order No. 155	22/09/1918	22/09/1918
Miscellaneous	Amendment No:2 To 61st. Divisional Artillery Order No:155	22/09/1918	22/09/1918
Miscellaneous	61st. Divisional Artillery Instructions No:18.	23/09/1918	23/09/1918
Miscellaneous	61st Divisional Artillery Instructions No:19.	25/09/1918	25/09/1918
Miscellaneous	61st. Divisional Artillery Instructions No:18	25/09/1918	25/09/1918
Miscellaneous	61st. Divisional Artillery Location Statement	26/09/1918	26/09/1918
Operation(al) Order(s)	61st Divisional Artillery Order No:156.	26/09/1918	26/09/1918
Map	18 PDR Barrage Map		
Miscellaneous	Amendment No:1 To 61st. Divisional Artillery Order No:156	27/09/1918	27/09/1918
Miscellaneous	61st. Divisional Artillery Instructions No.20.	29/09/1918	29/09/1918
Operation(al) Order(s)	61st. Divisional Artillery Order No:157.	28/09/1918	28/09/1918
Operation(al) Order(s)	61st. Divisional Artillery Order No:158.	29/09/1918	29/09/1918
Miscellaneous	4.5 Howitzer Tasks To Accompany 61 R.A. Order No 158		
Miscellaneous	61st. Divisional Artillery.	30/09/1918	30/09/1918
Miscellaneous	61st. Divisional Artillery Order No:158	29/09/1918	29/09/1918
Heading	61st Divisional Artillery War Diary For October 1918 Vol:30		
War Diary	Rill Works (W Of La Gorgue) 36 A. NE 1/20,000 Ref Map L.33 to Square	01/10/1918	03/10/1918
War Diary	Fontes	04/10/1918	06/10/1918
War Diary	Doullens Area	06/10/1918	07/10/1918
War Diary	Amplier	07/10/1918	08/10/1918
War Diary	Lagnicourt	09/10/1918	12/10/1918
War Diary	Avesnes-Lez-Aubert	12/10/1918	18/10/1918
War Diary	St. Aubert	19/10/1918	20/10/1918
War Diary	Haussy	21/10/1918	21/10/1918
War Diary	St. Aubert	22/10/1918	24/10/1918
War Diary	Montrecourt	25/10/1918	25/10/1918
War Diary	Vendegies	26/10/1918	31/10/1918
Operation(al) Order(s)	61st. Divisional Artillery Order No:159.	02/10/1918	02/10/1918

Type	Title	Date	Date
Miscellaneous	61st Divisional Artillery	02/10/1918	02/10/1918
Miscellaneous	Amendment No:1 To 61st Divisional Artillery Instructions No:1	19/09/1918	19/09/1918
Miscellaneous	61st Divisional Artillery Defence Instructions No:1		
Operation(al) Order(s)	61st. Divisional Artillery Order No:160.	03/10/1918	03/10/1918
Miscellaneous	March Table		
Miscellaneous	61st Divisional Artillery Administrative Instructions	03/10/1918	03/10/1918
Operation(al) Order(s)	61st Divisional Artillery Order No:161.	03/10/1918	03/10/1918
Miscellaneous	Entraining Table		
Miscellaneous	61st Divisional Artillery Administrative Instructions	04/10/1918	04/10/1918
Operation(al) Order(s)	61st. Divisional Artillery Order No:162.	07/10/1918	07/10/1918
Miscellaneous	March Table		
Miscellaneous	March Table	08/10/1918	08/10/1918
Miscellaneous	Amendment No:1 To 61st Divisional Artillery Order No. 162	07/10/1918	07/10/1918
Operation(al) Order(s)	61st Divisional Artillery Order No:163.	10/10/1918	10/10/1918
Map	Map		
Operation(al) Order(s)	61st Divisional Artillery Order No:164.	10/10/1918	10/10/1918
Operation(al) Order(s)	61st. Divisional Artillery Order No:165.	10/10/1918	10/10/1918
Miscellaneous	Administrative Instructions with reference To 61st Div. Artillery Order No. 165.		
Operation(al) Order(s)	61st. Divisional Artillery Order No. 166	11/10/1918	11/10/1918
Miscellaneous	61st Divisional Artillery Order No:166.	11/10/1918	11/10/1918
Miscellaneous	Relief Table To Accompany 61st Divisional Artillery Order No. 166		
Miscellaneous	61st. Divisional Artillery Instructions No:23.	12/10/1918	12/10/1918
Miscellaneous	61st. Divisional Artillery Instructions No:24	12/10/1918	12/10/1918
Miscellaneous	Amendment No:1 To 61st Divisional Artillery Location Statement	14/10/1918	14/10/1918
Miscellaneous	Landing Group XVII Corps Artillery	14/10/1918	14/10/1918
Operation(al) Order(s)	61st Divisional Artillery Order No:167.	14/10/1918	14/10/1918
Operation(al) Order(s)	61st. Divisional Artillery Order No:168.	15/10/1918	15/10/1918
Diagram etc	Diagram		
Operation(al) Order(s)	61st. Divisional Artillery Order No:169.	16/10/1918	16/10/1918
Miscellaneous	Amendment No:1 To 61st Divisional Artillery Order No:169.	17/10/1918	17/10/1918
Miscellaneous	61st. Divisional Artillery Instructions No:25.	17/10/1918	17/10/1918
Miscellaneous	XVII Corps Order No:169	18/10/1918	18/10/1918
Miscellaneous	61st Divisional Artillery	18/10/1918	18/10/1918
Diagram etc	Diagram		
Map	Map		
Operation(al) Order(s)	61st Divisional Artillery Order No:170.	20/10/1915	20/10/1915
Operation(al) Order(s)	61st, Divisional Artillery Order No:171.	20/10/1918	20/10/1918
Operation(al) Order(s)	61st. Divisional Artillery Order No:172.	23/10/1918	23/10/1918
Miscellaneous	61st Divisional Artillery	22/10/1916	22/10/1916
Miscellaneous	61st Divisional Artillery Order No. 172.	23/10/1918	23/10/1918
Miscellaneous	Amendment No.2 To 61st Divisional Artillery Order No. 172	23/10/1918	23/10/1918
Miscellaneous	Amendment No:3 To 61st Divisional Artillery Order No. 172.	23/10/1918	23/10/1918
Miscellaneous	61st Divisional Artillery Location Statement	23/10/1918	23/10/1918
Operation(al) Order(s)	61st. Divisional Artillery Order No. 173.	24/10/1918	24/10/1918
Operation(al) Order(s)	61st. Divisional Artillery Order No. 174.	25/10/1918	25/10/1918
Miscellaneous	61st Divisional Artillery Instructions No:26.	26/10/1918	26/10/1918
Operation(al) Order(s)	61st. Divisional Artillery Order No:176.	28/10/1918	28/10/1918
Miscellaneous	61st Divisional Artillery	27/10/1918	27/10/1918

Operation(al) Order(s)	61st Divisional Artillery Order No. 177	28/10/1918	28/10/1918
Miscellaneous	61st Divisional Artillery Order No:177.	28/10/1918	28/10/1918
Miscellaneous	XVII Corps Artillery Instructions No.1 on XVII Corps Order No. 173	28/10/1918	28/10/1918
Operation(al) Order(s)	61st. Divisional Artillery Order No:178.	30/10/1918	30/10/1918
Map	Issued In Conjunction With 61st D.A Order No. 178		
Map	Map		
Miscellaneous	61st Divisional Artillery	30/10/1918	30/10/1918
Operation(al) Order(s)	61st. Divisional Artillery Order No:178.	30/10/1918	30/10/1918
Operation(al) Order(s)	61st. Divisional Artillery Order No:179.	31/10/1918	31/10/1918
Heading	61st Divisional Artillery War Diary For November 1918 Vol:31		
War Diary	Vendegies	01/11/1918	03/11/1918
War Diary	St Aubert	04/11/1918	08/11/1918
War Diary	Vendegies	09/11/1918	14/11/1918
War Diary	Rieux	15/11/1918	15/11/1918
War Diary	Cambrai	16/11/1918	25/11/1918
War Diary	Wavans	26/11/1918	30/11/1918
Operation(al) Order(s)	61st. Divisional Artillery Order No:180.	01/11/1918	01/11/1918
Map	Map		
Operation(al) Order(s)	61st Divisional Artillery Order No:181.	07/11/1918	07/11/1918
Operation(al) Order(s)	61st. Divisional Artillery Order No:182.	13/11/1918	13/11/1918
Operation(al) Order(s)	61st Divisional Artillery Order No:1a.		
Miscellaneous	March Table		
Operation(al) Order(s)	61st Divisional Artillery Order No. 2a.	17/11/1918	17/11/1918
Operation(al) Order(s)	61st Divisional Artillery Order No:183.	20/11/1918	20/11/1918
Operation(al) Order(s)	61st. Divisional Artillery Order No:184.	22/11/1918	22/11/1918
Miscellaneous	61st Divisional Artillery Order No. 185	22/11/1918	22/11/1918
Miscellaneous	March Table		
Miscellaneous	Administrative Instructions with Reference To 61st Div. Artillery Order No. 185.		
Miscellaneous	61st Divisional Artillery	22/11/1918	22/11/1918
Miscellaneous	61st Divisional Artillery Order No:185	23/11/1918	23/11/1918
Miscellaneous	61st Division Artillery	23/11/1918	23/11/1918
Heading	61st Divisional Artillery War Diary For December 1918 Vol:32		
War Diary	Wavans	01/12/1918	05/12/1918
War Diary	Auxi-Le-Chateau	06/12/1918	12/12/1918
Miscellaneous	61st. Divisional Artillery	07/12/1918	07/12/1918
Miscellaneous	61st. Divisional Artillery	11/12/1918	11/12/1918
Heading	61st Divisional Artillery War Diary For January 1919 Vol:33.		
War Diary	Auxi-Le-Chateau (ref Map Sheet Lens II 1/100,000)	01/01/1919	31/01/1919
Miscellaneous	61st. Divisional Artillery.Location Of Units As On 3rd. January, 1919.	31/01/1919	31/01/1919
Heading	61st Divisional Artillery War Diary For February 1919 Vol:34		
War Diary	Auxi-Le-Chateau Sheet Lens 11 (1/10000)	03/02/1919	28/02/1919
Miscellaneous	61st Divisional Artillery	21/02/1919	21/02/1919
War Diary	Auxi-Le-Chateau Lens II 1/100,000	01/03/1919	30/04/1919
Miscellaneous	61st Divisional Artillery. Location Of Units	07/04/1919	07/04/1919
Miscellaneous	61st Divisional Artillery Location Of Units	25/04/1919	25/04/1919
Heading	61st Divisional Artillery 315 Army Brigade F.A. And Ho 521 Bo R.A.S.C. 61 Divl Lain War Diary May 1919 Volume 39		
War Diary	Auxi-Le-Chateau Lens II 1/100,000	06/05/1919	30/05/1919

WO 95/30388/1

61ST DIVISION

C. R. A.

July 1918 - 1919 MAY

WO 27

61st Div. Artillery
War Diary
— for —
July 1918

VOL 27

Army Form C. 2118.

WAR DIARY
OF
INTELLIGENCE SUMMARY.

61st Divisional Artillery

(Erase heading not required.)

Place	Date July	Hour	Summary of Events and Information	Remarks and references to Appendices
NOLINGHEM	1st		Our usual harassing fire was carried out by night. Several rounds were engaged with incendiary shell and complete failure. Experiments were made with a new variant of incendiary shell which gave poor results on percussion. Hun the fuse was forced to the very erratic. Enemy's artillery remained quiet, support howser harassing the usual activity. Green	
	2nd		Another quiet day, with the exception of a small concentration at 10.15 am on the area between Bosser and Amusoires. Our usual harassing fire was carried out and a successful shoot was undertaken with H.E. and incendiary shell against the houses in A.8.d. 0.3.v.e. Several fires were observed behind the enemy's line. Green	
	3rd		Hostile artillery was normal. There was some T.M. activity in the evening against our Right Brigade front. The 5th Artillery Horse show was held on the aerodrome ground S.E. of MRS and was a great success. Green	

WAR DIARY
or
INTELLIGENCE SUMMARY.
(Erase heading not required.)

Army Form C. 2118.

Place	Date	Hour	Summary of Events and Information	Remarks and references to Appendices
NOLINGHEM	4.E		The C.R.A. attended a conference at divisional H.Q. It was settled that in case of an enemy attack every line that would be defended and there would be no voluntary withdrawal from reserve line. Registration was carried out and the 106th Balloon observation was undertaken. About 7 am hostile artillery showed increased activity against our front line system. The Pojer Pillé area, Kru: the Hostile trenches were immediately subjected to a keen concentration & the enemy's fire ceased. It is thought that the enemy were using some captured 18 pr against us during the afternoon. Guns.	
"	5-K		Hostile Artillery was more quiet than usual. Sr VENANT, ROSSOR, S: FLORIS came in for a certain amount of attention. We carried out a shoot against enemy PERNG F.C. During the afternoon in consequence of movement having been seen there.	
		11 pm.	In co-operation with the Corps H.Q. in a few shoot against hostile batteries 18 pm. sniping selected targets with harassing fire. Guns.	

Army Form C. 2118.

WAR DIARY
or
INTELLIGENCE SUMMARY.
(Erase heading not required.)

Instructions regarding War Diaries and Intelligence Summaries are contained in F. S. Regs., Part II. and the Staff Manual respectively. Title pages will be prepared in manuscript.

Place	Date	Hour	Summary of Events and Information	Remarks and references to Appendices
MOLINGHEM	6th		A quiet day on the divisional front. The local harassing fire was carried out. Enemy's artillery remained very quiet.	
"	7th	1.30 a.m.	The divisional artillery supported a raid carried out by the 9th Northumberland Fusiliers in O.2.a. The raid was not very successful and no identification were obtained. Remainder of day passed quietly.	
		11 pm	We supported a raid carried out by the 1st East Yorks in O.2.c. No identifications were obtained. Gun.	
"	8th		Registration was carried out and harassing fire continued. Hostile artillery was normal. St VENANT area, area of fire brought into action.	
"	9th	1.30 a.m.	The divl. artillery supported a raid by the 18th D. of Yks in Q.8.c. The enemy's trenches were successfully entered but no identification were obtained.	
		9 pm	Two prisoners were captured in a shell hole opposite the	

WAR DIARY
or
INTELLIGENCE SUMMARY

(Erase heading not required.)

Army Form C. 2118.

Place	Date	Hour	Summary of Events and Information	Remarks and references to Appendices
MOULIN de JEM			left Brigade Head. Having been received from the division that the Artillery would be relieved by the 74th Div. Artillery on the nights of July 12th/13th & 13th/14th. C.R.A. Div. Hear. G.7. M.D. went over to First Army area to discuss some trench mortar experiments in open warfare.	Gun.
"	10th		O.R.A. 74th Division reconnoitred Battery positions with C.R.A. 61 Division. 61st Divisional Artillery Order No 136, giving details of relief, was issued. A very quiet day on the divisional front. Showery and with frequent heavy showers.	Gun.
		1.15 pm	We carried out a fire concentration in conjunction with the Corps Heavy Artillery against K.27.d. a.5.12. The usual fire passed quietly.	Gun.
"	11th		A dull showery day. Enemy's artillery very quiet during the day. Battery commanders + telephonists came up from the 74th Div. Artillery to commence taking over.	Gun.

Army Form C. 2118.

WAR DIARY
or
INTELLIGENCE SUMMARY.
(Erase heading not required.)

Instructions regarding War Diaries and Intelligence Summaries are contained in F. S. Regs., Part II. and the Staff Manual respectively. Title pages will be prepared in manuscript.

Place	Date	Hour	Summary of Events and Information	Remarks and references to Appendices
MOLINGHEM	12th		C.R.A. 74th Div. went round position of left group with C.R.A. 61st division.	
		2 pm	74th D.A.C. relieved 61st D.A.C. Detached section of 74th Div. A.C. relieved detached section b1c division Jun.	
	13th		A quiet day in the divisional front. Relief was completed, and Brigades billeted in their training area Sun.	
	14th	10 am	C.R.A. 61st division handed over to C.R.A. 74th division. R.H.Q. billetrus to ESTREÉ-BLANCHE. Jun.	
ESTREÉ-BLANCHE	15th		Arrival. Training was commenced.	
	16th		Training continued	
	17th 18th 19th 20th 21st		Training in section drill for open warfare was continued.	

Army Form C. 2118.

WAR DIARY
or
INTELLIGENCE SUMMARY.
(Erase heading not required.)

Instructions regarding War Diaries and Intelligence Summaries are contained in F. S. Regs., Part II. and the Staff Manual respectively. Title pages will be prepared in manuscript.

Place	Date	Hour	Summary of Events and Information	Remarks and references to Appendices
ESTREE-WAMIN	22ᵈ	2.30am	Orders were received from the Divisional Artillery to move to the WARLUS-CRUES area in the afternoon. Div Artillery Order No 132 was issued.	
PONT ASQUIN	23ᵈ		Brigade & Battery Commanders went forward to reconnoitre position to cover the army line.	
"	24ᵗʰ		R.O. Commanders went forward to reconnoitre position to cover the present line. The 306ᵗʰ Bde to cover the 1st Australian Division & The 307ᵗʰ Bde the 9ᵗʰ Division.	
"	25ᵗʰ	10.30pm	Orders were received from RA XV Corps for the Divisional Artillery to recon positions near the 26ᵗʰ to cover near HAZEBROUCK. So as to be near the position Div. Hdq. has to prepare MG. RA 5ᵗʰ Army visited Divisional Artillery & inspected units.	
"	26ᵗʰ		61 Div. Art less RAAR. T.M.B.'s and S.A.A. section 61 DAC marched to new area as per 61 Div Art Order No 135 306 Bde and 61 DAC were attached to 1ˢᵗ Australian Division. 307 Bde and Hdqt. 61 Div Train to 9ᵗʰ Division A.M.C.	

S E C R E T.   War Diary   Copy No: 38

61st. DIVISIONAL ARTILLERY ORDER NO: 131.

10th. July, 1918.

1. The 61st. Divisional Artillery is being relieved by the 74th. Divisional Artillery.

2. On relief the 61st. Divisional Artillery will withdraw to the ESTREE-BLANCHE area.

3. The relief will be carried out on the nights of July 12th/13th. and 13th/14th.
   Detached Sections of Batteries will be relieved on the first night and the remaining two Sections on the second night.

4. The 306th. Bde. R.F.A. will be relieved by the 44th. Bde. R.F.A., and the 307th. Bde. R.F.A. by the 117th. Bde. R.F.A.
   Guns will not be exchanged.

5. All details of relief will be arranged between Brigade Commanders concerned.

6. All documents, trench maps, photos, etc., will be handed over to incoming Units and receipts obtained.

7. Command of Units will pass on completion of a Unit's relief.

8. C.R.A. 61st. Division, will hand over to C.R.A. 74th. Divn. at 10 a.m. on July 14th.

9. The 74th. Divisional Artillery are sending forward Battery Commanders, one Officer and a proportion of telephonists per battery, on the afternoon of July 11th.

10. There will be no movement East of a line GUARBECQUE - BUSNES before 9.30 p.m. on either evening.

11. Sections relieving on the first night will proceed direct to Battery positions.
    Sections relieving on the second night will proceed to the wagon lines on the afternoon of July 13th.
    Guides from the 306th. Brigade will meet the 44th. Brigade at Road Junction, O.34.d.8.5., at 2 p.m. July 13th. to show relieving sections their wagon lines.
    Guides from the 307th. Brigade will meet the 117th. Brigade at LE PIRE, U.5.d.9.8., at 1 p.m. on the same date.

12. 61st. Divisional Artillery will leave behind:
    (a) One officer and one senior telephonist per Bde. H.Q. for 24 hours.
    (b) One officer and two telephonists per battery for 48 hours after the completion of relief.

13. Route for incoming Units will be by ECQUEDECQUES and LILLERS, and for outgoing Units by LILLERS and ST. HILAIRE.

14. The 61st. D.A.C. will be relieved by the 74th. D.A.C. at 2 p.m. July 12th.
    On relief the 61st. D.A.C. will march to the ESTREE-BLANCHE area.

15. D.T.M.O. 61st. Division, will hand over all 6" NEWTON MORTARS to D.T.M.O. 74th. Division, and will take over the Mortars at present with the 74th. Division.

- 1 -   16. Completion of/ P.T.O.

16. Completion of each portion of relief will be notified to this office by the code word "TURNIPS".

17. Further details of move of 61st. Divisional Artillery to the ESTREE-BLANCHE area, will be issued later.

18. ACKNOWLEDGE.

G.W. Meade
Major, R.A.,
Bde. Maj., 61 Div. Artillery.

Issued at 9am

Copy No:		
1 - 5.		306th. Bde. R.F.A.
6 - 10.		307th. Bde. R.F.A.
11 - 15.		330th. Bde. R.F.A.
16 - 20.		331st. Bde. R.F.A.
21 - 24.		61st. D.A.C.
25.		66th. D.A.C.
26.		D.T.M.O.
27.		61st. Division, 'G'
28.		61st. Division, 'Q'
29.		A.P.M., 61st. Division.
30.		4th. Divisional Artillery.
31.		5th. Divisional Artillery.
32.		74th. Divisional Artillery.
33.		66th. Divisional Artillery.
34.		R.A. XI Corps.
35.		H.A. XI Corps.
36.		28th. Bde. R.G.A.
37.		No.42 Squadron, R.A.F.
28 - 39.		War Diary.
40.		File.

SECRET. *War Diary* Copy No: 25

61st. DIVISIONAL ARTILLERY ORDER NO: 132.

22nd. July, 1918.

1. The 61st. Division is being transferred from the XI Corps to the XV Corps to-day, July 22nd., in accordance with March Table attached.

2. The following distances will be maintained between Units on the line of March.

   Between Batteries and Sections D.A.C. -- 100 yards.
   Between Artillery Brigades ------------ 500 yards.

   Vehicles of all kinds will leave gaps of 25 yards between Sections of six vehicles.

3. Units will report arrival in billets in new area.

4. Advance parties will meet the Staff Captain R.A. at ESTREE BLANCHE at 8.30 a.m. to-day.

5. R.A.H.Q. will close at ESTREE-BLANCHE at 2.30 p.m. and open at PONT ASQUIN (one mile due East of WARDREQUES Church) at the same hour.

6. ACKNOWLEDGE.

                                    G.W. Meade
                                    Major, R.A.,
                                    Bde.Maj., 61 Div. Artillery.

Issued at 8 a.m.

    Copy No.   1 - 5   306 Bde. RFA.
               6 - 10   307 Bde. RFA.
              11 - 14   61 D.A.C.
              15   D.T.M.O.
              16   No.1 Coy. 61 Div. Train.
              17   61 Div. 'G'.
              18   61 Div. 'Q'.
              19   A.D.M.S.
              20   D.A.D.V.S.
              21   A.P.M.
              22   R.A. XI Corps.
              23   R.A. XV Corps.
              24   R.A. 5th. Army Training Camp.
              25 - 26.   War Diary.
              27.   File.

MARCH TABLE issued with 61st. DIVISIONAL ARTILLERY ORDER NO: 138.

Serial No.	Unit.	From.	To.	Starting Point.	Time.	Route.	Remarks.
1.	306 Bde. RFA.	ENQUIN-les-MINES.	RACQUIGNEM.	Cross roads 1¼ miles N.W. of ENQUIN-les-MINES Church.	9 p.m.	ENQUINEGATTE - THEROUANNE.	
2.	307 Bde. RFA.	SERNY.	WARDRECQUES.	Road Junction ½ mile N.W. of SERNY CHURCH.	1 p.m.	BASSE BOULOGNE - THEROUANNE.	Not to cross the ECQUES - REBECQ Road before 3 p.m.
3.	61 D.A.C.	FLECHINELLE	WARDRECQUES.	Cross Roads ESTREE-BLANCHE.	2.15 p.m.	ESTREE-BLANCHE - THEROUANNE.	S.A.A. Section to LE HOCQUET.
4.	D.T.M.O.	ENQUIN-les-MINES.	To be notified later.	Under arrangements to be made by D.T.M.O.		As for Serial No.1.	To move by lorry.
5.	No.1 Co. 61 Div. Train.	ESTREE-BLANCHE.	To be notified by 61 Div. Train.	Cross Roads, ESTREE BLANCHE.	3.15 p.m.	THEROUANNE.	

S E C R E T.   Copy No: 27

War Diary

61st. DIVISIONAL ARTILLERY ORDER NO: 133.

26th. July, 1918.

Reference Sheet 36A. 1:40,000.
" 27. 1:40,000.

1. The 61st. Divisional Artillery, accompanied by No.1 Co., 61st. Divisional Train, will march to-day to new area in accordance with March Table attached.

2. The following distances will be maintained between Units on the line of march:-

   Between Batteries and Sections D.A.C. - - 100 yards.
   Between Artillery Brigades - - - - - - - 500 yards.

   Vehicles of all kinds will leave gaps of 25 yards between Sections of six vehicles.

3. On arrival in new areas, the 306th. Brigade R.F.A. will come under the 1st. Australian Divisional Artillery and the 307th. Brigade R.F.A. under the 9th. Divisional Artillery.

4. Completion of move will be reported to this office.

5. R.A.H.Q. will remain at PONT ASQUIN.

6. ACKNOWLEDGE.

G.W. Meade
Major, R.A.,
Bde.Maj., 61 Div. Artillery.

Issued at 3.15 pm.

Copy No.		
1 - 5.	306th. Bde. R.F.A.
6 - 10.	307th. Bde. R.F.A.
11 - 14.	61 D.A.C.
15.	D.T.M.O.
16 - 17.	No.1 Co. 61 Div. Train.
18.	61 Div. 'G'.
19.	61 Div. 'Q'.
20.	A.D.M.S.
21.	D.A.D.V.S.
22.	D.A.D.O.S.
23.	A.P.M.
24.	R.A. XV Corps.
25.	9th. Div. Artillery.
26.	1st. Australian Div. Artillery.
27 - 28.	War Diary.
29.	File.

MARCH TABLE for 26th July, 1913.

Serial No.	Unit.	From.	To.	Starting Point.	Time.	Route.	Remarks.
1.	306th. Bde. R.F.A.	RACQUINGHEM.	X roads, U.23.c.3.8.	BELLE CROIX.	4.30 p.m.	EBBLINGHEM - HAZEBROUCK Road.	Guides will meet Column at X Roads U.23.c.3.8.
2.	307th. Bde. R.F.A.	WARDRECQUES.	V.5.c.5.1.	PONT ASQUIN.	4 p.m.	EBBLINGHEM - STAPLE.	
3.	61 D.A.C.	A.23.b.	X Roads, U.22.d.4.9.	BELLE CROIX.	5.15 p.m.	EBBLINGHEM - HAZEBROUCK Road.	Guides will meet Column at X Roads U.22.d.4.9.
4.	No.1 Coy. 61 Div. Train.	B.2.c.	STAPLE.	PONT de CAMPAGNE.	To be fixed by O.C. No.1 Coy.	PONT de CAMPAGNE - RENESCURE - STAPLE.	Billets from Area Commandant.

SECRET.   Copy No: 28

War Diary

61st. DIVISIONAL ARTILLERY ORDER NO: 134.

Reference: Sheet 36A - 1:40,000.
         "   27 -   "
                                              30th. July, 1918.

1. The 61st. Division (less one Company 61st. Bn. M.G.C.) will be transferred by march route from XV to XI Corps area on night 31st. July/1st. August.
   Move to be carried out during darkness and to be completed by 5 a.m. 1st. August.

2. March Table for 61st. Divisional Artillery and No.1 Coy. 61st. Divisional Train, appended.

3. The following distances will be maintained on the line of march :-

   (a) Between Batteries, Sections D.A.C., Companies, Units and their transport, and transport of units when brigaded . . . . 100 yds.

   (b) Between Brigades of Artillery . . . . 500 yds.

   (c) Between Sections of 6 vehicles . . . . 25 yds.

4. Arrival in billets to be reported to R.A.H.Q., School ESTREE-BLANCHE, at 10 a.m., 1st August.

5. R.A.H.Q. will close at PONT ASQUIN at 10 a.m., 1st. Aug., and will reopen at ESTREE BLANCHE at the same hour.

6. Administrative Instructions attached.

7. ACKNOWLEDGE.

                                    [signature] Major
                                    for Captain, R.A.,
                                    Bde. Maj., 61 Div. Artillery.

Issued at 5.30 pm.

Copy No: 1 - 5.   306th. Bde. R.F.A.
          6 - 10.   307th. Bde. R.F.A.
         11 - 13.   61st. D.A.C.
         14.   S.A.A. Section.
         15.   D.T.M.O.
         16.   61st. Div. Train.
         17.   No.1 Coy. 61st. Div. Train.
         18.   61 Div. 'G'.
         19.   61 Div. 'Q'.
         20.   A.D.M.S.
         21.   D.A.D.V.S.
         22.   D.A.D.O.S.
         23.   A.P.M.
         24.   R.A. XV Corps.
         25.   R.A. XI Corps.
         26.   9th. Div. Artillery.
         27.   1st. Aust: Div. Artillery.
         28 - 29.   War Diary.
         30.   File.

MARCH TABLE to accompany 61st. Divisional Artillery Order No.134. of 30th. July, 1918.

Serial No.	Unit.	From.	To.	Starting Point.	Date.	Time.	Route.	Remarks.
1.	R.A.H.Q.	PONT ASQUIN.	ESTREE-BLANCHE.	-	1 Aug.	-	-	-
2.	306 Bde.	Wagon Lines.	ENQUIN-les-MINES.	Cross Roads Sh.27, U.22.c.7.9.	31 July.	11 p.m.	HERLINGHEM - BELLE CROIX - THEROUANNE.	Not to cross the BELLE CROIX cross roads before 1.30 a.m. 1st August.
3.	D.A.C. less SAA Section.	Wagon Lines.	FLECHINELLE.	do.	do.	11.30 p.m.	do.	
4.	307 Bde.	Wagon Lines.	SERNY and ESTREE-BLANCHE.	do.	31/1st.	12 M.N.	do.	
5.	No.1 Coy. Div. Train.	STAPLE.	ESTREE-BLANCHE.		1 Aug.	12.30 a.m.	do.	
6.	Sig. Sect. 61 D.A.C.	Wagon Lines.	FLECHINELLE.	Camp.	31st.	9 p.m.	THEROUANNE.	
7.	T.M. Bs.	Camp.	ENQUIN-les-MINES.	Camp.	31st.	9.30 p.m.	do.	

R.A.Q. 528/21.

ADMINISTRATIVE INSTRUCTIONS issued with 61 Div. Art Order 134.

1. The 61st Divisional Artillery will be billeted as follows in the ESTREE-BLANCHE Area.

       R.A.H.Q. .... ESTREE-BLANCHE.
       306 Bde. .... ENQUIN-les-MINES.
       307 Bde. .... SERNY and ESTREE-BLANCHE.
       61 D.A.C. .... FLECHINELLE.
       61 T.M.Bs. .... ENQUIN-les-MINES
       No.1 Coy
       61 Div Train..... ESTREE-BLANCHE.

All Units will occupy the billets which they evacuated on July 22nd.

Advance parties will be sent forward on the evening of July 31st, 1918.

A return of Billets occupied in the new area, will be rendered in DUPLICATE to this office by 12 noon on August 2nd, on the attached pro forma and each week subsequently by 9-0am on Thursdays.

2. LORRIES.
The following lorries will report as under by 4-0pm July 31st.

       R.A.H.Q. .... 2 lorries at B.8.a.5.7. Sheet 36.
       306 Bde. .... 2 lorries at U.24.c.2.7 Sheet 27.
       307 Bde. .... 2 lorries at V.5.c.1.5. Sheet 27.
       61 D.A.C. .... 2 lorries at U.18.b.1.4. Sheet 27.
       T.M.Bs. .... 4 lorries at A.24.a.2.7. Sheet 36.

306th, 307th Brigades and 61st D.A.C. will load one lorry each with tents and all area stores taken from WARDRECQUES Area; these will be sent during daylight on July 31st to Area Commandant WARDRECQUES.

These lorries will return to the Park on delivery of tents.

A N.C.O. and 3 men will be sent with each lorry to hand over tents etc., and will rejoin their own unit on the march at BELLE CROIX - A.13.a. central at 1-0am August 1st.1918.

R.A.H.Q., S.A.A. Section and T.M.Bs will return their tents by horse transport during the afternoon of July 31st.

Receipts for tents and trench shelters will be forwarded to this office, THE SCHOOL, ESTREE-BLANCHE.

The second lorry with Brigades and D.A.C. will be loaded with extra stores for transport to new area.

Lorries will make one journey only, and return to their Park on completion.

SUPPLIES.

3. **SUPPLIES.**

Supply wagons with rations for consumption on 1st Prox, will accompany units.

Locations for Refilling Points on August 1st will be notified later.

4. Baggage wagons will report to Units tonight.

5. **AMMUNITION.**

All units will march with full echelons and will report amount and nature of ammunition taken out of XV Corps Area by 12 noon August 1st.

Reports to be sent to R.A.H.Q., THE SCHOOL, ESTREE-BLANCHE.

6. **AMBULANCES.**

A horse ambulance will report at R.A.H.Q. at PONT ASQUIN at 11-0pm on July 31st and will be available for the use of 61st Divisional Artillery during the march, after the column has passed PONT ASQUIN.

It will march in rear of No.1 Coy., 61st Div. Train and will accompany the 61st Divisional Artillery until their arrival in the ESTREE-BLANCHE Area.

This ambulance will report on completion of march to 307th Brigade H.Q. at SERNY and return to its own unit on August 1st.

7. All billets and horse lines will be left clean; manure stacked at manure dump; latrines properly filled in and all cookhouse and other refuse burnt before leaving.

R.A.H.Q.
30.7.1918.

Major,
S.C.R.A., 61st Division.

CONFIDENTIAL

Vol 28

WAR DIARY.

61 Div Artillery

1st to 31st August 1918

Volume XXVIII

Army Form C. 2118.

WAR DIARY
or
INTELLIGENCE SUMMARY.
(Erase heading not required.)

Instructions regarding War Diaries and Intelligence Summaries are contained in F. S. Regs., Part II. and the Staff Manual respectively. Title pages will be prepared in manuscript.

Hour, Date, Place	Summary of Events and Information	Remarks and references to Appendices
ESTRÉE-BLANCHE 1st August 1918.	The move of the 61st Divisional Artillery from XV Corps Area to XI Corps Area was completed about 6 a.m. Rotten a long march. R.A.H.Q. opened at ESTRÉE BLANCHE at 10 a.m. Defence Instruction No 1 were issued. C.R.A. attended Lecture and Demonstration at LINGHEM by I.C. Training on training.	4th
2nd August	In rest. Training commenced. B.M. reconnoitred concentration areas in connection with Defence Instructions No 1. (1.8.18) Training continued.	4th
3rd August		4th
4th August	Warning Order received from the Division that the Divisional Artillery will be on the nights 6th/7th & 7th/8th August. C.R.A. & SCRA visited 5th D.A. relieve the 5th Division.	4th
5th August	C.R.A. inspected batteries. F.M. visits 5th DA & 74th DA & SCRA visits 74th DA in connection with the relief. 307 Brigade	4th

WAR DIARY
or
INTELLIGENCE SUMMARY.
(Erase heading not required.)

Army Form C. 2118.

Hour, Date, Place	Summary of Events and Information	Remarks and references to Appendices
5th August (continued)	are to relieve the 15th Bde R.F.A. (5th D.A.) & 30G Brigade are to relieve the 27th Bde R.F.A. (5th D.A.). 30G Brigade will come under CRA now the move of the 174th Divisional Artillery. 61st Divisional Artillery Order No 135 annexed. Training continued.	✓
6th August	C.R.A. attended a conference at 5th Div. H.Q. C.R.A. & B.M. visited H.Q. 5th D.A. about proposed formation to advance. Brief of 5th D.A. commences — the divisional front line, which is now being taken over, to the following line :- AIRE-MERVILLE CANAL to E of LE SART village. COURTEFROIE FARM (K27b). BOSHAM FARM (K21d) to F.L. about K16c3-1. In addition to the artillery covering the divisional front, the 5th D.A., 1 Army field Artillery Brigade & 2 18 pdr batteries are to come under C.R.A. 61st D.A. G.O.C.R.A. & Bates attended the conference when followed any details re re-inforcing artillery postheal, pace of arriving barrage etc were discussed. Relief of 5th D.A. commenced.	✓

Army Form C. 2118.

WAR DIARY
or
INTELLIGENCE SUMMARY.
(Erase heading not required.)

Instructions regarding War Diaries and Intelligence Summaries are contained in F.S. Regs., Part II. and the Staff Manual respectively. Title pages will be prepared in manuscript.

Hour, Date, Place	Summary of Events and Information	Remarks and references to Appendices
9th August 1918 ESTRÉE BLANCHE	Our Artillery (less 306 Bde which was coming into action under the 74th D.A. on the front S of the CANAL DE LA LYS) continued the relief of the 5th D.A. 307 Bde completed relief at 10 p.m. All 6 guns of B/307 were put into the forward section position. In view of the proposed operation the 5th D.A.C. was kept back to assist in carrying up ammunition & our D.A.C. doubled up with them on arrival. At 10 a.m. command of the Divisional front passed to G.O.C. 61st Division on completion of the infantry relief. During the morning the 74th Division reported having advanced their line & information was obtained indicating that the enemy were withdrawing, presumably with the object of straightening his line W. of MERVILLE. Arrangements were made for 182 Infantry Brigade & 184 Infantry Brigade, holding right & left Brigade fronts, to push forward during the evening and establish themselves in the enemy F.L. The Right & Left Groups put down a creeping barrage to cover advance by Right Brigade.(a) This was successful & the operation was gradually proceeded with. Only slight opposition was offered. C.R.A. issued orders for advance of some batteries to support forward move by infantry. C.R.A. & B.M.R.A. spent most of the day & stayed the night with 5th D.A. preparatory to taking over.	(a) Tracing of barrage appended.

WAR DIARY
or
INTELLIGENCE SUMMARY.
(Erase heading not required.)

Army Form C. 2118.

Hour, Date, Place	Summary of Events and Information	Remarks and references to Appendices
8th August 1918. J20 a 3-4 (Map Sheet 36 a 40,000) about 1 mile SSE W of THIENNES.	From 4am to 4.30am Right Group bombarded LE SART (K27c1.5) & the HALT (K27J); the Left Group engaged LOXTON HOUSE (K22c) and bombarded area about the roads junction on the MERVILLE-LAMOTTE Rd (K21c+d); following this the 183 I.Bde moved forward as divisional advance guard, 307 Bde RFA being affiliated as Advance guard artillery. The forward move was only gradual & entailed no move by the artillery. At 10am CRA 61st D.A. took over command of artillery covering 61st Divisional front from CRA 5th DA. The divisional artillery now consist of:— Right Group, 307 Bde RFA, Left Group 295 + 296 Bdes RFA, (59th D.A.) with cannons of O.C. 296 Bde R.F.A. H.Q. 59 D.A. & H.Q. 295 Bde RFA are out at rest. Our infantry having established their observatory on the line proposed on the 6th without any opposition for the proposed operation, all orders concerning it were cancelled and 61st DA left the area. Batteries were only slightly engaged during the day.	

Army Form C. 2118.

WAR DIARY
or
INTELLIGENCE SUMMARY.
(Erase heading not required.)

Instructions regarding War Diaries and Intelligence Summaries are contained in F.S. Regs., Part II. and the Staff Manual respectively. Title pages will be prepared in manuscript.

Hour, Date, Place	Summary of Events and Information	Remarks and references to Appendices
9th August 1918	A fine day. On receipt of orders from Division, Divisional Artillery Order No 136 was issued re-arranging Groups & co-ordinated of 183 I 13. & re-adjustment of Infantry Brigade boundaries. Harassing fire was maintained by day & night. Special attention being paid to MERVILLE & its approaches & the farms in the enemy's forward area. Hostile artillery activity was normal.	
10th August 1918	There was a morning haze which did not clear until about 11 am, after that the day was warm & sunny & visibility was very good. 12 6" NEWTON TMs were put in on our Divisional front to assist in proposed advance over to PLATE-BECQUE. (running through K 11 K 16 & MERVILLE). Divisional Operation Order No 137 was issued. Harassing fire was continued on selected targets.	
11th August 1918	At 4.15 am the operation referred to in Divisional Artillery Order No 137 was carried out but was not successful. Visibility was poor during the morning but improved as the day wore on. The weather was fine & hot. At different times during the afternoon & evening Divisional Artillery co-operated with the A.A. in shoots on the MERVILLE area, finishing at 8.30 pm with a Corps Crash on the	

Army Form C. 2118.

WAR DIARY
or
INTELLIGENCE SUMMARY.
(Erase heading not required.)

Instructions regarding War Diaries and Intelligence Summaries are contained in F.S. Regs., Part II. and the Staff Manual respectively. Title pages will be prepared in manuscript.

Hour, Date, Place	Summary of Events and Information	Remarks and references to Appendices
August 11th continued	COLLEGE. Harassing fire was also carried out on usual special attention being paid to be formed in the Enemy's forward area. Got put down the S.O.S at 9.45 pm at the Infantry's request for 6 mins. At 11.20 pm the area from COCHIN CORNER to CONEY COTTAGES was brought under fire at the request of the Infantry. Hostile artillery showed increased activity at night. CRA visited both groups and left Infantry Brigade Commander.	
August 12th	A fine day, very hot. A good deal of haze prevented good visibility until late in the afternoon. CRA visited HQ 307 Bde & OP at HAVERSKERQUE during the afternoon. BM visited both Infantry Brigades & Left Group & two batteries 296 Bde R.F.A. Harassing fire area carried out. Bursts of fire with gas shell were put also the ESTAIRE – VIEUX BERQUIN & NEUVILLE – NEUF BERQUIN Rds, on the area east of MERVILLE & on ROBERMETZ. Occasional spaceshoots on the COCHIN CORNER – CONEY COTTAGES area 6th carried out at the request of the Infantry.	
August 13th	CRA rode left group batteries. BM visited 307 HQ & A v B 307. Divisional Artillery Orders No 138 issued (also S.A. Instruction No.) & 139	

Army Form C. 2118.

WAR DIARY
or
INTELLIGENCE SUMMARY.
(Erase heading not required.)

Instructions regarding War Diaries and Intelligence Summaries are contained in F.S. Regs., Part II. and the Staff Manual respectively. Title pages will be prepared in manuscript.

Hour, Date, Place	Summary of Events and Information	Remarks and references to Appendices
August 13th continued	A fine hot day but visibility was not good until after 8.30pm on account of haze. The night & early groups co-operated with the H.A. during the day in a series of special shoots. One 6" Newton T.M. was taken forward at night & fired at an M.G. emplacement, & there was no further activity from this place afterwards. There was a decrease in early artillery fire during the 24 hours & the afternoon was very quiet, & harassing fire at night was normal	JM
Aug 14th	The C.R.A. visited the 61st S.A.C. at 4.20am the destructive barrage was put down on K16 b & d. 61st Brigade of artillery instructed No 2 Wagons. Both Groups again co-operated with the H.A. in shoots on the Merville area. Harassing fire was maintained chiefly on roads, tracks & bridges in the enemy's forward area. There was a marked decrease in hostile fire. The day was very hot & visibility has been owing to haze until the early evening. Brigadier J Bathurst G.O.C. No 40 was visited.	(a) See 61st S.A. Order No 139 appendix
Aug 15th	The C.R.A. visited the 31st D.A. with C.R.A. 29 & Div. left group Batteries co-operated with HA in shoots on CORHAM FARM and area east of the PLATE BECQUE	

Army Form C. 2118.

WAR DIARY
or
INTELLIGENCE SUMMARY.
(Erase heading not required.)

Instructions regarding War Diaries and Intelligence
Summaries are contained in F.S. Regs., Part II.
and the Staff Manual respectively. Title pages
will be prepared in manuscript.

Hour, Date, Place	Summary of Events and Information	Remarks and references to Appendices
August 15th Arrived	Usual enemy fire, reprisals normal and heavy shelling normal. 61st Div Arty instructions no 3 issued	M
August 16th	Left group batteries fires a 10 minutes barrage at 4.20 AM on line K11 d 03 - K11 c 95 03 pushing to +300 yds and creeping back by 100 yd steps to original line. D/296 carried out two shoots with balloon observation. Right Grs goes shoreing the day - normal at night. 61 Div Arty reconnoitred R24B5 corner	9th
August 17th	CRA visited batteries of right group (307 Bde) usual GOC Division left grup batteries fired a 16 minute barrage on K16, K16 c K17a and K17b 6" howitzer fired 69 rounds during the day. Hostile artillery less than usual	9th

WAR DIARY or INTELLIGENCE SUMMARY

Army Form C. 2118.

Hour, Date, Place	Summary of Events and Information	Remarks and references to Appendices
August 18th	At 4.45 am left gave batteries fired a 15 minute barrage on K23a r090, r17c and r17b. Changed to MERVILLE targets during the night by the enemy. Very extreme and then report between 2am and 7am. Every activity any 7am. At 4.30 am across PLATE BECQUE in K16 in K22, K28 and across PLATE BECQUE in K16. 43 Prisoners 189 I.R. ordered to K16. 61 Div Arty instructions to 6 rounds and the cancelled on account of any astonishment.	
August 19th	Advance continues Patrols crossed river BOURRE in K23 and K29. Boy little opposition any sort. A, B + C Batteries of 307 Bde move 1 section forward and B/307 move 1 Hrs forward. C/296 1 left gave own four guns forward. 61 Div Artillery Instructions No 7 issued.	

Army Form C. 2118.

WAR DIARY
or
INTELLIGENCE SUMMARY.
(Erase heading not required.)

Instructions regarding War Diaries and Intelligence Summaries are contained in F.S. Regs., Part II. and the Staff Manual respectively. Title pages will be prepared in manuscript.

Hour, Date, Place	Summary of Events and Information	Remarks and references to Appendices
August 20th	Enemy withdrawal continues. Merville taken. Our patrols had pushed to the line K36 B06 Caix C103. K30 a. Green Farm Point. An advance Brigade is pushed consisting of A and C 13 Batteries 276 Bde, 1 section of 2/h 96 under O/C left group, cooperating with G.O.C. 183 Infantry Brigade. C.R.A. 59th 9th (who are left front) sent its remaining batteries to the Artillery order to M1 in accord. 6 & 90 Hostile artillery was active. MERVILLE shelled in early morning with H.E and Gas. Batteries advanced with Brigade came in Harvest fire with batteries of left front within range	JW
August 21st		

Army Form C. 2118.

WAR DIARY
or
INTELLIGENCE SUMMARY.
(Erase heading not required.)

Instructions regarding War Diaries and Intelligence Summaries are contained in F. S. Regs, Part II. and the Staff Manual respectively. Title pages will be prepared in manuscript.

Hour, Date, Place	Summary of Events and Information	Remarks and references to Appendices
August 22 [?]	Our fire is directed against [farms?] and areas containing German machine gun nests. Shell held up an advance. One 18 pdr battery of the armoured artillery brigade in place under the direct command of the CRA battalion commander and the other 18 pdr battery in place under its [right?] battalion commander. Horse artillery actually reports on [forward?] areas so also normal. 61st Div battery moves to 142 and the [weekly?] location statements etc issued. Infantry attempt to advance along NEUF BERQUIN – ESTAIRES road and north of road. Little progress made. Enemy mounting sharply. Horse artillery cheerfully active. 61st D.A. reclks Rs 143 also 144 and 61 DA [supervision?] Ro 8 are issued.	[initials]
August 23 [?]		[initials]

Army Form C. 2118.

WAR DIARY
or
INTELLIGENCE SUMMARY.
(Erase heading not required.)

Instructions regarding War Diaries and Intelligence Summaries are contained in F.S. Regs., Part II. and the Staff Manual respectively. Title pages will be prepared in manuscript.

Hour, Date, Place	Summary of Events and Information	Remarks and references to Appendices
August 24th	A/296 Bde one gun put out of action by enemy known fire. Enemy withdrew to be holding line in front of ESTAIRES strongly. Many enemy M.S.S. found in NEUF BERQUIN. Our own and enemy fire normal.	
August 25th	Orders received for march 25-7/265. O/C 306 Bde turning o/c advance Artillery 59th Div Artillery to be withdrawn. 6.15" Howitzer Batts to be covered by 6.12" Div artillery also. 6.15" DG artillery due to 145 covered. Relief of 296 Bde RFA completed, 612 Siege Artillery now found into an advanced group under Colonel Burch 306 Bde, consisting of A/306, C/306, and a section of B/306, and a REAR GROUP	
August 26th		

WAR DIARY
or
INTELLIGENCE SUMMARY.
(Erase heading not required.)

Army Form C. 2118.

Hour, Date, Place	Summary of Events and Information	Remarks and references to Appendices
Aug. 26 & on board	Consisting of 3·7 Bde and remaining batteries and sections of 306 Bde. Hostile fire normal. 6·1·2· Divisional Artillery order no 147 issued. Order No 147 was issued in connection with an operation by 40th (the) Division on our Left flank.) Division and the Left Bn of our Advanced Guard Bde on 27th inst. The night passed quietly except that the enemy put over some gas shell in rear forward area	
August 27:	The light was very fair all day. At 10 a.m. the operation referred to in the preceding paragraph commenced and 27 minutes later the enemy barrage came down on our forward posts and the main road through NEUF BERQUIN. — mainly 77 mm field guns to 5" howitzers though some few 15 c.m. howitzer shells were reported. The 40th Div. Infantry were unable to reach their final	

WAR DIARY
or
INTELLIGENCE SUMMARY.
(Erase heading not required.)

Army Form C. 2118.

Instructions regarding War Diaries and Intelligence Summaries are contained in F.S. Regs., Part II. and the Staff Manual respectively. Title pages will be prepared in manuscript.

Hour, Date, Place	Summary of Events and Information	Remarks and references to Appendices
August 27th Cont.	object, and in consequence 15th Advanced Infantry Bde. were unable to cross the whs in front of the DICK BROOK owing to hostile MG fire from BOWERY COTTAGES and a small house at L.14.b.35.70. During the afternoon our Advanced Guard Batteries fired on various targets at the request of the Infantry. The enemy Artillery was very active on our forward areas.	
Night 27th/28th	Our Batteries carried out normal harassing fire on the tracks & roads leading to the enemy out post line.	
August 28th	The enemy put down a barrage on our Forward System, firing some 550 rounds 77mm of which 25% were gas, between 4 & 4.15 am. During the day our Batteries fired on various targets near the enemy outpost line and at night harassed roads and tracks in L.26.b and d, L.32.b and d, L.33.b and tracks leading to DIRK COTTAGES, TURTLE FARM in L.15.b. Many fires were seen at various points along the front. ESTAIRES CHURCH after burning all night collapsed on morning of 29th.	
August 29th	During the day successfully engaged MGs in L.26.a b and d and	

Army Form C. 2118.

WAR DIARY
or
INTELLIGENCE SUMMARY.
(Erase heading not required.)

Instructions regarding War Diaries and Intelligence Summaries are contained in F.S. Regs., Part II. and the Staff Manual respectively. Title pages will be prepared in manuscript.

Hour, Date, Place	Summary of Events and Information	Remarks and references to Appendices
August 29th continued	other targets at the request of Infantry. Between 1.30 & 3 pm some of our Advanced units fired in co-operation with 31 D.A. covering an operation by 49th Division on our left, while the remainder fired in conjunction with the attack and capture of OBUS COTTAGES and SKEETER CRISS localities by our Infantry. The enemy retaliation during the afternoon operations were very slight, and were maintained throughout the day except that about 10 pm 200 rounds 77 m.m. gas shell were fired into L.31.a.c. also L.25.c.d. Many this were again to be seen. Brig Gen R.G. OUSLEY. C.B. C.M.G. D.S.O. R.A proceeded on leave to ENGLAND. O.C. 306 Bde R.F.A. Lt Col E.M. BROOKE C.M.G. D.S.O. R.F.A. became A/C.R.A. 61. D.A. Instructions No 9 were issued.	
Night Aug 29/30.	During the night the Divisional front was extended to the NORTH. harassing fire was carried out the whole in forward area, an enemy relief being anticipated.	
Aug 30th	Very little artillery activity during the day. Some of our Advanced Guard units moved forward in support of our Infantry who were progressing towards ESTRÉES	

Army Form C. 2118.

WAR DIARY
or
INTELLIGENCE SUMMARY.
(Erase heading not required.)

Instructions regarding War Diaries and Intelligence Summaries are contained in F.S. Regs., Part II. and the Staff Manual respectively. Title pages will be prepared in manuscript.

Hour, Date, Place	Summary of Events and Information	Remarks and references to Appendices
August 30th continued	ammunition their units which advanced during daylight did so one or two vehicles at a time, and were in no way interfered with. They registered their new 3 in. mortars dark.	&c.
Night 30th/31st	Fire was again much in evidence behind the enemy lines. Harassing fire was carried out on roads & tracks.	&c.
August 31st	Our Batteries were more active today. LA GORGUE Church was reported by Infantry to be used by enemy observers and was engaged by our howitzers, also by the CORPS HEAVIES. Our Infantry continued their methodical advance, and during the night further forward moves were made by the Advanced Guard Infantry. Hostile Batteries were much more active on the favoured area :- a 10·5cm Howitzer Battery harassed our 18Pdr Batteries during midday. Our Batteries carried out harassing fire on roads & tracks: about midday the enemy were reported to be withdrawing from some of his forward positions: harassing fire was brought forward to ensure this. R.A. H.Q. moved to (J.21.c.70.15 mean) HOYERSACKARWE, 61 Division Advanced Headquarters.	

H Pryz
Capt. R.A.
Bde R.A. 61 Division

S E C R E T. (War Diary) Copy No:......
B.M.S. 40/9
1.8.18.

61st. DIVISIONAL ARTILLERY.

Ref: Sheet 36A.　**DEFENCE INSTRUCTIONS NO: I.**
1:40,000.

A. 1.　The Division is located as in Location Statement attached.

2.　Infantry Brigades, with present sections of the Div. Signal Coy. attached, will be referred to as follows :-

   ST. HILAIRE Bde.　- Bde. billeted at ST. HILAIRE - BOURECQ.
                     Bde. H.Q. - ST. HILAIRE.

   MAZINGHEM Bde.　- Bde. billeted at LAMBRES - QUERNES - LIETTRES.
                     Bde. H.Q. - ST. ANDRE FM., N.2.d.

   LINGHEM Bde.　- Bde. billeted at LINGHEM - FONTES.
                     Bde. H.Q. - FONTES.

3.　Should the formation of Inf. Bde. Groups become necessary, the following will be known as the Normal Formation of Groups :-

   182 Bde. Group ... ...　　182 Inf. Bde.
   (G.O.C. 182 Inf. Bde.) ..　No. 2 Sec. Div. Sig. Co.
                     "A" Co. 61st. Bn. M.G.C.
                     476 F. Co. R.E.
                     2/2 F. Amb.
                     No. 2 Co. 61st. Div. Train.

   183 Bde. Group... ...　　183 Inf. Bde.
   (G.O.C. 183 Inf. Bde.) ..　No. 3 Sec. Div. Sig. Co.
                     "B" Co. 61st. Bn. M.G.C.
                     478 F. Co. R.E.
                     2/3 F. Amb.
                     No. 3 Co. 61st. Div. Train.

   184 Bde. Group ... ...　　184 Inf. Bde.
   (G.O.C. 184 Inf. Bde.) .　No. 4 Sec. Div. Sig. Co.
                     "C" Co. 61st. Bn. M.G.C.
                     479 F. Co. R.E.
                     2/1 F. Amb.
                     No. 4 Co. 61st. Div. Train.

4.　The Division is in G.H.Q. Reserve, at 24 hours notice.

5.　As G.H.Q. Reserve, the Division may be called upon :-
     (a)　To move from XI Corps Area.
     (b)　To act as XI Corps Reserve in case of attack.

6.　Should it be necessary to form Brigade Groups suddenly, the following message will be sent from Div. H.Q. to all recipients of these Instructions :-

               "FORM BRIGADE GROUPS",
                     or
   "FORM BRIGADE GROUPS LESS Fd. COYS. R.E." etc.

   On receipt of the above message :
     (a)　Units as detailed in para. 3 (less any one or more units named in message) not now located in the areas of their Brigade Groups, will at once march to their pre-arranged rendezvous.

     (b)　H.Q. Div. Engineers will join Div. H.Q. if F. Coys. R.E. are detailed to form part of Groups.
     (c)　All other troops of the Division will stand fast.

B. Move of the Division from XI Corps Area.

1. The move will take place either :-
    (a) By March Route.
    (b) By Train.
    (c) By Bus.
    (d) A combination of any or all of (a) (b) (c).

2. In any of the above cases it will take place by Brigade Groups but in the case of a move by Strategical Train -
    (a) The M.G. Bn. will probably move as a complete Unit.
    (b) Half S.A.A. Section may be attached to two of the Inf. Bde. Groups.

3. (a) In the case of 1 (a), routes will be detailed when destination of troops is known.
   (b) In the case of 1 (b), if moved by strategical trains, the whole of the Division (less M.T.) moves by rail.
       The probably entraining stations are as follows :-
                                (1)   (2)
       184 Bde. Group. - LILLERS   or   ARQUES.
       182 Bde. Group. - BERGUETTE or   ST. OMER.
       183 Bde. Group. - AIRE   or   WIZERNES.

       Divisional Artillery at all three or any two of either (1) or (2). Probable Entraining Stations and order of entrainment of all units will be forwarded later.
       All the above stations have been reconnoitred.

   (c) In the case of 1 (c), the probable Embussing places are as follows :-
       <u>184 Bde. Group</u> - T.11.a.2.1. - T.15.a.3.7. - on the ST. HILAIRE - AUCHY-AU-BOIS road.
       <u>182 Bde. Group</u> - N.17.c.3.0. - N.4.d.0.5. - on the ST. HILAIRE - AIRE road.
       <u>183 Bde. Group</u> - N.29.c.7.0. - N.23.a.3.9. - on the ST. HILAIRE - AIRE road.
       Busses will face W. or S. in the case of a move S. or E., and E. or N. in the case of a move N.

C. Division acting as XI Corps Reserve in case of attack.

1. The tasks the Division will be prepared to carry out are as follows :-
   (a) <u>In the event of attack on the Corps on the immediate right of XI Corps.</u>
       (i) To extend the right flank of XI Corps along the NAVE R.
       (ii) To extend the right flank of XI Corps along the BUSNES-STEENBECQUE Line and hold L'ECLEME locality (V.3).
       (iii) To counter-attack towards MT. BERNENCHON and HINGES.

   (b) <u>In the event of attack against the centre of XI Corps.</u>
       To reinforce the junction between the right and left Divisions, either on the AMUSOIRES - HAVERSKERQUE Line or the BUSNES - STEENBECQUE Line.

   (c) <u>In the event of attack on the Corps on the immediate left of XI Corps.</u>
       (i) The extend the left flank of XI Corps from ESE: GD: DAM (K.2.a.4.0.) along the BOURRE R. and the BRAS-DE-LA BOURRE (K.2.a. - E.25.d. - D.24).
       (ii) To extend the left flank of XI Corps from LA-MOTTE-AU-BOIS along the canal running through D.18 and D.11.
       (iii) To counter-attack North-East to drive the enemy back across the canal in D.18 and D.11.

2. In order to be in a position to deal with any one or more of the situations as set forth in para.1 which may arise, the following <u>three Brigade Concentration Areas</u> have been selected:-

<u>Area "R"</u> - MIQUELLERIE - CORNET BRASSART - CORNET BOURDOIS.

<u>Area "C"</u> - ISBERGUES - LA ROUPIE - TREIZENNES.

<u>Area "L"</u> - STEENBECQUE - BOESEGHEM - THIENNES.

3. In case of necessity, Infantry Brigades (reinforced by one Machine Gun Company) may be ordered to move into one or more of the Concentration Areas mentioned in para.2.

4. Infantry Brigades (plus one M.G.Co. attached) will be prepared to move in accordance with Table "A" attached.

5. On the order "MAN BATTLE STATIONS" being received at Div. Art. H.Q. it will be sent out to Headquarters of all units in the following form :-
MAN BATTLE STATIONS aaa ST.HILAIRE Bde. to Area "R" aaa MAZINGHEM Bde. to Area "C" aaa Remainder at .... hours notice.
or
MAN BATTLE STATIONS aaa LINGHEM Bde. to Area "L" aaa Remainder at .... hours notice.
etc.

6. On receipt of the Order "MAN BATTLE STATIONS", etc(para.5):-
(a) The Infantry Brigade or Brigades affected will at once move in accordance with Table "A".
(b) The remainder of the Division will stand fast ready to move at the named "........hours" notice.

7. The Div. Artillery will be prepared to move and support the Infantry in any of the three tasks for which the Division has to be prepared (para.1).
The preliminary concentration of the Artillery will take place as under, and in accordance with Table "A" attached:

In case (a) or (b) of para.1, in an area East of FONTES on receipt of message "Concentrate FONTES".

In case (c) of para.1, in an area about BOESEGHEM (clear of roads) on receipt of message "Concentrate BOESEGHEM".

8. Instructions as regards reconnaissances to be carried out will be issued later.

9. ACKNOWLEDGE.

F.P.Wye.

Issued at. 9.p.m........

Captain, R.A.,
Bde.Maj., 61 Div.Artillery.

DISTRIBUTION.

Copy No.1 - 5.	306 Bde.RFA ☒	Copy No.19 -	61 Div. 'G'.
6 -10.	307 Bde.RFA ☒	20. -	R.A.XI Corps.
11 -14.	61 D.A.C. ☒	21. -	4th.Div.Art.
15.	D.T.M.O. ☒	22 -	5th.Div.Art.
16.	S.C.R.A. ☒	23 -	74th.Div.Art.
17.	R.O.R.A. ☒	24-25.	War Diary.
18.	O.i/c R.A.Sigs.	26.	File.

(Tracing showing Corps & Divisional Boundaries issued to (☒) only.)

TABLE 'A'.

SECRET.

Issued with 61st. D.A.
Defence Instructions No.1
(B.M.S.40/9 of 1.8.18.)

Unit.	From.	To.	Method.	Remarks.
ST. HILAIRE Bde., plus 'C' Coy. 61 Bn.M.G.C. (attached).	Present position	Area "R"	March Route.	Via HAM-EN-ARTOIS. Bde. Report Centre to HAM-EN-ARTOIS O.27.d.5.5.
MAZINGHEM Bde., plus 'A' Coy. 61 Bn.M.G.C. (attached).	Present position.	Area 'C'	March Route.	Via MOLINGHEM and LAMBRES. Bde. Report Centre to LA LACQUE I.31.a.7.7
LINGHEM Bde. plus 'B' Coy. 61 Bn.M.G.C. (attached).	Present position.	Area 'L'	Lorry.	LAMBRES - AIRE. Bde. Report Centre to I.8.b.6.1. In the event of circumstances rendering it desirable, lorries will be parked at LINGHEM at night.
Div. Artillery. 61 Div.Art. H.Q.	Present position. Present position.	NORRENT FONTES. (1) Area E. of FONTES. (2) Area BOESEGHEM.		Join 61 Div.H.Q. on move of Arty. On receipt of message "Concentrate FONTES". Routes as desired. On receipt of message "Concentrate BOESEGHEM". Routes as desired. Roads at BOESEGHEM to be kept clear.

SECRET.

61st. DIVISION.
LOCATIONS OF UNITS.

(To accompany 61 Div.Art. B.M.S.40/9 of 1.8.18 - Defence Instructions No.1.

61st. DIVISION H.Q.	NORRENT FONTES.
182 Inf.Bde.H.Q.	ST.ANDRE FARM, N.2.d.5.9.
2/6 Warwicks.	QUERNES.
2/7 Warwicks.	LAMBRES.
2/8 Worcesters.	Liettres.
L.T.M.B.	ST. QUENTIN.
183 Inf.Bde.H.Q.	FONTES.
9th.North Fus:	FONTES.
11th.Suffolks.	LINGHEM.
1st.E.Lancs.	do.
L.T.M.B.	do.
184 Inf.Bde.H.Q.	ST.HILAIRE.
2/5 Glosters.	do.
2/4 Oxfords.	do.
2/4 R.Berks.	BOURECQ.
L.T.M.B.	ST. HILAIRE.
1/5 D.C.L.I.(P).	BLESSY. M.11.b.
61 Bn.M.G.C.) A.B.C.D.Coys.)	WITTERNESSE.
C.R.E.	HAM. M.5.c.7.3.
476 Field Co.R.E.	" M.5.d.4.6.
478 do.	" M.5.c.5.5.
479 do.	" M.5.c.7.7.
A.D.M.S.	NORRENT FONTES.
2/1 Field Amb.	BOURECQ.
2/2 do.	LAMBRES.
2/3 do.	FONTES.
C.R.A.	ESTREE-BLANCHE.
306 Bde.R.F.A.	ENQUIN-LES-MINES.
307 do.	H.Q. & 2 Batteries - SERNY.) 2 Batteries -ESTREE-BLANCHE)
61 D.A.C.	FLECHINELLE.
T.M.Bs.	ENQUIN-LES-MINES.
61 Div.Train H.Q.	NORRENT FONTES.
No.1 Coy.	ESTREE-BLANCHE.
No.2 Coy.	LAMBRES (LA BEFORE FARM, N.9.a.9.9.)
No.3 Coy.	FONTES.
No.4 Coy.	ST.HILAIRE.

MOVE ON THE DIVISIONAL ARTILLERY BY STRATEGICAL TRAIN.

SERRE		AIRE or CASSEL		LILLERS or ARQUES	
BERGUETTE or ST.OMER					
Train.	Unit.	Train.	Unit.	Train.	Unit.
		23.	Headquarters R.A. D.A.C. Coy.Div.Train.	24.	H.Q. 306th.Bde.R.F.A. No.1 Sec.D.A.C. less 4 G.S. 16 limbered Amm.Wagons and teams. 'Y' T.M. Battery.
25.	H.Q. 307 Bde.R.F.A. No.2 Sec.D.A.C. less 4 G.S. 16 Limbd.Amm.Wagons & teams. 'Y' T.M. Battery.	26.	'C' Battery 307th.Bde.R.F.A. 1 G.S. 4 Limbd.Amm.Wagons and teams of No.2 Section D.A.C.	27.	'A' Bty. 306th.Bde.R.F.A. 1 G.S. 4 Limbd.Amm.Wagons & teams of No.1 Sec.D.A.C.
28.	'A' Bty 307th.Bde. R.F.A. 1 G.S. 4 Limbd.Amm.Wagons & teams of No.2 Section D.A.C.	29.	'D' Bty 307th.Bde. R.F.A. 1 G.S.Wagon 4 Limbd.Amm.Wagons of No.2 Section D.A.C.	30.	'B' Bty. 306th.Bde.R.F.A. 1 G.S. 4 Limbd.Amm.Wagons and teams of No.1 Sec. D.A.C.
31.	'B' Bty. 307th.Bde. R.F.A. 1 G.S. 4 Limbd.Amm.Wagons & teams of No.2 Section D.A.C.	32.	'D' Battery 305th.Bde.R.F.A. 1 G.S. 4 Limbd.Amm.Wagons No.1 Section D.A.C.	33.	'C' Battery 306th.Bde.R.F.A. 1 G.S.Wagon 4 Limbd.Amm. Wagons No.1 Section D.A.C.

S E C R E T.　　　　　　　　　　　　　B.M.S.340/9/1.

AMENDMENT NO. 1 to
61st. DIVISIONAL ARTILLERY INSTRUCTIONS NO:1.

Reference 61st. Divisional Artillery Instructions No:1 (B.M.S.40/9 of 1.8.18.)

Page 2, para. B, 3 (c), line 9, delete "or E."

　　　　　　　　　　　　　　　　F.P.Wye.
　　　　　　　　　　　　　　　　Capt. R.A.,
2.8.18.　　　　　　　　Bde. Maj., 61 Div. Artillery.

To all recipients of
61 D.A. Instructions No.1.

S E C R E T.   B.M.S. 40/9/2.

                    AMENDMENT NO: 2 to
             61st. DIVISIONAL ARTILLERY INSTRUCTIONS NO: 1.

    Reference 61st. Div. Artillery Defence Instructions
No.1, page 2, para. B.3 (b).

    The probable Entraining Stations will be amended to
read as follows :-

                                (1)   (2)
        184 Brigade Group.   LILLERS   or   ARQUES.
        183   "   "   BERGUETTE or   ST. OMER.
        182   "   "   AIRE   or   WIZERNES.

                                        for Capt. R.A.,
                                Bde.Maj., 61 Div. Artillery.

3.8.18.

To all recipients of
61 D.A. Defence Instructions No.1.

S E C R E T.   War Diary

B.M.S. 40/9/3.

To all recipients of
61 Div. Artillery Defence
Instructions No.1.

    The attached Table of probable Entraining Stations and order of entrainment, is forwarded with reference to 61st. Div. Artillery Defence Instructions No.1 (B.M.S. 40/9 dated 1.8.18.)

    Please acknowledge.

                             F.P.Wye.
                             Capt. R.A.,
                Bde.Maj., 61 Div. Artillery.

4.8.1918.

SECRET. (War diary)　　Copy No: 26

61st. DIVISIONAL ARTILLERY ORDER NO: 135.

5th. August, 1918.

Ref: Map Sheet 36A. 1:40,000.

1. The 61st. Division commenced relief of 5th. Division in the Left Sector, XI Corps Front, on 4th. instant.
   Relief of Division (less Artillery) to be completed by 6 a.m. on 7th. instant.
   The Artillery relief to be completed by 10 a.m. on 8th. inst.

2. Movement Table attached.

3. The following distances will be maintained between Units and parts of units on the march :-
   (a) Between Batteries and Sections D.A.C. - - 100 yds.
   (b) Between Brigades - - - - - - - - - - - 500 yds.
   (c) Between each section of 6 vehicles - - - - 25 yds.

4. All documents relating to the Sector, Battery Boards, Trench maps, aeroplane photographs and S.O.S.Rifle Grenades, will be taken over from Units on relief.

5. Guns will not be exchanged.

6. Brigade Signal Officers and Battery Commanders will go forward to new positions on 6th. instant and remain.

7. 306th. Brigade, R.F.A., will relieve 27th. Brigade, R.F.A., 5th. Divisional Artillery, now under orders of 74th. Divisional Artillery, and will come under orders of C.R.A. 74th. Division, on completion of relief.

8. On 7th. instant, 307th. Bde. R.F.A. will take over and provide detachments for Anti-Tank guns in action at :-
   (1) 1 15-pdr. at J.36.c.75.55.
   (2) 1 18-pdr.(worn) at J.30.a.8.0.

9. Command will pass on completion of relief, which will be reported to R.A.H.Q. 5th.D.A., 74th.D.A. and 61st.D.A. by code word "BELGIUM".

10. All details of reliefs to be arranged direct between Units concerned.

11. Relief of Trench Mortars will be carried out under arrangements made direct between D.T.M.Os. concerned.

12. The 306th. Bde. and 307th. Bde. will each detail 1 18-pr. with limber, team and limber gunner, to report to H.Q. 61 D.A.C. at I.8.c.5.0. at 10 a.m. on 8th. inst. These two guns will form a section to be used for training purposes. Details of training arrangements will be notified later.

13. The C.R.A. 61st. Division, will take over command of Artillery covering 61st. Division from C.R.A. 5th. Division, at 10 a.m. 8th. instant, at which hour R.A.H.Q. will close at ESTREE BLANCHE and open at I.20.a.2.4.

14. ACKNOWLEDGE.

T.Wye.

Capt. R.A.,
Bde.Maj., 61 Div. Artillery.

Issued at 7.p.m.

61st. DIVISIONAL ARTILLERY ORDER NO. 135.

12th. August, 1918.

DISTRIBUTION.

Copy No. 1 - 5.	306 Bde. R.F.A.
6 - 10.	307 Bde. R.F.A.
11 - 14.	61 D.A.C.
15.	D.T.M.O.
16.	R.A. XI Corps.
17.	5th. Div. Artillery.
18.	74th. Div. Artillery.
19.	31st. Div. Artillery.
20.	61 Division 'G'.
21.	61 Division 'Q'.
22.	A.P.M.
23.	D.A.D.O.S.
24.	D.A.D.V.S.
25.	A.D.M.S.
26 - 27.	War Diary.
27.	File.

MOVEMENT TABLE to accompany 61st. Div. Artillery Order No.135 of 5.8.1918.

Serial No.	Date.	Unit.	From.	Route.	To Wagon Lines at	Remarks.	Night.	Relieves.	In action at	Remarks.
1	6th.	1 Sec.of: A/305. B/305. C/306. D/306.	ENQUIN-les-MINES.	FONTES – BERGUETTE.	O.16.d.7.3. O.23.a.9.5. O.12.c.1.6. P.1.c.8.2.8	3 Lines available for staging at O.15.d.3.6.	6/7th.	Section of 119 Bty. 120 " 121 " 37 "	J.34.d.3.3. P.10&35.11. P.3.b.6.5. P.9.c90.60.	No movement E.of GUARBECQUE – BUSNES before 9 p.m. Relief to be completed by daylight 7th.inst.
2	6th.	1 Sec.of: A/307. B/307. C/307. D/307.	SERNEY.	Via.AIRE.	M.34.c.5.6. I.35.d.4.6. I.29.d.0.9. I.34.a.7.9.		6/7th.	1 Sec.of: 4/15. 52 Bty. 80 Bty. D/15.	J.28.c.0.5. J.23.c.55.60. J.35.b.8.8. J.30&60.95.	No movement in forward area before 9 p.m. Relief to be completed by daylight 7th.inst.
3	7th.	61 D.A.C. HQ. No.1 Sec. No.2 Sec. SAA Sec.	FLECHI-NELLE.	Road June: M.26.d.5.9. ST.QUENTIN-AIRE – WIDDEBRUCQ.	I.8.c.5.0. I.7.b.2.3. I.7.d.2.2. I.7.c.3.2.	Not to pass Road June: I.13.d.05.50 before 12 noon.		HQ.5 D.A.C. Sec. " Sec. " Sec. "		Completion of relief to be reported direct to 61 Div.Qr.
4	7th.	306 Bde. less 1 Sec.per Battery.	Wagon Lines.	FONTES – BERGUETTE.	H.Q. – P.1.b. 35.15.	As above.	7/8th.	B.HQ.27th. Bde.RFA. Remainder of 119 Bty. 120 " 121 " 37 "	P.1.b.3515. J.34.c.0.3. P.3.d.39.D8 P.3.c.95.87 P.9.c.90.60.	No movement E.of GUARBECQUE – BUSNES before 9 p.m. Relief to be completed by daylight 8th.instant.

MOVEMENT TABLE (continued).

Seri-al No.	Date.	Unit.	From.	Route.	To Wagon Lines at	Remarks.	Night. Relieves.	In action at.	Remarks.
5	7th.	307 Bde. less 1 Sec. per Battery.	Wagon Lines.	ST. QUENTIN (H.32.b.)- AIRE- Bridge H.29b.95.30.	H.Q. I.36.d.2.1. Batteries as Serial No.2.	Not to pass 7/8th. Drawbridge H.29.b.9530 before 1 pm	B.H.Q. 15th Bde. R.F.A. Remainder of: A/15. 52nd. Bty. 80th. " D/15.	J.21.a.2.6. J.33.b.8.2. J.33.c.05.55. J.35.d.45.00. J.27.c.80.80.	No movement in Forward area before 9 p.m. Relief to be completed by daylight 8th. instant.
6	7th.	T.M.Bat-teries.	Billets.	Via AIRE.	Under arrangements made by D.T.M.O.				
7	8th.	R.H.Q.	ESTREE-BLANCHE	Via AIRE.	—	—	R.H.Q. 5th. Div.	I.20.a.2.4.	

R.A.Q. 528/25.

ADMINISTRATIVE INSTRUCTIONS
with reference to 61 Div.Art. Order No. 135.
----

1. Wagon lines will be located as under :-

306 Bde.	H.Q.	P.1.b.35.15
	A.Bty	O.16.d.7.3.
	B. "	O.22.a.9.5.
	C. "	O.12.c.1.6.
	D. "	P.1.c.8.2.
307 Bde.	H.Q.	I.36.d.3.1.
	A Bty	I.34.a.5.6.
	B "	I.35.d.4.6.
	C "	I.29.d.0.9.
	D. "	I.34.a.7.9.
61st D.A.G.	H.Q.	I.8.b.5.0.
	No.1.Sect.	I.7.b.2.3.
	No.2.Sect.	I.7.d.2.2.
	S.A.A.Sect.	I.7.c.3.2.

2. Lorries.

The following lorries will report as under :- for surplus stores and baggage.

R.A.H.Q. 2 lorries at School ESTREE BLANCHE 8.0 am 8th Aug
306 Bde. 1 lorry at B.H.Q. ENQUIN LES MINES at 10. am 7th August.
307 Bde. 1 lorry at B.H.Q. SERNY at 10. am 7th Aug.
D.A.C. 1 lorry at H.Q. FLECHINELLE at 10 am 7th
T.M. Arrangements to be notified later.

3. Supplies. Supply wagons with rations for consumption on 8th will march with No. 1 Coy. 61 Div. Train and deliver to units on arrival in new area.
All baggage wagons will report to No. 1 Coy. 61 Div. Train by 12 noon on Aug. 8th.

4. Ammunition. All Units will march with full echelons – 61st A.R.P. is situated at FORESTERS HOUSE I.25.c.2.5. and will be started by 61st D.A.C.

5. Tents. All tents, trench shelters, and area stores will be returned to Area Commandant ESTREE BLANCHE. Receipts for tents etc. together with a certificate from the Area Commandant that billets have been left in a satisfactory condition will be forwarded to R.A.H.Q. on Aug. 8th.

6. Billets. All billets and horse lines will be left clean, manure tightly stacked at manure dumps, latrines cleaned, cookhouse and other refuse burnt before leaving.

R.A.H.Q.,   S.C.R.A. 61st Div.
61st Div.,
5th August 1918.

J. Huff. Capt.
for Major.

S E C R E T.   W.X.

B.M.S. 2/88.

AMENDMENT NO:1
- to -
61st. DIVISIONAL ARTILLERY ORDER NO: 135.
----

1. <u>Serial Nos. 2 & 5.</u>

   Cancel "No movement in forward area before 9 p.m." in final remarks column.

2. <u>Serial No. 3.</u>

   First Remarks column for "12 noon" read "1 p.m."

3. <u>Serial No. 5.</u>

   Under "Route" cancel "Bridge H.29.b.95.20", and substitute "BOESEGHEM, THIENNES, and Ferry I.28.d."
   Cancel "Not to pass Drawbridge, etc." in first remarks column, and substitute "Head of column to pass cross roads I.15.a. at 1 p.m.".

4. ACKNOWLEDGE.

                                              F. Phye
                                          Capt. R.A.,
6.8.1918.   Bde. Maj., 61 Div. Artillery.

<u>To all recipients of 61 D.A. Order No. 135.</u>

War Diary

S E C R E T.

B.M.S. 2/89.

AMENDMENT NO: 2
- to -
61st. DIVISIONAL ARTILLERY ORDER NO:135 of 5/8/1918.

Para.12 of the above Order is cancelled.

A.P.Wye.

7.8.18.

Capt. R.A.,
Bde. Maj., 61 Div. Artillery.

To all recipients of 61 D.A. Order No.135.

SECRET.   Copy No: 27

61st. DIVISIONAL ARTILLERY ORDER NO: 136.

8th. August, 1918.

1. The following Infantry reliefs are being carried out to-night 9/10th. August:-

   (a) The 182 Inf. Bde. will relieve all troops of 183 and 184 Infantry Brigades, on the line they now hold from the LYS CANAL as far North as the BOURRE River. At the same time 184 Inf. Brigade will relieve any troops of 183 Inf. Brigade North of the River.

   On completion of relief the boundaries between 184 Inf. Brigade on the left and 182 Inf. Brigade on the Right, will be the BOURRE River (inclusive to 182 Inf. Brigade) from the present front posts to a point about K.15.a.3.2., thence to the present boundary at K.14.b.1.5.

   (b) The 183 Inf. Brigade will be in Divisional Reserve with H.Q. at SPRESIAND Camp, J.14.b.

2. The Line of Retention will remain as at present, viz:- From the Southern Divisional Boundary about J.36.b.9.1. to road at K.26.c.1.3. thence along our old front line to K.15.d.3.3. thence to K.15.b.5.0. - K.9.d.9.6. - K.10.a.0.2. - K.10.a.8.5. to K.4.a.6.0.

3. In consequence of para.1, the Artillery covering the front will be rearranged as follows from 8 p.m., 9.8.18 :-

   RIGHT GROUP - O.C. 307 Brigade, R.F.A.
   A/307 Bty. R.F.A.
   B/307 "   "
   C/307 "   "
   D/307 "   "
   C/296 "   "

   will cover Right Infantry Brigade front.

   LEFT GROUP - O.C. 296 Brigade, R.F.A.
   A/295 Bty. R.F.A.
   B/295 "   "
   C/295 "   "
   D/295 "   "
   A/296 "   "
   B/296 "   "
   D/296 "   "

   will cover front of Left Infantry Brigade.

4. Officer i/c R.A. Signals will arrange the necessary signal communications in conjunction with Brigade Signal Officers.

5. Groups will keep a Senior Liaison Officer with their respective Infantry Brigade H.Q. and also a liaison Officer with each Battalion in the Line on their front.

6. The S.O.S. Barrage will be arranged with B.-Gs. Commanding Infantry Brigade and O.C. Div.M.G. Battalion.

7. ACKNOWLEDGE.

F.P.Wye.
Capt.R.A.,
Bde.Maj., 61 Div. Artillery.

DISTRIBUTION. P.T.O.

DISTRIBUTION.

Copy No.	1 - 5.	295 Brigade. R.F.A.
	6 - 10.	296 Bde. R.F.A.
	11 - 15.	307 Bde. R.F.A.
	16.	61 Div. 'G'.
	17.	R.A. XI Corps.
	18.	51st. Div. Art.
	19.	74th. Div. Art.
	20.	182 Inf. Bde.
	21.	183 Inf. Bde.
	22.	184 Inf. Bde.
	23.	H.A. XI Corps.
	24.	C.B.S.O., XI Corps.
	25.	28th. Bde. R.G.A.
	26.	61st. D.A.C.
	27 - 28.	War Diary.
	29.	File.

S E C R E T.   61st. D.A. No. R.G.1.

61st. DIVISIONAL ARTILLERY GROUP.

LOCATION STATEMENT - 9 Aug.1918.

Ref: Sheet 36A N.E. Edition 7.

Unit.	Location.	Wagon Lines.
61st. R.A. Headquarters.	I.20.a.3.4.	
RIGHT GROUP.		
307 Bde. R.F.A., H.Q. (rear)	J.21.a.20.60.	I.35.d.20.10.
" " " " (Adv:)	J.23.c.05.90.	
A/307 (6 guns)	J.29.a.7.3.	I.27.d.90.20.
B/307 (6 ")	J.23.c.50.60.	I.35.d.30.70.
C/307 (6 ")	J.35.d.3.0.	I.29.a.40.40.
D/307 (6 Hows.)	J.30.a.6.8.	J.31.b.60.30.
LEFT GROUP.		
296 Bde. R.F.A., H.Q.	D.27.b.20.75.	I.11.b.30.55.
A/296 (6 guns)	K.2.c.30.40.	I.5.c.5.4.
B/296 (6 ")	K.2.c.80.70.	I.3.d.2.4.
C/296 (4 ")	J.10.b.45.35.	I.3.d.3.8.
(2 ")	J.11.b.60.40.	
D/296 (4 Hows.)	J.11.c.14.22.	I.11.a.6.3.
(2 ")	K.13.a.50.60.	
A/295 (6 guns)	K.3.c.7.4.	C.15.d.5.2.
B/295 (6 ")	K.2.d.4.7.	C.27.d.5.3.
C/295 (6 ")	J.12.a.75.80.	C.28.d.9.4.
D/295 (6 Hows.)	J.6.c.30.60.	C.16.d.9.9.
295 Bde. R.F.A. H.Q.	-	C.16.c.8.9.
59th. Div. Art. H.Q.	-	C.29.d.4.1.
59th. D.A.C. H.Q.	-	I.5.b.5.3.
61st. D.A.C. H.Q.	-	I.8.c.5.0.
61st. D.T.M.O., H.Q.	-	I.16.c.50.30. (Billet 43, THIENNES.)
59th. D.T.M.O.	-	C.30.d.80.05.
Y/61 T.M.B. (1 6" NEWTON)	K.25.b.45.50.	
(1 ")	K.25.b.45.55.	
(1 ")	K.20.a.65.35.	
(1 ")	K.20.b.15.50.	
59 T.Ms. (1 6" NEWTON)	K.10.c.65.00.	
(1 ")	K.10.c.45.05.	
(1 ")	K.16.a.40.90.	

Spencer Batchelor.
Lieut.R.A.,
R.O., 61st. Div. Artillery.

9.8.1918.

S E C R E T.

61 D.A.No.R.G.1.

AMENDMENT to
61st. Divisional Artillery Location Statement
of 9 Aug.1918.

LEFT GROUP.
    296 Bde.R.F.A.,H.Q.   Delete "D.27.b.20.75"

                and substitute "D.30.c.80.60. Chateau."

Spencer Batchelor.
Lieut. R.A.,
10.8.1918.   R.O., 61 Div. Artillery.

To all recipients of 61 D.A.Location Statement
    dated 9.8.1918.

MESSAGES AND SIGNALS.

Army Form C. 2121
(In pads of 100.)

Prefix...... Code......m.	Words	Charge	This message is on a/c of:	Recd. at......m
Office of Origin and Service Instructions	Sent At ......m To ...... By		......Service. (Signature of "Franking Officer")	Date...... From ...... By ......

TO { Right Group 31 X.A   XI Corps RA
     Left Group   74 D.A   X ? M.O

Sender's Number.	Day of Month	In reply to Number.	AAA
RAG 1/4/2	10		

61	DA	Order	No 137
para 11	plus	6	hours
15	minutes	aaa	acknowledge

From 61 X A
Place
Time 7:40 pm

The above may be forwarded as now corrected   (Z)

Censor.   Signature of Addressor or person authorised to telegraph in his name

* This line should be erased if not required.

Order No. 1625 Wt. W3253/ P 511 27/2 H. & K. Ltd (E. 2634)

War Diary

S E C R E T.   R.A.G.1/6/1.

AMENDMENT NO: 1
to
61st. DIVISIONAL ARTILLERY ORDER NO; 137
of 10.8.1918.
----

1. Our Infantry having established a post at K.22.a.3.3. this afternoon, the Right Group 18-pr. Barrage will be amended as follows :-

    The Right or South-western boundary of the Barrage will now run K.22.a.55.95 to K.22.d.3.8.

    D/307 will barrage the road from K.22.c.80.85 to K.22.d.20.45. throughout the operation.

2. Para. 7 of the above Order is cancelled.

    6-in. T.M. Programme will be as arranged between B.G.C. 184 Inf. Brigade and 61 D.T.M.O., and published in 184 Inf.Bde. Operation Order.

F.P.Wye
Capt. R.A.,
Bde.Maj., 61 Div. Artillery.

10.8.1918.

To all recipients of 61 D.A.Order No.137.

SECRET.   Copy............

61st. DIVISIONAL ARTILLERY ORDER NO: 137.

Ref: Sheet 36A.N.E.-1:20,000,   10th. August, 1918.
    & attached Barrage Maps.

1. On 11th August, at an hour to be notified later, the 184th.
    Inf. Bde. will cross the PLATE BECQUE and establish a Bridge-head
    on the general line K.22.b.7.7. (LES PURESBECQUES incl:) - houses
    at K.17.a.6.6. (incl:) - PLATE BECQUE at approximately K.11.c.7.2.

2. The 182nd. Inf. Bde., conforming to the above, will push for-
    ward its left in close touch with the 184th. Inf. Bde. and establish
    itself on the general line K.22.c.0.5. - K.22.b.7.7.

3. The Field Artillery covering the front of the 61st.
    Division and 12 T.Ms. assisted by 2 18-pr. and 2 4.5" How. Batteries
    of the 31st. Divisional Artillery will provide the barrage for the
    above operation.

4. C/296 will come under the orders of O.C. Left Group, for the
    operation.

5. The 18-pr. Barrage will open on the RED LINE shown on the
    attached map, and will move forward in lifts of 100 yards until
    the Brown Line - Protective Barrage - is reached.
    Rate of fire throughout - Rapid.

    Ammunition :-
        From Zero to Zero plus 3 mins. - AX 101 Fuze.
        "   Plus 3 mins. - end of
                          Operation.   - A. 30% graze.

    Note: Right Group will fire A throughout.

6. The 4.5" How. Barrage of 31st. Divisional Artillery and Left
    Group Batteries will open on the RED LINE and will move forward in
    lifts of 100 yards, except that as each locality marked in GREEN
    on the map, thus ⌒ , is reached, one Battery will be concen-
    trated on it for 2 minutes using 50% Delay Fuzes, after which the
    Howitzers of the Battery detailed resume their place in the Barrage.

    D/307, Right Group, will barrage the LA MOTTE - MERVILLE Road,
    as shewn in RED on attached Map, from Zero to plus 4 minutes.
    As shewn in BLUE from Plus 4 mins. onwards.

    Rate of fire throughout - Rapid.

    Ammunition :-
        From Zero to Zero plus 9 mins. - BX. 101 Fuze.
        From plus 9 mins. onwards   - - BX. 106 Fuze.

7. Trench Mortars will follow the Barrage programme for 4.5" Hows.
    up to a range of 1200 yards from the guns when they will stop.

    Rate of fire throughout - 4 rounds per gun per minute.

8. Batteries will be prepared to continue or re-open the Protective
    (Final) Barrage if ordered to do so by B.Gs. Commanding Infantry
    Brigades, through Liaison Officers, who will call on Groups direct.
    The latter will at once inform R.A.H.Q.

                                - 1 -   P.T.O.

9. From Zero onwards, Batteries of 31st. Divisional Artillery will be under the tactical control of O.C. Left Group, 61st. Div. Artillery.

10. Watches will be synchronised at 184 Infantry Brigade Headquarters, J.4.c.7.5., at 7 p.m. to-night.

11. Zero hour will be notified as ...... hours and ...... minutes plus of 10 p.m. (viz: 7 a.m. = plus 9 hours.)

12. ACKNOWLEDGE.

L.P. Nye
Capt. R.A.
Bde. Maj., 61 Div. Artillery.

Issued at ...6 p.m.....

DISTRIBUTION.

Copy No.	1 - 5.	Right Group.
	6 - 14.	Left Group.
	15 - 19.	31st. Div. Art.
	20 - 21.	182 Inf. Brigade.
	22 - 24.	184 Inf. Brigade.
	25.	61 Div. 'G'.
	26.	R.A. XI Corps.
	27.	74th. Div. Art.
	28.	28th. Bde. R.G.A.
	29 - 30.	War Diary.
	31.	File.

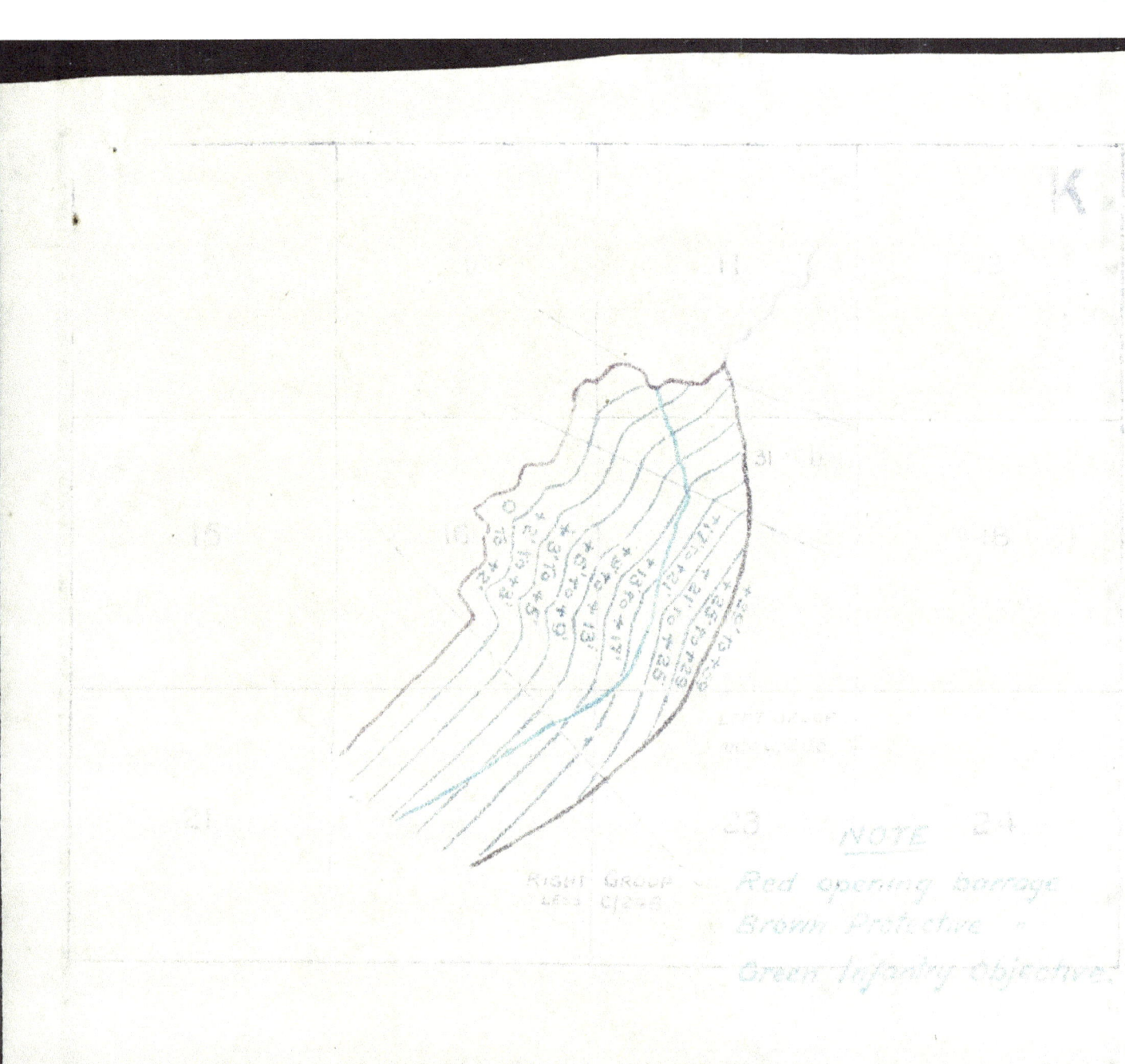

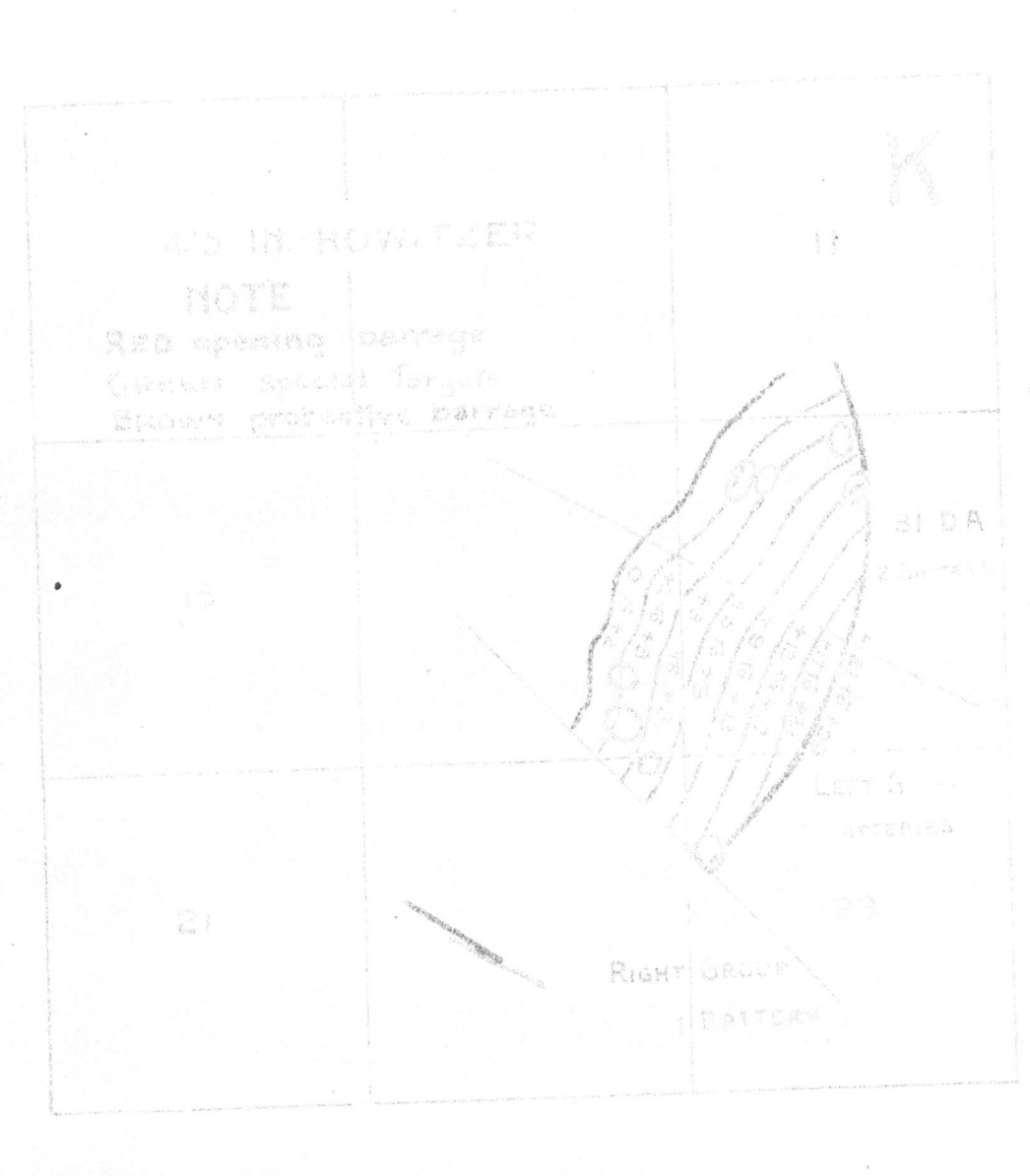

REFERENCE.

Black :- Lifts.

Red :- Opening barrage.

Brown :- Protective barrage.

Green :- Objective

○ :- Posts to be established.

Blue :- Protective barrage for capture of COURTEFROIE FM.

Barrage arranged by 5th D.A. to cover advance of 182 I.B. troops on evening 7/8/18

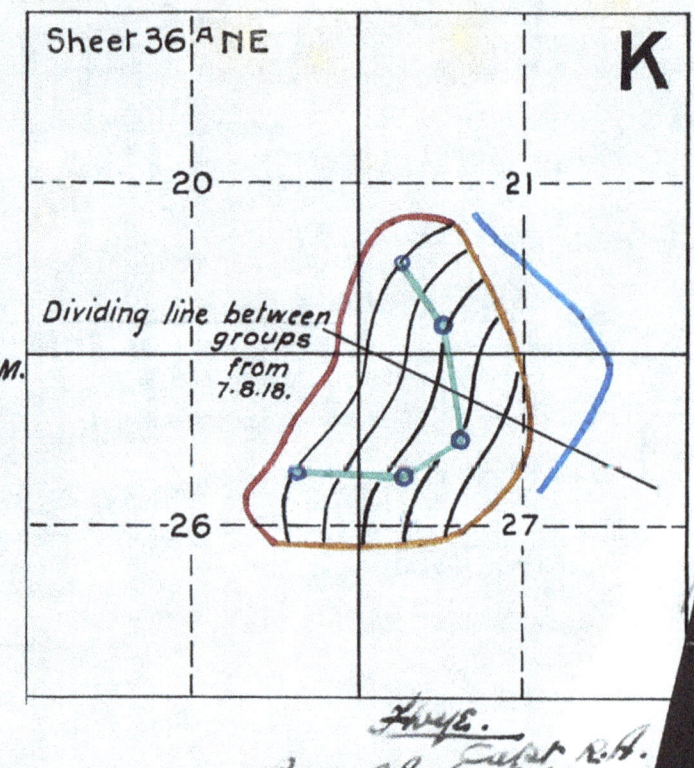

SECRET. War Diary Copy No: 28

61st. DIVISIONAL ARTILLERY ORDER NO: 138.

13th. August, 1918.

1. (a)　The 183rd. Infantry Brigade is relieving the 184th. Inf. Brigade in the left (ARREWAGE) Section of the Divisional front on night 14/15th. instant, and in addition 183rd. Inf. Brigade will take over from 182nd. Inf. Brigade, the front from the BOURRE River to the LA MOTTE - MERVILLE Road exclusive.

(b)　The Boundary between Brigades will then be as follows:-

　　The LA MOTTE - MERVILLE Road from the front post line to the building at K.14.b.1.5, - K.13.b.9.9, - K.17.central (all inclusive to the Right - LE SART - Brigade.)

(c)　On relief the 184th. Inf. Brigade will be in Divisional Reserve with H.Q. at STEENBECQUE.

2.　In consequence of para.1 (b) above, the Artillery covering the front will be rearranged as follows from 5 a.m. 14.8.18.

　　RIGHT GROUP.　O.C. 307th. Brigade, R.F.A.

　　　　307 Brigade, R.F.A.
　　　　　　covering Right Infantry Brigade front.

　　LEFT GROUP.　O.C. 296th. Brigade, R.F.A.

　　　　295th. Brigade, R.F.A.
　　　　296th.　　"　　"
　　　　　　covering left Infantry Brigade front.

3.　ACKNOWLEDGE.

　　　　　　　　　　　Capt. R.A.,
　　　　　　　　Bde.Maj., 61 Div. Artillery.

Issued at 12 noon.

DISTRIBUTION.

Copy No.	Recipient
1 - 5.	295 Brigade, R.F.A.
6 - 10.	296 Brigade, R.F.A.
11 - 15.	307 Brigade, R.F.A.
16.	61 Div. 'G'.
17.	R.A. XI Corps.
18.	31st. Div. Art.
19.	74th. Div. Art.
20.	182 Inf. Brigade.
21.	183 Inf. Brigade.
22.	184 Inf. Brigade.
23.	H.A. XI Corps.
24.	C.B.S.D. XI Corps.
25.	28th. Bde. R.G.A.
26.	61 D.A.C.
27.	61 D.T.M.O.
28 - 29.	War Diary,
30.	File.

SECRET

AMENDMENT NO: 2
61st, DIVISIONAL ARTILLERY ORDER NO: 138 of 13.8.18.

Reference above Order, para. 2, line 2 :

    For "14.8.18."

    Read "15.8.18."

ACKNOWLEDGE.

                          Spencer Bulcher
                          for Capt. R.A.,
                    Bde. Maj., 61 Div. Artillery.

14.8.18.

To all recipients of 61 D.A. Order No. 138.

SECRET   War Diary   Copy No: 24

61st. DIVISIONAL ARTILLERY ORDER NO: 139.

13th. August, 1916.

1. In order to facilitate the gradual establishment of a system of Infantry Posts to form a Bridge-head on the Eastern side of the PLATE BECQUE, on the front of the Left Infantry Brigade between BRIDGE HOUSE - K.16.d.18.63 - and the Northern Divisional Boundary through VIERHOUCK, the Artillery will by bombardment, barrages and harassing fire, weaken the enemy defences in the area.

2. Maps showing areas to be dealt with is attached.

3. At noon daily the Artillery programme will be issued giving tasks for 24 hours from 8 p.m. to 8 p.m. following day.

4. Groups will be notified by wire of any special tasks ordered by R.A. XI Corps.

5. Arrangements are being made for cooperation of C.H.A.

6. ACKNOWLEDGE.

P. Nye.
Capt. R.A.,
Bde.Maj., 61 Div. Artillery.

Issued at 3.30 p.m.

DISTRIBUTION.

Copy No:	1 - 5.	Right Group.
	6 - 14.	Left Group.
	15.	R.A. XI Corps.
	16.	59th. Div. Art.
	17.	31st. Div. Art.
	18.	74th. Div. Art.
	19.	61 Div. 'G'.
	20.	H.A. XI Corps.
	21.	C.B.S.O.
	22.	28th. Bde. R.G.A.
	23.	61 D.T.M.O.
	24 - 25.	War Diary.
	26.	File.

SECRET.   War Diary   Copy No: 24

61st. DIVISIONAL ARTILLERY INSTRUCTIONS NO: 1.

R.A.C.1 - 13.8.18.

Reference 61st. Div. Artillery Order No.139 of 13.8.18.

Tasks for 24 hours, 8 p.m. 13.8.18 to 8 p.m. 14.8.18, will be as follows :-

1. **HARASSING FIRE - NIGHT.**
   Normal harassing fire will be carried out night 13/14th. instant.

2. **BARRAGE.**
   At 4.20 a.m. 14.8.18, Left Group will carry out following barrage :-

   (a) 6 - 18-pr. Batteries :
       Starting Line, the PLATE BECQUE from K.16.d.2.6. to K.16.b.70.65.

       Zero to plus 2 mins.   Starting line.   Ammn: AX 101 Fuze.
       plus 2 to plus 4 "   Lift 100 yds.   "   AX 106   "
       plus 4 to plus 6 "   Lift 100 yds.   "   A 30% graze.
       plus 6 to plus 10 "   Starting line   "   50% AX 101 Fuze
                                                     50% A.

       Rates of Fire :
       Zero to plus 2 mins.   Intense.
       Plus 2 to plus 6 mins.   Rapid.
       "   6 "   " 10 "   Intense.
       Stop.

   (b) 2 - 4.5" Howitzer Batteries:
       Zero to plus 10 mins. Standing barrage from K.16.d.3.5. to KENNET FARM.

       Rate of fire - Rapid.

       Ammunition   - BX 106 Fuze.

   (c) 6" Trench Mortars will cooperate under orders of D.T.M.O.

3. **BOMBARDMENTS & HARASSING FIRE - DAY.**

   (a) 18-prs. will harass the area barraged at intervals during the day.

   (b) 4.5" Hows. will bombard areas A & B. Time as convenient between 5 a.m. and 8 p.m., ammunition 200 rounds, and will harass areas C, E, J & Q. at intervals during the day.

   (c) Trench Mortars programme will be arranged by D.T.M.O.

4. The 6" Howitzers are firing 100 rounds on both BRIDGE HOUSE and KENNET FARM.

5. No troops will be within 400 yards of BRIDGE HOUSE or KENNET FARM between 5 a.m. and 8 p.m.

6. ACKNOWLEDGE.

J.P. Wys
Capt. R.A.
Bde. Maj., 61 Div. Artillery.

13.8.18.

P.T.O.

DISTRIBUTION.

Copy No.	1 - 5.	Right Group.
	6 - 14.	Left Group.
	15.	R.A. XI Corps.
	16.	59th. Div. Art.
	17.	31st. Div. Art.
	18.	74th. Div. Art.
	19.	61 Div. 'G'.
	20.	H.A. XI Corps.
	21.	C.B.S.O.
	22.	28 Bde. R.G.A.
	23.	61 D.T.M.O.
	24 - 25.	War Diary.
	26.	File.

MESSAGES AND SIGNALS.

Army Form C. 2121.
(In pads of 100.)

Prefix	Code	m.	Words	Charge	This message is on a/c of:	Recd. at ...... m.
Office of Origin and Service Instructions.			Sent		.... Service.	Date ....
....			At .... m.			From ....
....			To		(Signature of "Franking Officer.")	By ....
			By			

TO { Right Group
      Left Group
      61 Division G (for information) }

Sender's Number.	Day of Month.	In reply to Number.	AAA
G.S.734	13		

Concentration	to-day	13th	May inst
1	1.40 p.m.	rapid	B
5 minutes	rapid	C north	A to B
2	2.50 p.m.	ditto	B
3 minutes	rapid	ditto	B
3.31 p.m.	rapid	J	1 round
gun	4	4.41 p.m.	HILTON
MILL	5.1 p.m.	5 minutes	rapid
3	5 p.m.	min	road
7 M.G.	5 minutes	rapid	ewep
A to B	at	100 yards	a
minute	6	7 p.m.	rate
A	1 round	crash	7
8.10 p.m.	gun	A	1 round
crash	8	11.50 p.m.	gun
A	1 round	crash	are
night	where	possible	

From	61	Div.	Arty.
Place			
Time			

The above may be forwarded as now corrected.   (Z)   F.P.Wye.

Censor.   Signature of Addressor or person authorised to telegraph in his name.

* This line should be erased if not required.

War Diary

SECRET.   Copy No: 29

61st. DIVISIONAL ARTILLERY ORDER NO: 140.

Ref: Sheet 36A.N.E.
     1:30,000.

1. The 61st. Divisional Artillery is responsible for
N.F., A.N.F. and G.F. calls in the following area :-

   Northern Boundary.
       Follows Corps Boundary from front line about
       K.11.b.8.4. to L.7.c.00.45.

   Southern Boundary.
       From front line along grid line through K.34 and
       K.35.central to K.36.a.0.0.

   Eastern Boundary.
       L.7.c.00.45. - L.19.c.0.0. - K.24.c.0.0. - K.36.a.0.0.

   Boundary between Right & Left Groups.
       LA MOTTE - MERVILLE Road to K.29.a.0.9. - K.29.b.0.0.
       to K.30.a.0.0.

2.   ACKNOWLEDGE.

                                          F.P. Nye
                                          Capt. R.A.,
                                Bde.Maj., 61 Div. Artillery.

14-8-18

DISTRIBUTION.

      Copy No: 1 - 5.   Right Group.
               6 - 14.   Left Group.
              15.   C.B.S.O.
              16.   R.A. XI Corps.
              17.   H.A. XI Corps.
              18.   59th. Div. Art.
              19.   31st. Div. Art.
              20.   74th. Div. Art.
              21.   42nd. Squadron, R.A.F.
              22.   A.L.O., 42nd. Sqn. R.A.F.
              23.   28th. Bde. R.G.A.
              24.   40th. Balloon Coy. R.A.F.
              25.   5th. Observation Group.
              26.   'U' Section, Sound Rangers.
              27.   61st. Div. 'G'.
              28 - 29.   War Diary.
              30.   File.

SECRET.   Copy No: 24

61st. DIVISIONAL ARTILLERY INSTRUCTIONS NO: 2.

14th. August, 1918.

Reference 61st. Divisional Artillery Order No.139 of 13.8.18.
Artillery tasks, 7 p.m. 14/8/18 to 8 p.m. 15/8/18, will be as follows :-

1. **BARRAGE. 14.8.18.**
   7.3 p.m. to 7.6 p.m. Left Group.
   From K.16.d.30.45 to K.16.b.90.45.
   Rate of Fire - Rapid.
   Ammunition :-   18-pr. A. 10% graze.
                   4.5" How. BX - 106 Fuze.

2. **HARASSING FIRE - NIGHT.**
   (a)   Normal harassing fire will be carried out during night 14/15th. inst.

   (b)   Normal amount of ammunition to be expended on night harassing fire will be 15 rounds per gun.

3. **BARRAGE. 15.8.18.**
   At 4.20 a.m. 15.8.18, Left Group will carry out the following barrage :-
   (a)   6 - 18-pr. Batteries :
   Starting line from K.16.b.80.75 to K.11.c.95.25.

   Zero to plus 2 mins.   Starting line - Ammn. 106 Fuze.
   Plus 2 mins. to plus 4 mins. Lifts 100 yds.   "   "
      " 4 "   "   "   6 "   "   100 "   "   A. 10% graze.
      " 6 "   "   " 10 "   Starting line.   "   A. "   "
   Stop.

   (b)   2 - 4.5" Howitzer Batteries:

   Zero to Zero plus 10 mins. Standing Barrage from K.17.a.3.6. to
                                                    K.17.b.2.9.
   Rate of fire - Rapid.
   Ammunition -   BX. 106.

4. **BOMBARDMENTS & HARASSING FIRE - DAY.**
   LEFT GROUP.
   (a)   18-prs. will harass the area barraged, and areas J & C, at intervals during the day.
      4.5" Hows. will bombard houses in areas E - 150 rounds, and F - 50 rounds, and will harass areas C & W at intervals.

   (b)   T.M. programme as arranged by D.T.M.O.

5. 6" Howitzers are firing 150 rounds on group of ruins area 'D' during the day.

6. Groups and D.T.M.O. to acknowledge.

Spencer Batchelor
for Capt. R.A.,
Bde. Maj., 61 Div. Artillery.

DISTRIBUTION - As for 61 D.A. Instructions No.1.

SECRET.   Copy No: 24

61st. DIVISIONAL ARTILLERY INSTRUCTIONS NO: 3.

War Diary

15th. August, 1918.

Reference 61st. Divisional Artillery Order No.139 of 13.8.18.
Artillery Tasks, 8 p.m. 15.8.18 to 8 p.m. 16.8.18, will be as follows :-

1. **HARASSING FIRE - NIGHT.**
   Normal harassing fire will be carried out during night 15/16th. instant.

2. **BARRAGE.** 16.8.18.
   At 4.20 a.m. Left Group will carry out following barrage :-
   (a)   6 - 18-pr. Batteries.
         Starting Line from K.11.d.0.3. to K.11.b.95.03.

Zero to Zero plus 2 mins.	Starting Line.	Ammn. AX 106.
Plus 2 mins. to " 4 "	Starting Line, plus 300 yds.	" 2/3rds. A 10% graze; 1/3rd. AX.106.
" 4 " " " 6 "	Starting line, plus 200 yds.	do. do.
" 6 " " " 8 "	Starting line, plus 100 yds.	do. do.
" 8 " " "10 "	Starting line.	do. do.

   Rate of fire - Rapid.

   (b)   2 - 4.5" How. Batteries.

Zero to plus 2 mins	Area F to S.	Ammn: BX 106 throughout.
Plus 2 mins. to plus 4 mins.	K to K.17.c.7.7.	
" 4 " " " 6 "	U to M.	
" 6 " " "10 "	D to E.	

   Rate of fire - Rapid.

3. **BOMBARDMENT.**
   LEFT GROUP.
   (a)   4.5" Howitzers will bombard areas F, G & S.
         Ammunition - 100 rounds per area.
   (b)   6" T.Ms. will fire 50 rounds on area H, under arrangements to be made by D.T.M.O.

4. **HARASSING FIRE - DAY.**
   LEFT GROUP.
   18-prs. will harass the areas A, J, C, D, at intervals during the day.

5. 6" Hows. are firing 100 rounds on Area E and on area L.

6. Our trenches are not being cleared on 16.8.18.

7. Groups and D.T.M.O. to acknowledge.

                                    F.P.Wye.
                                    Capt. R.A.,
15.8.1918.   Bde.Maj., 61st. Div. Artillery.

Distribution as for 61 D.A. Instructions No.1.

SECRET.   Copy No: ..24..

61st. DIVISIONAL ARTILLERY INSTRUCTIONS NO: 4.

16th. August, 1918.

Reference 61st. Divisional Artillery Order No.139.
Artillery Tasks, 8 p.m. 16.8.18 to 8 p.m. 17.8.18, will be as follows :-

1. **HARASSING FIRE - NIGHT.**
   Normal harassing fire will be carried out during night 16/17th. inst.

2. **BARRAGE - 17.8.18.**
   At 6 a.m. Left Group will carry out the following barrage :-
   (a) <u>6 - 18-pr. Batteries.</u>

Zero to plus 4 mins.	K.16.d.15.45 to K.16.b.80.45.	Ammn. AX.106 Fuze.
Plus 4 mins to Plus 6	Lift 100 yards.	" A 10% graze.
" 6 " " " 8	Lift 100 "	" " " "
" 8 " " " 12	K.17.a.0.4. to K.17.b.1.9.	" AX. 106 Fuze.
" 12 " " " 14	Lift 100 yards.	" A. 10% graze.
" 14 " " " 16	" 100 "	" A. " "

   Rate of fire - Rapid.

   (b) <u>2 4.5" How. Batteries.</u>
   As per attached Tracing.
   Ammunition 106 Fuze BX.
   Rate of fire - Rapid.

3. **BOMBARDMENT.**
   LEFT GROUP.
   (a) 4.5" Hows. will bombard areas A, C, D, J.
   50 rounds on each.
   (b) 6" T.Ms. will fire under arrangements to be made by D.T.M.O.

4. **HARASSING FIRE - DAY.**
   LEFT GROUP.
   18-prs. will harass the areas F, G, H, S, at intervals during the day.

5. 6" Howitzers are firing 250 rounds on areas W, N, O, P, during the day. Firing to be finished by 7 p.m.

6. Our trenches will not be cleared on 17.8.18.

7. Groups and D.T.M.O. to acknowledge.

F.P.Wye.

Capt. R.A.,
Bde.Maj., 61 Div. Artillery.

<u>DISTRIBUTION</u> as usual.

			K	L
		4.5 Howitzer Barrage 6 a.m. to 6.16 a.m. 17.8.18		
		11	12	
			18	
		+11. +9. +11. +10. +12. +9. +16. +8. +12. +9. +7. +9. +12. +10. +5. +9. +8. +6. Zero +2. +4.	Sheet No 36 A N.E. 1.20.000 Reference :- 61. D.A. Instructions No 4 of 16.8.18

S E C R E T.   Copy No: 24

61st. DIVISIONAL ARTILLERY INSTRUCTIONS NO: 5.

Reference 61st. Divisional Artillery Order No.139.

Artillery Tasks, 8 p.m. 17.8.18 to 8 p.m. 18.8.18.

1. HARASSING FIRE - NIGHT.
   Normal harassing fire will be carried out during night 17th/18th. instant.

2. BARRAGE - 18.8.18.
   From 4.45 a.m. to 5 a.m., Left Group will carry out the barrage shown on attached tracing.
   Ammunition - 18-prs.
      Zero to plus 14 mins.   AX.106.
      Plus 14 to plus 15 mins. A Smoke (if wind favourable.)
   Rate of fire - RAPID.

   Ammunition - 4.5" Hows. - BX.106 throughout.
   Rate of fire - RAPID.

3. BOMBARDMENT.

   (a) 4.5" Howitzers, Left Group, will bombard areas J, C, W, O,- 50 rounds on each.

   (b) 6" NEWTON T.Ms., Area F, and 2 houses about K.17.a.65.90. - 30 rounds each.

4. HARASSING FIRE - DAY.
   Left Group will harass areas N, W, O, P, Q, with 18-prs. at intervals during the day.

5. 6" Howitzers are firing 50 rounds on each of the following areas: D, L, E, G, S.

6. None of our trenches or posts are being cleared on 18.8.18.

7. Groups and D.T.M.O. to acknowledge.

                                        F.P.WYE
                                        Capt. R.A.,
                                        Bde.Major, 61 Div. Artillery.

16.8.1918.

DISTRIBUTION as for 61st. D.A. Instructions No.1.

K.

4.5 Hows Left Group

ZERO to +4'
+4' to +8'
+8 to +12'
+12 to +15'

+13' to +15'
+10' to +13'
+7 to +10'
+4 to +7'
+2 to +4'
0 to +2'

16

22   23

To accompany 61 D.A. Instructions Nº 5   Sheet 36ª N.E
4.5" How. Barrage —   1/20.000
18 Pdr.   "   —

War Diary

S E C R E T.

R.A.G.1/1.

AMENDMENT NO: 1
to
61st. DIVISIONAL ARTILLERY INSTRUCTIONS NO: 5.
of 17.8.18.

1. Paras. 3, 4, 5, & 6 are cancelled.

 There will be no artillery fire within 800 yards of the PLATE BECQUE between 5 a.m. and 7 p.m. 18.8.18., except in case of S.O.S. or at special request of the Infantry.

2. Groups and D.T.M.O. to acknowledge.

F.P. Wye.
Capt. R.A.,
Bde.Maj., 61 Div. Artillery.

17.8.18.

To all recipients of 61 D.A. Instructions No.5.

War Diary

S E C R E T.   R.A.G.1/1.

To all recipients of
61 D.A. Instructions No. 6
of 18.8.1918.
----

1.   61st. Divisional Artillery Instructions No.6 of 18.8.1918 are cancelled with the exception of para.1, Harassing Fire - Night.

2.   Groups and D.T.M.O. to acknowledge.

F.P.WYE.

Capt. R.A.,
Bde.Maj., 61 Div.Artillery.

18.8.1918.

SECRET.   War Diary   Copy No: 24

61st. DIVISIONAL ARTILLERY INSTRUCTIONS NO: 6.

Reference 61st. Divisional Artillery Order No.139.

Artillery Tasks 8 p.m. 18.8.18 to 8 p.m. 19.8.18.

1. **HARASSING FIRE - NIGHT.**
    Normal harassing fire will be carried out during night 18/19th. instant.

2. **BARRAGE - 19.8.18.**
    (a) From 4.45 a.m. to 5.1 a.m. Left Group 18-pr. Batteries will carry out the barrage shown on attached tracing.

    Ammunition :
    Zero to plus 4 mins.   AX delay fuze.
    Plus 4 mins. to plus 16 mins. A 10% graze.
    Rate of fire :
    Zero to plus 4 mins.   Rapid.
    Plus 4 mins. to plus 14 mins. Normal.
    " 14 "   "   "   16 "   Rapid.

    (b) 4.5" How. Batteries, Left Group, will at the same time concentrate on areas as follows :-
    Zero to plus 4 mins.   Areas D & E.
    Plus 4 mins. to plus 8 mins.   "   K & L.
    "   8 "   "   " 12 "   "   Q, X & Y.
    " 12 "   "   " 16 "   "   Z & V.

    Ammunition: BX.
    Rate of Fire :
    Zero to plus 4 mins.   Rapid.
    Plus 4 mins. to plus 14 mins. Normal.
    " 14 "   "   "   16 "   Rapid.

3. **BOMBARDMENT.**
    (a) 4.5" Howitzers, Left Group, will bombard areas J, C, W, O 50 rounds on each.

    (b) 6" NEWTON T.Ms., Area F, and 2 houses about K.17.a.65.90. 30 rounds each.

4. **HARASSING FIRE - DAY.**
    Left Group will harass areas N, W, O, P, Q, with 18-prs. at intervals during the day.

5. 6" Howitzers are firing 50 rounds on each of the following areas: D, L, E, G, S.

6. None of our trenches or posts are being cleared on 19.8.18.

7. Groups and D.T.M.O. to acknowledge.

A.P.Wye.
Capt. R.A.,
Bde.Maj., 61 Div. Artillery.

18.8.1918.

DISTRIBUTION as for 61st. D.A. Instructions No.1.

REFERENCE of D.A. Instructions No 6
18 Pdr. Barrage 19-8-18
Sheet 36A N.E.   1/10,000

Reference 61.D.A. Instructions N°6
18 Pdr. Barrage 19-8-18
Sheet 36A. N.E. 1/20,000

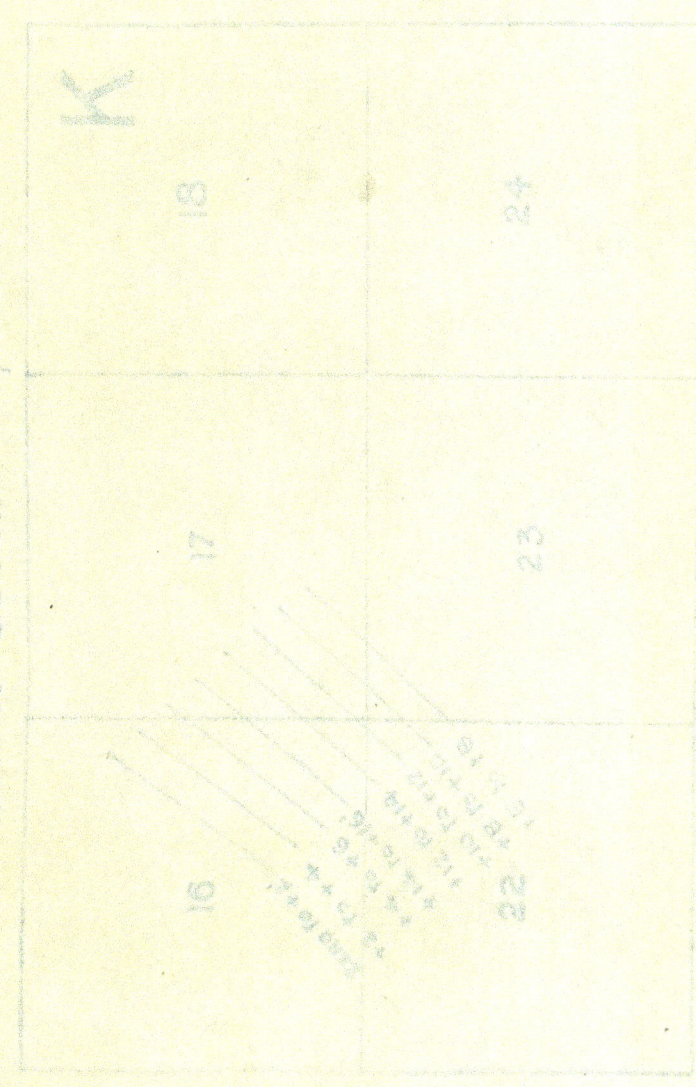

War Diary

SECRET.   Copy No: 22

61st. DIVISIONAL ARTILLERY INSTRUCTIONS NO: 7.

1. **AMMUNITION.**

   In the event of hostile gas shelling prior to or during an attack, rendering the setting of fuzes for time shrapnel difficult, 106 fuzes with H.E. will be used.

   For this purpose a reserve of 100 H.E. with No.106 fuzes will be kept with every 18-pr. in action, not to be drawn upon except in case of emergency.

2. Groups to ACKNOWLEDGE.

[signature]

Major,
for Bde.Maj., 61 Div. Artillery.

19.8.1918.

Copy No:		
1 - 5.	Right Group.	19. R.A. XI Corps.
6 -14.	Left Group.	20. 31st. Div. Art.
15 -17.	D.A.C.	21. 74th. Div. Art.
18.	D.T.M.O.	22-23. War Diary.
19.	61 Div. 'G'.	24. File.

(Copies for War Diary)

Right Group.

B.M.13/23   18

Detail one Section of A/307 to take up advanced positions in following area K.25 - K.26 - K.30 - K.31 or K.32 during to-night or tomorrow morning 19th inst, time to be selected by you aaa Report new location of section to RUBU and to this office aaa Confirming telephone conversation

From WUGU.

                              (Sd.)   F.WYE.
                                     Capt.

SECRET.   Copy No: ....

61st. DIVISIONAL ARTILLERY ORDER NO: 141.

20th. Aug. 1918.

1. (a) The Division is now on the General Line K.36.b.0.5. - COLLEGE K.23.d.5.6. thence road running North of VIERHOUCK - in touch with 74th. Division on the right and 31st. Division on the left.

   (b) The enemy is withdrawing, but it is uncertain to what position he has decided to retire.

2. The 74th. Division has been ordered to advance and to endeavour to reach the line of the LAWE River to-day.

3. The Advance Guard of the Division composed as under :

   G.O.C. 183rd. Inf. Bde.
   A & C Batteries, 296 Bde. R.F.A.
   1 Section D/296 Bde. R.F.A.
   2 Secs. F.Co.R.E.
   1 M.G.Co.
   183rd. Inf. Bde.
   Portion of Field Ambulance.

   will push forward boldly and endeavour to establish itself on the General Line LOUNGE House - (L.32.b.6.8.) - CHAPELLE DUVELLE - TROMPE Bridge - RUE MONTIGNY to-day.
   Touch will be established with the 74th. Division on the Right, but G.O.C. 183rd. Inf. Bde. will be responsible for forming a Defensive Flank protecting his own left.
   If the enemy is not encountered the Advance Guard will continue the forward movement within the boundaries allotted to the Division until touch with the enemy is established.
   Boundaries are as follows :-
   Southern Boundary - The LYS Canal.
   Northern Boundary - VIERHOUCK - COCHIN CORNER (excl.) - L.15.a.0.0. - thence along grid line due East.

4. O.C. 296th. Brigade, R.F.A. will command the Advance Guard Artillery and will report at once to G.O.C. 183rd. Inf. Bde.

5. C.R.A. 59th. Division will take over command of Left Group (less Units of 296 Bde. R.F.A. mentioned in para.3) from O.C. 296th. Bde. R.F.A., forthwith.

6. (a) The two rear Sections of B & D Batteries, 295 Bde. R.F.A. will move forward and join their Advanced Sections in action, in accordance with verbal orders given by C.R.A. to O.C. Left Group this afternoon.

   (b) No other Artillery moves will take place for the present, the policy being for the Artillery units other than those mentioned in para.3, to remain covering the Main Line of Retention.

   (c) Where possible Groups will be prepared to put down a barrage to protect the advancing Infantry.

- 1 -

P.T.O.

7. All remain Units of the Division are standing fast, except that one Battalion 184 Inf. Bde. will move to the Main Line of Retention of the Left Section vacated by 183 Inf. Bde. and will come temporarily under the orders of G.O.C. 183rd. Inf. Bde.

8. The Main Line of Retention remains as at present.

9. The 59th. Divisional Artillery will arrange ammunition supply for Advance Guard Artillery.

10. ACKNOWLEDGE.

F.P.WYE.

Capt. R.A.,
Bde.Maj., 61 Div. Artillery.

Issued at 7.15 p.m.

DISTRIBUTION.

Copy No.	
1 - 8.	59th. Div. Art.
9 - 13.	Right Group.
14 - 17.	O.C. Adv: Guard Artillery.
18.	183rd. Inf. Bde.
19.	61.Div. 'G'.
20.	61 Div. 'Q'
21.	R.A. XI Corps.
22.	31st. Div. Art.
23.	74th. Div. Art.
24.	XI Corps H.A.
25.	XI C.B.S.O.
26.	42nd. Squad: R.A.F.
27.	A.L.O. 42 Squad.R.A.F.
28.	5th. Observation Group.
29.	'U' Sound Rangers.
30 - 31.	War Diary.
32.	File
33.	61 D.T.M.O.
34.	61 D.A.C.
35.	28th. Bde. R.G.A.
36.	40th. Balloon Coy.R.A.F.

War Diary

SECRET.   Copy No: 35

61st. DIVISIONAL ARTILLERY ORDER NO: 142.

Ref: Map 36A. 1:40,000.   22.8.1918.

1. The following moves are taking place to-day, August 22nd. and to-night Aug. 22/23rd.
   They will be completed by dawn 23rd. August.

   (a) The 184 Infantry Brigade will take over and be responsible for the defence of the Main Line of Retention, with Brigade Headquarters at J.4.c.7.5.
   1 Battalion will occupy the Right Section with 2 Coys. in the Line and 2 Coys. in Support in K.13.c. and d.
   1 Battalion will occupy the Left Section with 2 Coys. in the Line, and 2 Coys. in Support about CHAPRILLE BOOM.
   1 Battalion will be in reserve at SPRESIANO CAMP.

   (b) The 182 Infantry Brigade will be withdrawn into Reserve and will be disposed as follows :-

Brigade Headquarters	- STEENBECQUE.
1 Battalion	- do,
1 Battalion	- VILLORBA CAMP.
1 Battalion	- LA LACQUE.

   (c) The O.C., 61st. Machine Gun Battalion will detail one Company for the Defence of the Main Line of Retention under the orders of the G.O.C., 184 Infantry Brigade.
   The remaining 2 Coys. and Bn.H.Qrs. will be at HAVERSKERQUE

2. The Right and Left Groups, 61 Div. Artillery (less Batteries attached to Advance Guard Infantry Brigade) will be at the disposal of G.O.C. 184 Infantry Brigade for purposes of Artillery support in event of emergency.

3. Each Group will keep a senior liaison officer with 184 Inf. brigade, and also a liaison officer with the Battalion which they cover.

4. ACKNOWLEDGE.

                                           F.P. Wye
                                           Capt. R.A.,
                                    Bde.Maj., 61 Div. Artillery.

Issued at 6.30 pm.

DISTRIBUTION.

Copy No.				
1 - 8.	59th. Div. Art.		27.	A.L.O. 42 Squad. RAF
9 - 13.	Right Group.		28.	5th. Observation Gp:
14 - 17.	O.C. Adv:Guard Arty.		29.	'U' Sound Rangers.
18.	183rd. Inf. Bde.		30.	61 D.T.M.O.
19.	61 Div. 'G'		31.	61 D.A.C.
20.	61 Div. 'Q'		32.	28 Bde. R.G.A.
21.	R.A. XI Corps.		33.	40 Balloon Coy. RAF
22.	31st. Div. Art.		34.	184 Inf. Bde.
23.	74th. Div. Art.		35-36.	War Diary.
24.	H.A. XI Corps.		37.	File.
25.	C.B.S.O.			
26.	42nd. Squad. R.A.F.			

SECRET.   61st. D.A. No.R.G.1.

61st. DIVISIONAL ARTILLERY GROUP.

LOCATION STATEMENT - 22.8.1918.

Ref: Sheet 36A.

Group.	Unit.	Location.	Wagon Lines.	Fwd. Wagon Lines.
	61st. R.A.H.Q.	I.20.a.3.4.		
RIGHT GROUP. O.C.307 Bde.RFA.	H.Q. 307 Bde.	J.21.a.20.60.	I.36.d.20.10.	
	A/307 (4 guns) (2 ")	J.29.c.30.80. J.30.d.60.20.	I.27.d.90.20.	
	B/307. (4 ")	J.23.c.50.60. J.30.d.50.80.	I.35.d.30.70.	
	C/307. (4 ") (2 ")	J.35.d.30.00. K.31.a.70.90.	I.29.a.40.40.	
	D/307. (5 Hows) (1 ")	J.30.a.60.80. K.26.c.50.08.	J.31.b.60.30.	
LEFT GROUP. C.R.A. 59 D.A.	H.Q.	D.30.c.80.60.	I.11.b.30.60.	
	A/295. (4 guns) (2 ")	E.19.a.80.80. E.20.a.95.10.	C.16.d.30.30.	D.26.b.95.75.
	B/295. (6 ")	K.2.d.40.70.	C.28.d.80.60.	D.27.a.10.50.
	C/295. (4 ") (2 ")	J.12.a.70.75. K.14.b.18.35.	C.27.d.50.30.	D.25.b.00.10.
	D/295. (6 Hows)	E.26.d.40.00.	C.16.d.80.80.	D.26.d.15.80.
	B/296. (6 guns)	K.2.c.80.75.	I.3.d.30.40.	K.14.a.80.35.
	D/296. (4 Hows)	K.13.a.28.40.	I.11.a.20.60.	J.8.a.20.20.
ADVANCE GUARD ARTY: Attd:183 Inf.Bde.	A/296. (4 guns) (2 ")	K.22.d.2.9. K.9.central.	D.26.d.70.30.	K.14.a.85.40.
	C/296. (4 ") (2 ")	K.21.a.95.05. K.14.b.7.9.	I.6.d.00.40.	K.8.c.40.45.
	D/296. (2 Hows.)	K.22.d.2.4.	I.11.a.20.60.	J.8.a.20.20.

61 D.T.M.O. H.Q.		I.16.c.20.20.	59 D.T.M.O. HQ.	C.30.d.80.05.
Y/61 T.M.B. HQ.		K.13.b.80.80.	59 T.M.B. HQ.	K.8.d.05.65.
" (1 6" NEWTON)		K.21.b.2.3.	(2 6" NEWTONS)	K.11.a.35.35.
" (1 ")		K.25.b.45.50.	(2 ")	K.10.d.15.95.
" (1 ")		K.25.b.45.55.	(1 ")	K.10.b.20.00.
" (1 ")		M.28.d.2.3.	(2 ")	K.16.a.10.20.
			(1 ")	K.16.a.05.10.
			(2 ")	K.15.d.35.40.
			(1 ")	K.15.d.20.55.
61st. D.A.C. H.Q.		I.8.c.5.0.	306 Bde.RFA.H.Q.	P.1.b.35.15.
59th. D.A.C. H.Q.		I.5.b.5.3.	(Under orders of C.R.A. 74 D.A.	
			295 Bde.RFA.H.Q.	C.16.c.8.9.

22.8.1918.

Lieut. R.A.,
R.O., 61st. Div. Artillery.

SECRET.   Copy No:........ 36

            61st. DIVISIONAL ARTILLERY ORDER NO: 143.

Ref: Map sheet 36A.N.E. 1:20,000.   23rd. Aug. 1918.

1.   The front at present held by the Division will be extended to
   the North to the grid line K.4.central - L.5.central - thence in
   a straight line to G.11.a.0.0.
        This line will form the Northern administrative and tactical
   boundary of XI Corps and 61 Division.

2.   The left defensive flank of the line as at present held by the
   Advance Guard Brigade will be brought forward, in continuation of
   the front line, to the boundary above described.

3.   120th. Infantry Brigade, 40th. Division, on the left, established itself on night 22/23rd. on the line of the road COCHIN CORNER
   (L.7.c.8.2.) inclusive - PONT RONDIN, and to-day, 23/8/18, at 4 p.m.
   will move forward from the above road and establish itself on the
   line BISHOP'S CORNER (L.3.a.5.0.) - BECKET CORNER (F.26.central).

4.   At the same hour, the Advanced Guard Brigade will extend to
   the North-East in co-operation with 120th. Infantry Brigade, and
   will push forward strong battle patrols to the line NEUF BERQUIN -
   RUE MONTIGNY - X Roads L.3.c.8.5. - BISHOP'S CORNER L.3.c.5.0.

5.   On completion of the above operation, or at such a time as may
   be notified later, responsibility for the area south of the new
   boundary line will be assumed by G.O.C. 61 Division.

6.   XI Corps Counter-Battery and harassing fire boundary will run
   due East from L.14.central, from midnight 23/24th. August.

7.   The Artillery of XV Corps, now covering the new front, will
   continue to do so until 10 a.m. August 24th.

8.   The present dispositions of 61 Div.Art. will remain in force
   until further notice.

9.   ACKNOWLEDGE.

                                            F.P.Wye.
                                            Capt. R.A.,
                                            Bde.Maj., 61 Div.Artillery.
Issued at 12 noon

                              DISTRIBUTION.

Copy No. 1 - 8. 59th. Div. Art.   26.   42nd. Squad.R.A.F.
         9 - 13. Right Group.   27.   A.L.O. 42 Squad.R.A.F.
        14 - 17. O.C. Adv.Guard Arty.   28.   5th.Observation Group.
        18.   183rd. Inf. Bde.   29.   'U' Sounder Rangers.
        19.   61 Div. 'G'.   30.   61 D.T.M.O.
        20.   61 Div. 'Q'.   31.   61 D.A.C.
        21.   R.A. XI Corps.   32.   28 Bde.R.G.A.
        22.   31st. Div. Art.   33.   40 Balloon Coy.R.A.F.
        23.   74th. Div. Art.   34.   184 Inf. Bde.
        24.   H.A. XI Corps.   35-36. War Diary.
        25.   C.B.S.O.   37.   File.

War Diary

S E C R E T.   Copy No. 36

61st. DIVISIONAL ARTILLERY ORDER NO: 144.

Ref. Map 36A. 1/40,000.   23rd. Aug. 1918.

1. The 184th. Infantry Brigade is relieving the 183rd. Infantry Brigade in the Advance Guard Brigade Area on the nights 24/25th and 25/26th August, as under :-

   (a) One battalion 184th Infantry Brigade will relieve one battalion 183rd Infantry Bde. on the night 24/25th. Aug.
       (The battalion of 184th Inf. Bde. located in the Advance Guard Brigade Area will come under the orders of G.O.C. 183rd Inf. Bde. until completion of relief.
       Similarly, the battalion of 183rd Inf. Bde. located in the Intermediate Brigade area will come under the orders of G.O.C. 184th. Inf. Bde.)

   (b) Remainder of 184th Inf. Bde. will relieve remainder of 183rd Inf. Bde. on the night 25/26th. inst.

2. On relief, the 183rd. Inf. Bde. will take over the dispositions of 184th. Inf. Bde. and be responsible for the defence of the Main Line of Retention.

3. The nucleus garrison of four companies will be maintained in the Main Line of Retention during the relief.

4. The G.O.C. 184 Inf. Bde. will take over command of Advance Guard on completion of the above mentioned reliefs.

5. ACKNOWLEDGE.

                                        F.P. Wye.
                                        Capt. R.A.,
                                Bde. Maj., 61st. Div. Artillery.

Issued at 11 p.m.

DISTRIBUTION.

Copy No.	Recipient
1 - 8.	59th. Div. Art.
9 - 13.	Right Group.
14 - 17.	O.C. Adv: Guard Arty:
18.	183rd. Inf. Bde.
19.	61 Div. 'G'.
20.	61 Div. 'Q'.
21.	R.A. XI Corps.
22.	31st. Div. Art.
23.	74th. Div. Art.
24.	H.A. XI Corps.
25.	C.B.S.O.
26.	42nd. Squad, R.A.F.
27.	A.L.O. 42 Squad. R.A.F.
28.	5th. Observation Gp:
29.	'U' Sound Rangers.
30.	61 D.T.M.O.
31.	61 D.A.C.
32.	28th. Bde. R.G.A.
33.	40 Balloon Coy. R.A.F.
34.	184th. Inf. Bde.
35 - 36.	War Diary.
37.	File.

War Diary

SECRET.   Copy No: 26

61st. DIVISIONAL ARTILLERY INSTRUCTIONS NO: 8.

23rd. Aug. 1918.

1. **AMMUNITION.**

    (a)   Group Commanders will arrange for all vacated Field Battery positions in their area to be cleared of ammunition, except as stated in para.1 (b).

    (b)   Group Commanders may at their discretion order 100 rounds per gun, boxed ammunition, to be maintained at those positions covering the MAIN LINE OF RETENTION, to which their forward units would be withdrawn in the event of a defensive action.
    A list of these positions and any alterations will be sent to Staff Captain, R.A., 61 Division.

2. ACKNOWLEDGE.

                                            F.P.Nye
                                            Capt. R.A.,
                                    Bde.Maj., 61 Div. Artillery.

DISTRIBUTION.

Copy No.		
1 - 5.	Right Group.
6 - 13.	Left Group.
14 - 16.	O.C. Adv: Guard Arty.
17 - 18.	61 D.A.C.
19.	61 D.P.M.O.
20.	61 Div. 'G'.
21.	61 Div. 'Q'.
22.	R.A. XI Corps.
23.	31 Div. Art.
24.	74th. Div. Art.
25 - 26.	War Diary.
27.	File.

(Copies for War Diary)

Left Group.
61 Div. 'G'.

B.M.19/24   24

Advance C and D Batteries 296 Bde. R.F.A. to new positions within 5000 yards of present front outpost line aaa Batteries to move forward by sections each section to be completely in action before move of next section commences aaa Addressed Left Group repeated 61 Divn. 'G'.

From WUGU.

War Diary

SECRET.   Copy No: 40

61st. DIVISIONAL ARTILLERY ORDER NO: 145.

25th. Aug. 1918.

1. The 306th. Brigade, R.F.A., will relieve 296 Brigade, R.F.A. to-night 25/26th. instant, in accordance with Table attached.

2. The 18-pr. Anti-Tank gun on charge of 296 Bde. R.F.A. will be taken over by 306th. Bde. R.F.A. who will provide the necessary guard and will be prepared to find detachments in case of emergency.

3. Details of relief to be arranged between Units concerned.

4. B/306 (less 1 Section) and D/306 (less 1 Section) will come under orders of O.C. Left Group, on completion of relief.

5. Completion of relief to be wired to this office by code word "PAPER".

6. Administrative instructions attached.

7. ACKNOWLEDGE.

                                    Captain R.A.,
                        Bde. Maj., 61 Div. Artillery.

Issued at 7 p.m.

DISTRIBUTION.

Copy No.	Recipient
1 - 8.	59th. Div. Art.
9 - 13.	Right Group.
14 - 17.	O.C. Adv: Guard Arty.
18 - 22.	306th. Bde. R.F.A.
23.	183rd. Inf. Bde.
24.	184 Inf. Bde.
25.	61 Div. 'G'.
26.	61 Div. 'Q'.
27.	R.A. XI Corps.
28.	31st. Div. Art.
29.	74th. Div. Art.
30.	H.A. XI Corps.
31.	C.B.S.O.
32.	42nd. Squad. R.A.F.
33.	A.L.O. 42 Squad. R.A.F.
34.	5th. Observation Group.
35.	'U' Sound Rangers.
36.	61 D.T.M.O.
37.	61 D.A.C.
38.	28th. Bde. R.G.A.
39.	40th. Balloon Coy. R.A.F.
40 - 41.	War Diary.
42.	File.

P.T.O.

TABLE ISSUED WITH 61st. DIVISIONAL ARTILLERY ORDER NO.745.

Serial No.	Relieving Unit.	Unit relieved.	Remarks.
1.	H.Q. 306 Brigade.	H.Q. 296 Bde.	O.C. 306th. Brigade becomes O.C. Advanced Guard Artillery on completion of relief.
2.	A/306.	A/296.	A/296 on relief proceeds to Wagon Lines.
3.	C/306.	C/296.	C/296 " " "
4.	1 Section D/306.	1 Section D/296.	Sect. D/296 " " "
5.	B/306 (less 1 Section)	B/296.	To action at J.6.a.7.7. (1 Section remains in new wagon lines for Training.) Withdraws to Wagon Lines.
6.	D/306 (less 1 Section.)	D/296 (less 1 Section.)	To action at J.11.c.14.22. Withdraws to Wagon Lines.

306th Brigade
61st D.A.C.
59th D.A.
61st Division 'Q'

61st Div. Art. R.A.Q.539/2

Reference 61st Div. Art. Order No.145.

1. **AMMUNITION.**

306th Brigade will take over all ammunition in the Battery Positions taken over and occupied in the 59th Div Art Area.

Amounts taken over by natures by each Battery will be reported to these Headquarters as soon as possible. A.R.P's are as follows :-

(1). Dump at K.8.a.0.7. for Artillery covering Advanced Guard and B/306.

(2). D/306 draw by decauville railway to DUNCAN Station from 61st A.R.P. at LE FORET J.25.c.2.7.

Demands for ammunition to be sent to the Officer i/c 61st A.R.P. by 1-0pm for issue the following day.

2. **WAGON LINES.**

306th Brigade batteries will occupy lines adjoining the wagon lines of the corresponding battery of 296th Brigade tonight and occupy the wagon lines at present occupied by 296th Brigade on that Brigade marching out of the area.

They will take over all tents and area stores now on charge of 296th Brigade.

3. **SUPPLIES.**

Refilling Point is at PONT DE THIENNES I.21.a.7.3. at 11-0am tomorrow 26th, and until further orders.

4.

59th Div. Arty will forward to 61st Div. Arty a list of all dumps of ammunition in 59th Div Arty Area giving number of rounds and nature of ammunition left in each dump.

This will not include the ammunition taken over in Battery Positions occupied by any Section or Battery of 306th Brigade.

306th Brigade and 61st D.A.C. will report amount of ammunition brought into 61st Div. Area.

R.A.H.Q.
August 25th, 1918.

Major,
S.C.R.A., 61st Division.

SECRET.   Copy No: ....40....

61st. DIVISIONAL ARTILLERY ORDER NO: 146.

26th. Aug. 1918.

1. (a) The O.C. Right Group will take over command of the Artillery covering the MAIN LINE OF RETENTION at 8 p.m. on 26.8.18.

   (b) The Artillery covering the MAIN LINE OF RETENTION will then be known as the REAR GROUP.

2. On relief the H.Q. 59th. Div. Art. will go to STEENBECQUE.

3. (a) The 61st. D.T.M.O. will detail one Battery to take over T.M. positions covering Left Section MAIN LINE OF RETENTION from D.T.M.O. 59th.D.A., relief to be completed by 8 p.m. on 26.8.18.

   (b) Details to be arranged by D.T.M. Officers.

   (c) T.Ms. will not be exchanged.

   (d) On completion of relief, 61 T.M.Batteries will then be disposed as follows :-

   Right Section MAIN LINE OF RETENTION :.
   1 T.M. Battery, less 1 Section.

   Left Section MAIN LINE OF RETENTION :.
   1 T.M. Battery, less 1 Section.

4. 295 Brigade R.F.A., will withdraw from action to Wagon Lines on night 26/29th. at 8 p.m.
   All Battery Boards, aeroplane photos, secret maps, to be handed over to O.C. REAR GROUP.

5. (a) The advanced Sections of A and C Batteries will be withdrawn to their Main Battery Positions at J.29.c.8.8. and J.35.d.3.0. by 8 p.m. 26.8.18.

   (b) B/307 will move from present positions as follows :-
   4 guns to J.10.b.45.35.
   2 guns to J.11.b.6.4.
   Guns to be in action in new positions by 8 p.m. 26.8.18.

6. D.T.M.O. will send a N.C.O. and 2 men to take over portion of LA MOTTE CHATEAU from H.Q. 59th.D.A. on afternoon 26.8.18, and to remain as wardens.

7. O.C. REAR GROUP will arrange to send a senior Liaison Officer to 183 Infantry Brigade H.Q. and a liaison officer to each battalion covering the MAIN LINE OF RETENTION in the event of a battle.

8. Completion of reliefs to be wired to this office by code word "TOK".

9. ACKNOWLEDGE.

                                        Capt. R.A.,
                                        Bde.Maj., 61 Div. Artillery.

Issued at 6.30 a.m.

DISTRIBUTION.

Copy No. 1	- 8.	59th. Div. Art.
9	- 13.	Right Group.
14	- 17.	O.C. Adv. Guard Artillery.
18	- 22.	306th. Bde. R.F.A.
23.		183rd. Inf. Bde.
24.		184 Inf. Bde.
25.		61 Div. 'G'.
26.		61 Div. 'Q'.
27.		R.A. XI Corps.
28.		31st. Div. Art.
29.		74th. Div. Art.
30.		H.A. XI Corps.
31.		C.B.S.O.
32.		42nd. Squadron R.A.F.
33.		A.L.O. 42 Squad. R.A.F.
34.		5th. Observation Group.
35.		'U' Sound Rangers.
36.		61 D.T.M.O.
37.		61 D.A.C.
38.		28th. Bde. R.G.A.
39.		40th. Balloon Coy. R.A.F.
40	- 41.	War Diary.
42.		File.

S E C R E T.   Copy No: 16

War Diary

61st. DIVISIONAL ARTILLERY ORDER NO: 147.

26th. Aug. 1918.

Ref: Map sheet 36A.N.E. 1:20,000.

Information. 1. The enemy is holding a line from the road junction NEUF BERQUIN (L.14.d.7.2.) - RUE MONTIGNY and along the LAUDIC BROOK through BOWERY COTTAGES - L.2.c.1.1.

Intention. 2. Tomorrow, August 27th., at a Zero hour to be notified later, the Advanced Guard Brigade will attack, in conjunction with troops of the 40th. Division on our left, with the object of advancing the left flank of our present line forward to the line L.14.d.5.4. - RUE MONTIGNY - RUE PROVOST.

Objective. 3. The objective and northern boundary are shown on map attached.

Action by 40th. Divn. 4. (a) The 119th. Infantry Brigade (40th. Division) are attacking at Zero from the North astride the BECKET CORNER - BISHOP'S CORNER Road, and will make good the line of road as far south as BISHOP'S CORNER inclusive. This attack will be followed by special mopping up parties, who will turn Westward and clear the area between the LAUDICK and the above road. A special party will, in addition, be told off to capture BOWERY COTTAGES.

(b) This attack will be carried out behind a creeping barrage which will finally remain as a protective barrage about 300 yards South of and parallel to the line BOWERY COTTAGES - RUE PROVOST - PRINCE FARM. At Zero plus 90, this protective barrage will commence to roll up from West to East.

5. During the above operation, there will be a standing barrage mixed with smoke on the line of the LAUDICK from L.1.b.65.25. to L.14.b.7.7. This barrage will remain on this line till Zero plus 72, when it will be continued by the Advanced Guard Artillery, on the frontage to be attacked, till Zero plus 90.

Method of Attack. 6. The attack of the Advanced Guard Brigade will commence at Zero plus 90, and will be carried out by two Companies pivoting with their right at L.14.d.5.4.
The attack will be made in conjunction with troops of the 120th. Infantry Brigade advancing from the direction of DENVER, and who will take over the line BOWERY COTTAGES - RUE PROVOST - BISHOP'S CORNER.

7. (a) Tasks for 18-pr. Batteries, Advanced Guard Artillery, are shown on the attached Barrage map.

Time.	Ammunition.	Rate of Fire.
Zero to plus 30 mins.	A Smoke.	Battery salvo followed by B.F. 10 seconds.
Plus 30 to plus 70	AX 106.	Normal.
" 70 " " 85	A 10% graze.	"
" 85 " " 90	" "	INTENSE.
" 90 " " 121	" "	RAPID.
" 121 " " 145	50% AX 106.	Normal.
	50% A 10% graze.	

1.   P.T.O.

(b) Tasks for 4.5" Howitzers (Section of D/306 and Section D/307 Bde. R.F.A.) are as follows, vide tracing attached:-

	Time.	Objective.	Ammn.	Rate of Fire
D/306.	Zero to plus 32 mins.	Sweep the LAUDICK Stream from L.8.d. 2.2. to L.8.d. 45.00	BX 106.	RAPID.
	Plus 32 to plus 90.	Concentrate on areas 1 to 6 alternately.	BX 106.	RAPID.
	" 90 " " 94	Areas 5 & 6.	"	INTENSE.
	" 94 " " 100	" 2 & 4.	"	RAPID.
	" 100 " " 106	Area 3.	"	"
	" 106 " " 109	Areas 1 & 12.	"	"
	" 109 " " 145	" 11 & 12.	"	Normal.

Section D/307 Bde. R.F.A.

Time	Objective	Ammn	Rate of Fire
Zero to plus 32 mins.	Sweep the LAUDICK STREAM L.8.d. 45.00 to L.14.b.7.7.	BX	RAPID.
Plus 32 to plus 90.	Concentrate on Areas 7 to 12 alternately (there will be no fire on Area 7 after plus 80 mins.)	BX	RAPID.
" 90 " " 94	Area 9.	BX 106.	INTENSE.
" 94 " " 100	" 8 & 10.	"	RAPID.
" 100 " " 106	" 8.	"	"
" 106 " " 109	" 10.	"	"
" 109 " " 145	" 8 & 10.	"	NORMAL.

8. D.T.M.O. will arrange with O.C. 184 Infantry Brigade for cooperation of the 6" NEWTON in action near PULLET FARM.

9. The signal that various objectives have been reached will be three WHITE Very lights fired in quick succession.

10. O.C. Advanced Guard Artillery will arrange S.O.S. lines in accordance with para. 9, 61 Div. Order No. 194, Copy No. 4 forwarded to him herewith.

11. O.C. Advanced Guard Artillery will arrange for synchronization of watches of his Units and Section D/307.

12. ACKNOWLEDGE.

F.P.Kyle.
Capt, R.A.,
Bde. Maj., 61 Div. Artillery.

Issued at 7.45 p.m.

DISTRIBUTION.

Copy No.		
1 - 5.	O.C. Adv: Guard Arty.
6 - 7.	O.C. Rear Group.
8.	61 Divn. 'G'.
9.	R.A. XI Corps.
10 - 11.	31st. Div. R.A.
12.	74th. Div. R.A.
13 - 14.	D.T.M.O.
15.	51 D.A.C.
16 - 17.	War Diary.
18.	File.

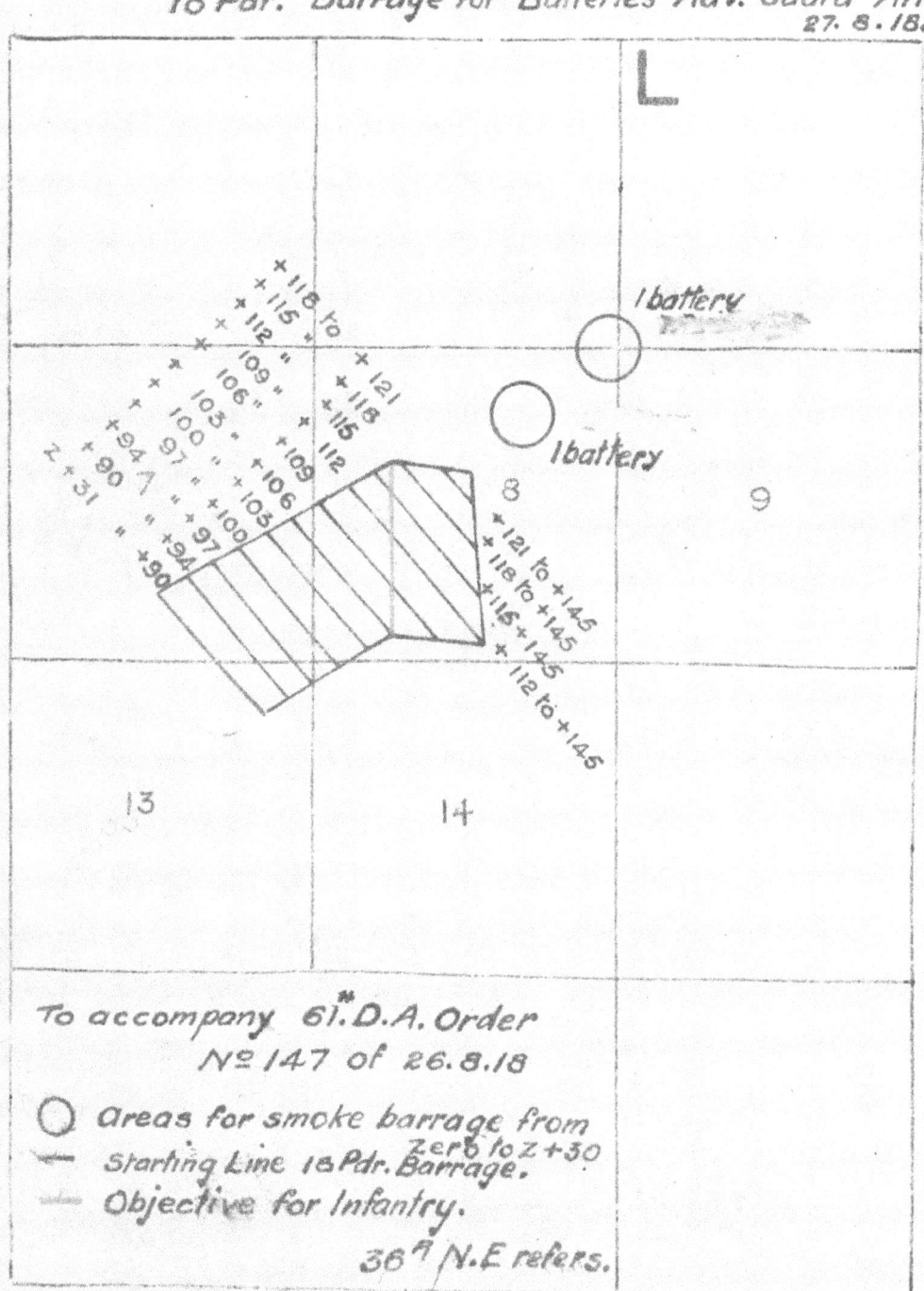

L

| 2 | 3 | 4 |

4.5" Howitzer Task 27/8/18

| 8 | 9 | 10 |

ZERO to
Z.T.2
D/306
D/307

| 14 | 15 | 16 |

—— Barrage Line

Ref: Map Sheet 36ᵃ NE 1:20000

To accompany 61/D.A. Order No 147
of 26/8/18

AMENDMENT TO

61st Divisional Artillery Order No. 157.

26th August, 1918.

The numbered map squares on the 18 pounder Barrage Map issued with 61st Divisional Artillery Order No. 147 dated 26th August, 1918, should read 9, 10, 14, and 15.

Captain, R.A.,
Bde. Major 61st Div. Art.

To all recipients of 61st Div. Arty. Order No. 147.

SECRET.   Copy No. 28

61st DIVISIONAL ARTILLERY INSTRUCTIONS NO: 9.

29th August, 1918.

1. The front at present held by the Division will be extended tonight August 29th/30th, Northwards to the grid line K.4.central - L.5.central.

   This line will, from the hour of relief, form the Northern Administrative and Tactical boundary of the XI Corps and 61st Division, continuing in a straight line to G.11.a.0.0.

2. The 184th Infantry Brigade and attached troops will relieve the 120th Infantry Brigade (40th Division) South of the above line tonight.

3. Command of the area taken over will pass to G.O.C., 184th Infantry Brigade on completion of relief.

4. ACKNOWLEDGE.

                                   F. P. Wye
                                   Captain,
                                   Bde-Major, R.A., 61st Div Arty.

DISTRIBUTION.

Copy No. 1.- 4   O.C. Advanced Guard Artillery.
         5 - 11 O.C., Rear Group.
        12- 14   D.T.M.O. 61st Div.
         15   D.A.C. 61st Div.
         16   'G'
         17   R.A. XI Corps.
         18   C.B. S.O. XI Corps.
         19   H.A. XI Corps.
         20   R.A. 31st Division.
         21   R.A. 59th Division.
         22   28th Bde, R.G.A.
         23   42nd Squadron, R.A.F.
         24   A.L.O. 42nd Squadron, R.A.F.
         25.   40 Balloon Section, R.A.F.
         26   5th Observation Group.
         27   'U' Sound Rangers.
        28- 29   War Diary.
         30   File.

SECRET.   Copy No. 23

61st DIVISIONAL ARTILLERY INSTRUCTIONS NO: 10.

1. **AMMUNITION.** (Advanced Guard Artillery).

   The following amounts of ammunition per gun will be kept at Battery Positions :-

   18pr Batteries. - 300 rds 45% A, 40% AX, 5% AT, 10% A Smoke.

   4.5" How Bty. - 175 rds BX.
   50 rds B. Gas.
   15 rds B. Smoke.

   Positions which Units vacated during advance will be cleared of all ammunition before more is drawn from A.R.P. or D.A.C.

                                   [signature]
                                   Captain, R.A.,
   30.8.1918.   Bde-Major, 61st Div. Artillery.

DISTRIBUTION.

Copy No.		
1 - 6		Advanced Guard Artillery.
7 - 13		Rear Group.
13 - 16		D.A.C.
17		D.T.M.O.
18		61st Div 'G'
19		61st Div 'Q'
20		R.A. XI Corps.
21		R.A. 59th Divn.
22		R.A. 31st Divn.
23 - 24		War Diary.
25		File.

SECRET.   Copy No. 33

61st. Divisional Artillery Order No. 148.

30th. August, 1918.

1. B/306 and D/306 (less 1 Section) will come under orders of O.C. Advanced Guard Artillery forthwith.

2. 61st. Divisional Artillery will be disposed as follows :-

    306th. Bde. forms Advanced Guard Artillery.
    307th. Bde. forms Rear Group and covers the MAIN LINE of RETENTION.

3. MAIN LINE of RETENTION remains the same.

4. ACKNOWLEDGE.

                                        F.P. Nye.
                                        Captain, R.A.
Issued at 12-30 pm   Bde. Major, 61st. Div. Artillery.

    Copy No. 1 - 5 306 Bde.
             6 -10 307 Bde.
            11-13   D.T.M.O.
            14-16   D.A.C.
            17   61st. Div. G.
            18   61st. Div. Q.
            19   R.A., XI Corps.
            20   R.A., 31st. Div.
            21   R.A., 59th. Div.
            22   XI Corps H.A.
            23   XI Corps C.B.S.O.
            24   28 Bde. R.G.A.
            25   182 Inf. Bde.
            26   183 Inf. Bde.
            27   184 Inf. Bde.
            28   42 Squad. R.A.F.
            29   A.L.O., 42 Squad. R.A.F.
            30   40 Balloon Sec. R.A.F.
            31   5th. Observation Group.
            32   'U' Sound Rangers.
            33-34   War Diary.
            35   File.

Army Form W.3091.

Cover for Documents.

Nature of Enclosures.

61ˢᵗ Divisional Artillery.

War Diary
— for —
September 1918.

VOL: 29.

Notes, or Letters written.

Army Form C. 2118.

WAR DIARY
or
INTELLIGENCE SUMMARY.
(Erase heading not required.)

Instructions regarding War Diaries and Intelligence Summaries are contained in F.S. Regs., Part II. and the Staff Manual respectively. Title pages will be prepared in manuscript.

Hour, Date, Place	Summary of Events and Information	Remarks and references to Appendices
1st September 1918. CROIX MARAISSE	A fine day, visibility was fair. 61st Divisional Artillery Order No. 148 were covered. The advance guard artillery harassed the neighbourhood of SAILLY-SUR-LA-LYS & E. of ESTAIRES. The last mentioned was shelled by our infantry today. Hostile artillery was on the whole quiet & was firing at long range. Fires & explosions were observed still behind the enemy's lines, especially in the direction of ARMENTIÈRES. GR	
2nd September 1918.	Divisional Artillery Order No. 150 was issued. The Pepper Group carried out of reconnaissance of the F1 area. The advance guard artillery was sent up during the day. Harassing fire was maintained by day & night especially in the direction Y having Erquinghem of SAILLY-SUR-LA-LYS. Hostile artillery activity was mostly captured to our forward lines W of the LYS. GR The weather was fine & visibility good.	
3rd September 1918.	A fine day but good visibility. Forward movement of advanced guard artillery was continued. Hostile artillery activity showed an occasional increase on forward areas. Our harassing fire by night & day was maintained. Fires were burning in Erquinghem, and two behind the enemy's lines. DA order No.151 issued GR	

Army Form C. 2118.

WAR DIARY
or
INTELLIGENCE SUMMARY.
(Erase heading not required.)

Instructions regarding War Diaries and Intelligence Summaries are contained in F.S. Regs., Part II. and the Staff Manual respectively. Title pages will be prepared in manuscript.

Hour, Date, Place	Summary of Events and Information	Remarks and references to Appendices
4th September 1918	A very hot day with some haze. Advanced sections were pushed up to the NW bank of the LYS to support our infantry advanced guards in preparation to our crossing the river. Hostile artillery fairly active especially in the neighbourhood of SAILLY-SUR-LA-LYS at night. Harassing fire by us were maintained. There was an increase in hostile aerial activity. DA instructions NO 11 issued.	
5th September 1918	Another hot day with some haze. The LYS RIVER was crossed early in the morning & Bos kept the whole of the advanced guard artillery ((60 fdr guns) was across. There was a considerable increase in hostile artillery activity. Our harassing fire was maintained. The HQ RA moved to new (Bailey) positions.	
6th September 1918	A fine day, but some haze to the morning; in the afternoon visibility was good. Batteries were moved up to the BOG JST came up to cover the outpost line of resistance. Hostile activity was made, any especially in the forward areas & about SAILLY. The advanced guard artillery carried out harassing fire during the day & night. eRA - Brigade Major visited battery positions.	

Army Form C. 2118.

WAR DIARY
or
INTELLIGENCE SUMMARY.
(Erase heading not required.)

Instructions regarding War Diaries and Intelligence Summaries are contained in F.S. Regs., Part II. and the Staff Manual respectively. Title pages will be prepared in manuscript.

Hour, Date, Place	Summary of Events and Information	Remarks and references to Appendices
6th Sept 1918 (contd)	306 Regt was ordered to move to trenches NW of Pont LYS in order to conn O.L.R. 9R.	
7th September 1918.	Heavy showers during the day; visibility was fair. Our opposed (enemy) artillery increased their activity, especially in harassing fire about FLEURBAIX. Hostile artillery was active & there was considerable shelling of back areas at night with S.A. Hows & H.V. guns. B.R.	
8th September 1918	Another showery day with poor intervals during which visibility was fair. Harassing fire was maintained by the Advanced Guard Artillery at an increased rate throughout. Little arty fire was not so active. B.R.	
9th September 1918. RAHQ closed at the CROIX MARRAISE & reopened at the RILL WORKS (L 33.b – W of LA GORGUE) at 10 a.m.		
RILL WORKS (L 33.b N of LA GORGUE)	Heavy showers came down at frequent intervals throughout the day & visibility was poor. Our harassing fire was carried out as usual to forestall enemy's & hostile artillery was fairly quiet. SR	

(73989) W4141–163. 400,000. 9/14. H.&J.Ltd. Forms/C. 2118/10.

WAR DIARY
or
INTELLIGENCE SUMMARY.
(Erase heading not required.)

Army Form C. 2118.

Instructions regarding War Diaries and Intelligence Summaries are contained in F.S. Regs., Part II. and the Staff Manual respectively. Title pages will be prepared in manuscript.

Hour, Date, Place	Summary of Events and Information	Remarks and references to Appendices
10th September 1918.	A small operation by the right flank battalion was supported by our artillery. B.A. instructions No 13 & B.A order No 132 were issued. In addition to the usual harassing fire several concentrations in conjunction with 60 pdr & 6" hows. were carried out during the day. Hostile artillery was quiet during the day but active at night. A fine day with good visibility. SNR	
11th September 1918.	Heavy rain during the morning but clearing in the afternoon. Concentration shoots were again carried out, in addition to harassing fire, & several observed destruction shoots gave good results. Hostile fire was normal. B.A. instruction No 14 was issued. SNR	
12th September 1918.	An operation by our infantry was supported by the divisional artillery & our line was advanced slightly on the right. All objectives were not held; a counter attack succeeding in regaining JUNCTION POST. My heavy rain hindered the infantry. The new attitudes brought the enemy in addition to several concentration shoots harassing fire was carried out as usual & several other targets were engaged with observation during the day. Hostile artillery was fairly active on forward areas by day but slower & silenced at night. SNR	

WAR DIARY
or
INTELLIGENCE SUMMARY.
(Erase heading not required.)

Army Form C. 2118.

Hour, Date, Place	Summary of Events and Information	Remarks and references to Appendices
September 12th (continued)	After heavy rain all the morning the weather cleared in the afternoon & there was considerable aerial activity in back areas. Three Enemy aeroplanes captured in ESTAIRES & SAILLY-SUR-LA-LYS.	
September 13th 1918	The C.R.A. returned from leave & Col. Brooke accompany returned to resume his command of 306 Bde R.F.A. Another day of heavy showers. On such days by A.G. Artillery concentrations being fired on nine different occasions in addition to observed shoots & harassing fire. Hostile artillery was normal, there was some heavy shelling of LAVENTIE By A.59 How Battery & two Aeroplanes & 6 batteries by Aeroplane. 6%D.A. fired 10,153 rounds S.A.A.	
September 14th 1918	A clearing day. The C.R.A. visited Cops. (Artys) in the morning & Colt Brigades & some of the batteries in the afternoon. S.A. Instructions No 15 % issued. Harassing fire & concentrations No 96	

WAR DIARY
or
INTELLIGENCE SUMMARY.
(Erase heading not required.)

Army Form C. 2118.

Hour, Date, Place	Summary of Events and Information	Remarks and references to Appendices
September 14th 1918 (about)	Was carried out as usual by 6A A.G. Artillery & several observed shoots gave good results. Hostile artillery showed an increase. Forward areas & a corresponding decrease in back areas. LAVENTIE came in for considerable attention. There was some form of enemy SOS (suspected) registered by EA 4 53/347 (Artillery position was heavily shelled at 6h evening). No casualties. S.R.	
September 15th 1918.	CRA & BM visited Batteries & OPs. A fair day but good visibility. Enemy gave Artillery carried out harassing fire as usual. Effects unknown. There was no decrease in hostile artillery activity during the day. Enemy activity showed a big increase. S.R.	
September 16th 1918.	The day was fine with much wind, & visibility was good. Guns. In night there was very heavy rain. C.R.A & B.M. went round front line area & night demands had in the evening. Harassing fire was carried out as usual & selected targets	

WAR DIARY or INTELLIGENCE SUMMARY.

(Erase heading not required.)

Army Form C. 2118.

Hour, Date, Place	Summary of Events and Information	Remarks and references to Appendices
16th September 1918	Hostile activity was less during the day but increased considerably at night. Specially heavy shelling near pill boxes between LAVENTIE & NOUVEAU MONDE. In the afternoon a pill box at 2/307° pierced blew up (due to a stray shell arriving) & the only occupant Pnr D.H Harman was killed. A very big increase in Aerial activity was noticeable. D.A Instruction No 7 was issued. The relief of the Advanced Guard Artillery (307 Bde) by 306 Bde was completed. SR	
17th September 1918	A fine day. In the afternoon & evening's hostiles's heavy guns shelled any too great activity on enemy's. Unusually a relief in intrapress. Hostile artillery showed considerable activity. There was a increase in enemy aerial activity. A concentration shoot on FLEURBAIX was carried out in the morning. C.R.A & B.M. went round all our areas in the morning. SB	

Army Form C. 2118.

WAR DIARY
or
INTELLIGENCE SUMMARY.
(Erase heading not required.)

Instructions regarding War Diaries and Intelligence Summaries are contained in F.S. Regs., Part II. and the Staff Manual respectively. Title pages will be prepared in manuscript.

Hour, Date, Place	Summary of Events and Information	Remarks and references to Appendices
18th September 1918.	A fine day with good visibility. CRA went to Corps HQ in the morning & inspected wagon lines in the afternoon. Active harassing fire was maintained throughout the 24 hours & some 40 targets were engaged. A considerable shoot in conjunction with HA on a battery position at H.22.a.8.8. at 4 p.m. (EWE of Flesquieres went (100?) Hostile artillery was quieter in the morning but increased considerably in the afternoon & night firing was normal. Mainly 4.2" shells & heavy's 5.9" & 8" for very long range. Batteries were again shelled in the evenings. Was a fine afternoon. SP.	
19th September 1918	A fine day. Harassing fire was carried out as usual. Hostile artillery was somewhat quieter. The area N of the River LYS & S of CROIX DU BAC received constant attention, & it was apparently registered on at our troops in the early morning. General activity. Intelligence issued Defence Instructions No.1. SP.	
20th September 1918	A fair day with good visibility. Harassing fire was carried out by day	

Army Form C. 2118.

WAR DIARY
or
INTELLIGENCE SUMMARY.
(Erase heading not required.)

Instructions regarding War Diaries and Intelligence Summaries are contained in F.S. Regs., Part II. and the Staff Manual respectively. Title pages will be prepared in manuscript.

Hour, Date, Place	Summary of Events and Information	Remarks and references to Appendices
20th September 1918 continued	ady. Hostile artillery was quieter. Three batteries went up to our lines during the day. C.R.A. went round forward areas. 92	
21st September 1918.	A fine day. Our harassing fire was actively maintained. Hostile artillery was fairly active. Some enemy registration was apparent during the day with our Cruests. Two explosions occurred in BOIULY-SUR-LA-LYS. 92	
22nd September 1918.	The day was a fair one until 3.30 p.m. when heavy rain came on. A high wind blew in gusts throughout the day. C.R.A. and round forward areas. Our harassing fire "maintained" & some wire cutting attempted about Eau Junction Post (H22.a) gully was prevented very good results & the shoot was curtailed. A section of A/130 G. was (?) (moved) in the early morning from its position to N of LAVENTIE & fired 200 rounds during the day on selected targets, returning to its position at night. 6" NEWTONS engaged in wire cutting. EB

WAR DIARY
or
INTELLIGENCE SUMMARY.
(Erase heading not required.)

Army Form C. 2118.

Hour, Date, Place	Summary of Events and Information	Remarks and references to Appendices
22nd September 1918 -continued)	Hostile artillery was considerably quieter. B.A. Order No 154 issued. A memo received for XI Corps B.A. Orders No 153 and issued.	
23rd September 1918.	A showery morning but with a high gusty wind leaving C.E.A. unobserved. Wagon Wounds S.C.R.P. 8/ B.M. went up to 183 Inf Bde H.Q. and 9.S.O.I. in reference to corps with reference to proposed minor operation. B.A. Instructions No 18 issued. Orders harassing fire continued 1.6" Newtons engaged in wire cutting. Area shoots were carried out on BARTLETTE Fm. JUNCTION POST & vicinity, in accordance with para 1 B.A. instructions No 18. Hostile artillery showed however activity in the morning, a fair number of shell and shrapnel were carried out, & there was a considerable amount of hyp air burst wire wards ranging. A fire broke out in FLEURBAIX in the afternoon. Weather cleared in the afternoon & evening. Fire (night). Cols. 307 Bde went into line from wagon W.Co. (per B.A. O.D.N. (No 154)	

WAR DIARY
or
INTELLIGENCE SUMMARY.
(Erase heading not required.)

Army Form C. 2118.

Instructions regarding War Diaries and Intelligence Summaries are contained in F.S. Regs., Part II and the Staff Manual respectively. Title pages will be prepared in manuscript.

Hour, Date, Place	Summary of Events and Information	Remarks and references to Appendices
September 24th 1918	A fine bright day. Battery took up positions with reference to capture of BARTLETTE. CRA ordered harassing fire continued & wire cutting by 6" NEWTONS. The gas projector operation on BARTLETTE FM & JUNCTION POST was carried out at 11.15 pm + own artillery co-operated. SD. Hostile shelling was about normal. Aerial activity was vy great.	
September 25th 1918	Showing early but clearing to a fine day later. CRA attended G.O.Cs (Bri:) conference in the afternoon. The afternoon found BARTLETTE FM & JUNCTION POST postponed for 24 hours. SD. Harassing fires carried out & wire cutting by our 4.5 How battery & 6" NEWTONS. Hostile artillery was somewhat quieter. There was less aerial activity. BM rode & conferred with O.C. 183 Inf. Bde in the morning. S.A. Withdrawn NO 19 as used.	
September 26th 1918	A fine day. In addition to the usual harassing fire wire cutting was carried out during the day by our 4.5 How battery & 6" NEWTONS. At 10.10 pm an operation by 183 Infantry brigade	

WAR DIARY
or
INTELLIGENCE SUMMARY.
(Erase heading not required.)

Army Form C. 2118.

Instructions regarding War Diaries and Intelligence Summaries are contained in F. S. Regs., Part II. and the Staff Manual respectively. Title pages will be prepared in manuscript.

Place	Date	Hour	Summary of Events and Information	Remarks and references to Appendices
	26th Sept/18 (contd)		was carried out & both BARTLETTE FM & JUNCTION Post were captured. The artillery fire barrage in support. Hostile artillery was general. D.A. Order No 20 issued.	
	27th Sept/18		The enemy counter-attacked in the early hours of the morning & recaptured the posts mentioned by us on the previous night. A fine day. C.R.A. attacked 90 C.F.A.(Howitzer) Batteries in the morning. Harassing fire actively carried out. Hostile counter-fire artillery activity was less.	
	28th Sept/18		Heavy rain in the morning had cleared by mid-day for later. C.R.A. captured went Brigade commanding the Infantry Brigade in the opening of their attacks. Supt Commanding artillery. D.A. Order No 157 issued. Several concentrations were carried out as well as the usual harassing fire. A shot fed barrage was put down by us at 9 pm for the purpose of ascertaining if the Germans were still there, as it was observed that they kept a watch during the hours. This result was that very many coloured lights were put up. There was a rather decrease in hostile artillery fire & many aircraft were out also.	
	29th Sept/18		Concentrations & harassing fire was carried out actively all day. V.T.M's cut up. Hostile artillery was keener-normal. Aerial activity was marked on both sides. D.A. Order No 158 issued. A fine day.	

Army Form C. 2118.

WAR DIARY
or
INTELLIGENCE SUMMARY.
(Erase heading not required.)

Instructions regarding War Diaries and Intelligence Summaries are contained in F.S. Regs., Part II. and the Staff Manual respectively. Title pages will be prepared in manuscript.

Hour, Date, Place	Summary of Events and Information	Remarks and references to Appendices
30th October 1918	Consolidation was continued. Heavy shelling throughout the day. The enemy operation was supported by our barrage on the early morning Y JUNCTION Pit was taken & an advance made to the right of the Divisional front. Protective barrages were put down on several occasions. A number of concentration shoots were carried out. Harassing fire was as usual. Hostile artillery was active on our F.L. system in the morning + the ROUGE DE BOUT also received counterbattery attention. Aerial activity practically nil. CRA + BM captured with negative capacity 10+ of Bar in the evening. G.O.C. 5th Army with RAH on a tr afternoon. BM visits brigades in an afternoon.	

Spencer Batchelor
Lieut
R.O. R.A. 61st Sn. Battery for
CRA 61st Div Artillery

SECRET.   Copy No. 33

61st. Divisional Artillery Order No. 148.

30th. August, 1918.

1. B/306 and D/306 (less 1 Section) will come under orders of O.C. Advanced Guard Artillery forthwith.

2. 61st. Divisional Artillery will be disposed as follows :-

    306th. Bde. forms Advanced Guard Artillery.
    307th. Bde. forms Rear Group and covers the MAIN LINE of RETENTION.

3. MAIN LINE of RETENTION remains the same.

4. ACKNOWLEDGE.

F.T.Nye
Captain, R.A.
Bde. Major, 61st. Div. Artillery.

Issued at 12-30 pm

```
Copy No. 1 - 5  306 Bde.
         6 -10  307 Bde.
         11-13  D.T.M.O.
         14-16  D.A.C.
         17     61st. Div. G.
         18     61st. Div. Q.
         19     R.A., XI Corps.
         20     R.A., 31st. Div.
         21     R.A., 59th. Div.
         22     XI Corps H.A.
         23     XI Corps C.B.S.O.
         24     28 Bde. R.G.A.
         25     182 Inf. Bde.
         26     183 Inf. Bde.
         27     184 Inf. Bde.
         28     42 Squad. R.A.F.
         29     A.L.O., 42 Squad. R.A.F.
         30     40 Balloon Sec. R.A.F.
         31     5th. Observation Group.
         32     'U' Sound Rangers.
         33-34  War Diary.
         35     File.
```

War Diary

SECRET. R.G.1.

AMENDMENT No.2, to
61st DIVISIONAL ARTILLERY LOCATION STATEMENT - 31.8.1918.

The following amendments are made to 61st
D.A. Location Statement :-

REAR GROUP.	Location.	Wagon Lines.
B/307.		J.10.b.3.1.
C/307.		J.33.d.9.5.
D/307. (6 hows)	J.30.a.60.80.	J.36.a.9.1.

ADVANCED GUARD
ARTILLERY.

C/306	(2 guns)	WOAD FARM, K.28.c.	K.14.b.30.80.
	(4 guns)	L.25.a.7.8.	
D/306	(2 hows)	K.23.b.6.4.	
	(4 hows)	K.24.d.3.7.	

1.9.1918.

Captain, R.A.,
Bde-Major, 61st Div. Artillery.

War Diary

SECRET.　　　　　　　　　　　　　　　　　　　R.G. 1.

AMENDMENT No.1, to
61st DIVISIONAL ARTILLERY LOCATION STATEMENT - 31.8.18.

The following amendments are made to 61st D.A. Location Statement :-

REAR GROUP.

C/307 Bde Wagon Lines - J.33.d.9.5.

F.P. Wye.

R.A.H.Q.
31.8.1918.
　　　　　　　　　　　　　　　　　Captain, R.A.,
　　　　　　　　　　　　　　　Bde-Major, 61st Div Arty.

SECRET.

Copy No ...33...

61st DIVISIONAL ARTILLERY ORDER NO: 149.

September 1st, 1918.

1. The 307th Brigade, R.F.A. will relieve 306th Brigade, R.F.A. as follows :-

    2/9/18. A/307   relieves   A/306 Bde, R.F.A.

    3/9/18. C/307   "   C/306   "

    4/9/18. HQ/307 Bde R.F.A., relieves HQ/306 Bde, R.F.A.
             B/307 relieves B/306 Bde, R.F.A.
             1 Sec.)   (1 Sec.
             D/307)   "   (D/306   "

    5/9/18. Remainder   Remainder
             D/307   "   D/306   "

2. H.Qs. and Batteries 306th Brigade, R.F.A. will take over and occupy the same positions as units of 307th Bde, R.F.A., except that :-

    B/306 will put 4 guns into position at J.12.a.7.7. instead of at J.10.b.45.35.

3. The relief of Batteries of the Advanced Guard Artillery will be carried out, gun for gun.

4. No guns will be exchanged.

5. The 306th Bde. will place 3 subaltern officers at the disposal of 307th Bde; these will include the officers at present doing liaison with the Infantry Battalions.

6. Remaining details of relief to be arranged by Bde. Commanders concerned.

7. ACKNOWLEDGE.

Issued at 11.30 am

P. WYE.
Captain, R.A.,
Bde-Major, 61st Div. Artillery.

DISTRIBUTION.

Copy No.				
1 - 5	306 Bde.	23	XI Corps C.B.S.O.
6 -10	307 Bde.	24	28 Bde, R.G.A.
11- 13	D.T.M.O.	25	182 Inf Bde.
14- 16	D.A.C.	26	183 Inf. Bde.
17	61 Div 'G'	27	184 Inf. Bde.
18	61 Div 'Q'	28	42 Squad. R.A.F.
19	R.A. XI Corps.	29	A.L.O. 42 Squad. R.A.F.
20	R.A. 31 Div	30	40 Balloon Sec. R.A.F.
21	R.A. 59 Div	31	5th Observation Group.
22	XI Corps H.A.	32	'U' Sound Rangers.
		33-34	War Diary.
		35	File.

SECRET.   R.G.1.

AMENDMENT NO.7 to 61st DIVISIONAL ARTILLERY LOCATION STATEMENT - 31.8.18

The following amendments are made to 61st Div. Arty Location Statement :-

Unit.	Location.	Wagon Lines.
307th Bde H.Q.	} Occupy positions } in readiness at :-	K.24.d.3.6.
A/307.		K.23.a.2.4.
B/307.		K.24.d.7.9.
C/307.		K.18.d.0.5.
D/307.		K.23.e.7.1.

ADVANCED GUARD ARTILLERY,

A/306.	(4 guns)	L.13.d.20.40.
	(2 guns)	L.15.d.35.40.
B/306.	(2 guns)	L.11.c.1.4.
	(4 guns)	L.10.c.2.8.
C/306.	(2 guns)	L.28.b.00.60.
	(4 guns)	L.27.b.20.40.
D/306.	(3 hows)	L.20.b.70.95.
	(2 hows)	L.16.a.6.9.

61st T.M. H.Q.   J.10.a.6.5.

61st D.A.C. HQ.   J.21.a.20.60.

T.Pwye

Captain, R.A.
Bde-Major, 61st Div. Artillery

2.9.1918.

SECRET.   Copy No............ 54

61st DIVISIONAL ARTILLERY ORDER No. 150.

September 2nd 1918.

1. (a) The 307th Bde. R.F.A. at present covering the Main LINE OF RETENTION will advance at once to positions of readiness East of the BOURRE RIVER about LES PURESHECQUE.

   (b) 307 Bde. R.F.A. will be in new locations by 4 pm and will notify arrival to this office by code word "AUTUMN".

   (c) 307 Bde. R.F.A. will march with an interval of 1 hour between Batteries.

2. (b) Units of 306 Bde. R.F.A. on relief will come under orders of O.C. 307 Bde. R.F.A. until passing of Brigade Commands, when the units of 307 Bde. R.F.A. which are not in action will come under orders of O.C. 306 Bde. R.F.A. until completion of relief.

3. The O.C. D.A.C. will take over and provide guards at once on ANTI-TANK guns now in action at :-

   (a) J.36.c.3.7.   ) From 307 Bde. R.F.A.
   (b) J.30.d.75.05   )

   (c) K.14.d.30.70.   From B/306 Bde. R.F.A.

3. (c). The relief referred to in 61 D.A. Order No. 149 will be carried out as therein stated.

4.   ACKNOWLEDGE.

                                              F.P.Wye.
Issued at... 1 am ..
                                          Captain, R.A.,
                                     Bde. Major 61st Div. Arty.

DISTRIBUTION.

Copy No.		
1 - 5	306 Bde.	23 XI Corps C.B.S.O.
6 - 10	307 Bde.	24 26 Bde. R.G.A.
11-13	D.T.M.O.	25 182 Inf. Bde.
14-16	D.A.C.	26 183 Inf. Bde.
17	61 Div. "G"	27 184 Inf. Bde.
18	61 Div. "Q"	28 42 Squadron R.A.F.
19	R.A. XI Corps.	29 A.L.O. 42 Squad R.A.F.
20	R.A. 31 Div.	30 40 Balloon Sec R.A.F.
21	R.A. 59 Div.	31 5th Observation Group.
22	XI Corps H.A.	32 "Q" Sound Rangers.
		33 61 Div. Train.
		34-35 War Diary.
		36 File.

SECRET.   Copy No. ....

61st DIVISIONAL ARTILLERY ORDER NO: 151.

September 3rd, 1918.

1. (a). The 306th Brigade, R.F.A. Wagon Lines will march on 4.9.1918 under Brigade arrangements to new lines, to be selected by units concerned, close to the Road from ACHEN CROSS to L.11.c.35.85.

   (b). 2 hours interval will be maintained between batteries and 400 yards between Sections of Batteries on the march.

2. (a). The 61st D.A.C. will march on 4.9.1918 under arrangements by O.C. via "The VIA ROMA" to new lines about ITCHEN FARM, (K.10.d.)

   (b). The following distances will be maintained on the line of march.

   Between Sections, D.A.C.   100 yards.
   Between Sections of 6 vehicles   25 yards.

3. Arrival in new locations to be notified by code word "WARRIOR".

4. Administrative Instructions appended.

5. ACKNOWLEDEG (61st D.A.C. & 306th Bde R.F.A. only).

Issued at 7-30pm.

F.P. WYE.
Captain, R.A.,
Bde-Major, 61st Div. Artillery.

DISTRIBUTION.

Copy No.		
1 - 5	306th Bde, R.F.A.	
6 - 10	307th Bde, R.F.A.	
11 - 13	D.T.M.O.	
14 - 16	D.A.C.	
17	61st Div. 'G'	
18	61st Div. 'Q'	
19	R.A. XI Corps.	
20	R.A. 31st Div.	
21	R.A. 59th Div.	
22	XI Corps H.A.	
23	XI Corps C.B.S.O.	
24	28th Bde, R.G.A.	
25	182nd Inf. Bde.	
26	183rd Inf. Bde.	
27	184th Inf. Bde.	
28	42nd Squadron, R.A.F.	
29	A.L.O. 42nd Squad. R.A.F.	
30	40 Balloon Section, R.A.F.	
31	5th Observation Group.	
32	'U' Sound Rangers.	
33	11th Balloon Coy.	
34 - 35	War Diary.	
36	File.	
37	61st Div. Train.	
38	No.1 Coy., 61st Div. Train.	

S E C R E T.   Copy No ...24...

61st DIVISIONAL ARTILLERY INSTRUCTIONS NO: 11.

1. 61st D.A. Instructions No. 10 are cancelled.

2 (a) During present operations Batteries will keep one wagon load of ammunition per gun dumped at the Battery Position.

   (b) The echelon will be kept full.

3. Batteries may have a forward Wagon Line consisting of gun limbers and Firing Battery Wagons, at the discretion of Bde. Commanders.

4. Positions which units vacate during the advance will be cleared of all ammunition before more is drawn from D.A.C.

                                            S.P. Hyde
                                            Captain R.A.,
4.9.1918.   Bde-Major, 61st Div. Artillery.

DISTRIBUTION.

    Copy No. 1 - 6   306th Brigade, R.F.A.
             7 -13   307th Brigade, R.F.A.
            13 - 16 D.A.C.
            17   D.T.M.O.
            18   61st Division 'G'
            19   61st Division 'Q'
            20   R.A. XI Corps.
            21   R.A. 59th Divn.
            22   R.A. 31st Divn.
            23 - 24 War Diary.
            25   File.

SECRET.   R.G.L.

61st DIVISIONAL ARTILLERY,
LOCATION STATEMENT,
September 5th.

Group.	Unit.	Location.	Wagon Lines.
	R.A.H.Q.	J.21.c.70.15.	J.21.c.70.15.
ADVANCED GUARD ARTILLERY.	307th Bde HQ.	G.13.b.6.4.	L.10.d.9.6.
	A/307 (3 guns).	G.23.d.5.7.	L.17.d.2.7.
	(2 guns).	G.23.a.2.1.	"
	B/307 (4 guns)	G.16.a.7.7.	L.11.c.
	(2 guns)	G.17.c.4.6.	"
	C/307 (4 guns)	G.28.a.8.4.	L.23.b.4.8.
	(2 guns)	G.29.a.0.5.	"
	D/307 (4 hows)	G.22.a.70.15.	L.10.d.4.3.
	(2 hows)	G.22.b.8.5.	"
BRIGADE IN READINESS.	306th Bde HQ.	L.11.d.25.75.	L.10.a.60.95 to L.11.c.30.90.
	A/306 (6 guns)	L.10.a.60.95 to L.11.c.30.90.	
	B/306 (6 guns)		
	C/306 (6 guns)		
	D/306 (6 hows)		
	61st D.A.C. HQ.	K.7.d.9.0.	K.10.d.
	61st T.M. H.Q.	J.10.a.9.3.	
	X/61 T.M.B.	K.8.d.05.65.	
	Y/61 T.M.B.	K.13.b.80.80.	

5.9.1918.

F.P.Wye Capt R.A.
for R.O.R.A., 61st Divn.

S E C R E T.

R.A., XI Corps.
C.B.S.O., XI Corps.
61st. Division "G".
11th. Balloon Coy.

R.G.1.

AMENDMENTS TO LOCATIONS.
61st. DIVISIONAL ARTILLERY - 5.9.18.

Advanced Guard Artillery.	Location.	Wagon Lines.
A/307 (3 guns)	G.20.d.5.8.	G.14.c.2.3. (forward lines)
B/307 (4 guns)	G.10.b.3.2.	G.9.d.3.5. (do. do.)
C/307		G.19.a.95.50. (do. do.)
D/307 (4 Hows)	G.15.b.3.8.	

Lieut-Colonel,
C.R.A., 61st. Division.

7th. Sept. 1918.

S E C R E T.   R.O.1.

AMENDMENTS TO LOCATIONS.
61st. DIVISIONAL ARTILLERY - 5.9.18.

Advanced Guard Artillery.		Location.	Wagon Lines.
A/307	2 Guns	C.23.c.5.2.	-
B/307			C.8.d.1.9.(forward lines)

Lieutenant,
R.O.R.A., 61st. Division.

9th. Sept. 1918.

To all recipients of R.O.1 of 5.9.18.

SECRET.   Copy No. 10

61st DIVISIONAL ARTILLERY INSTRUCTION No 13.

AMMUNITION.   1.   The following amounts of Smoke and Incendiary Shell will, as far as possible, be maintained by Batteries in their Echelons :-

       18 pdr. Batteries .... A Smoke 60 rounds.
                                                A.T.   16 rounds.

       4.5 "How. batteries ....; B Smoke 36 rounds.
                                               B.T.   12 rounds.

TELEPHONE   2.   (a) Several complaints have been received that units
LINES.   are recovering field cables in use, and that lengths are being cut out of working lines.
          Although salvage or derelict cable is essential, yet this must on no account be done before ascertaining that the lines are spare and no longer required.

       (b) All lines must be clearly labelled at least every 440 yards.

       (c) Orders will be issued to all units to this effect and disciplinary action will be taken against anyone found cutting lengths out of or reeling up working lines.

       3. ACKNOWLEDGE.

10-9-18.
                                                 Captain, R.A.,
                                       Bde.Major R.A. 61st Div.

DISTRIBUTION.

       Copy No. 1   306 Bde. R.F.A.
               2   307 Bde. R.F.A.
               3   61st Div. "G"
               4   61st D.A.C.
               5   61st D.T.M.O.
               6   R.A. XI Corps.
               7   R.A. 59th Divn.
               8   40th Div. "G" (for R.A.).
               9   28th Bde. R.G.A.
              10)
              11) War Diary.
              12   File.

SECRET.

SECRET.   Copy No. 24

61st. DIVISIONAL ARTILLERY ORDER No. 152.

10th. Sept. 1918.

1. One 18-pdr. Battery 306th. Brigade R.F.A. to be detailed by O.C., 306th. Bde. R.F.A. will come under orders of O.C., Advanced Guard Artillery (307th. Bde. R.F.A.) forthwith.

2. Details to be arranged between Bde. Commanders concerned.

3. ACKNOWLEDGE.

F.P. WYE
Captain, R.A.,
Bde. Major, 61st. Div. Artillery.

Copies to

1 - 2	306 Bde. R.F.A.
3	307 Bde R.F.A.
4	61 D.T.M.O.
5 - 6	61st D.A.C.
7	61st. Div. G.
8	61st. Div. Q.
9	R.A., XI Corps.
10	R.A., 59 Divn.
11	40 Div G for R.A.
12	H.A., XI Corps.
13	C.B.S.O., XI Corps.
14	28th. Bde. R.G.A.
15	182 Inf. Bde.
16	183 Inf. Bde.
17	184 Inf. Bde.
18	42 Squad. R.A.F.
19	A.L.O., 42 Squad. R.A.F.
20	11th. Balloon Coy. R.A.F.
21	5th. Observation Group.
22	11th. Sound Rangers.
23	No. 1 Coy, 61st. Div. Train.
24 - 25	War Diary.
26	File.

AMENDMENTS TO LOCATIONS.
61st. DIVISIONAL ARTILLERY - 5.9.18.

Unit.	Locations.	Wagon Lines.
R.A.H.Q.	L.33.b.3.7.	L.33.b.3.7.
D/306 Bde.	-	L.11.a.6.8.
61st D.A.C. HQ	L.20.c.7.0.	

10th. Sept. 1918.

[signature]
Lieutenant,
R.O.R.A., 61 Division.

To all recipients of R.G.1 of 5.9.18.

S E C R E T.

AMENDMENT No. 1
to 61st. D.A. Instructions No. 11.

Para 2(a) is cancelled and the following substituted :-

"During the present phase in the operations, Batteries of the Advanced Guard Artillery will keep two wagon loads of ammunition per gun dumped at the gun positions - exclusive of Smoke, Gas and Incendiary shell ordered to be dumped for special purposes."

A.P. Wye

Captain, R.A.,
Bde. Major, 61st. Div. Artillery.

10th. Sept. 1918.

To all recipients D.A. Instructions No. 11.

61st DIVISIONAL ARTILLERY INSTRUCTION No. 14.

DAILY INTELLIGENCE REPORTS

1. The importance of full reports being given by Brigades does not seem to be fully realised.

2. It is very necessary that as much information as possible should be given as regards :-

    (a) Our own shelling and observation of same.
    (b) Ground observation from O.Ps.
    (c) Hostile shelling; area shelled; calibre; from what direction and number of rounds.

    It is from these three items being systematically given by all units in the line, that higher formations are greatly assisted in forming a correct estimation of the situation and of the enemy's intentions, and also as regards the third item, if this information is given fully it helps the Counter Battery Staff to an enormous extent to locate hostile batteries, and so save our own casualties and damage to material.

    Many details of information which may seem inessential to batteries, may form a link with other information received by higher formations, to complete a chain of evidence as to enemy intentions and it is therefore imperative that the reports in question should be as full as possible with regard to the above mentioned items.

    At times such as the present when there is a partial return to moving warfare it is more than ever necessary to glean as much information as possible as to the enemy movement and his intentions, and this can only be done effectually if everyone co-operates in doing his best to enable the very fullest information to be conveyed to Army Intelligence.

3. Attention is called to the necessity of sending in early information of events, as they occur.

    The practice which has gradually grown up during Trench Warfare of collecting information and transmitting it in bulk at the end of a fixed period has shown itself to be entirely unsuitable and inadequate to the needs of the more mobile form of warfare which now obtains and which is likely to continue.

    The German Staff has publicly recognized the superiority of our Intelligence and it is the duty of everyone to endeavour not only to maintain this superiority but to increase it.

    While it is understood that it may be difficult to give reports as fully now as in the time of trench warfare, it must be realized that it is essential that no effort should be spared to make them as full as possible and an improvement must be shown on the meagre reports of the last few weeks if our information is to be of any use to the Army. There have been a few notable exceptions but on the whole the reports have been of little practical use to those to whom they are rendered.

F. P. Wye.

Captain, R.A.,
Bde. Major 61st Div. Arty.

11th September, 1918.

DISTRIBUTION.

Copies No.		
1 to 5	306 Bde. R.F.A.
6 to 10	307 Bde. R.F.A.
11 to 14	61st D.A.C.
15 to 17	61st D.T.M.O.
18	61st Division "G"
19	File.
20 - 21	War Diary.
22	R.A. XI Corps.
23	R.A. 66th Divn.
24	R.A. 59th Divn.

SECRET. R.G.1.

61st. DIVISIONAL ARTILLERY.
LOCATION STATEMENT.
September 12th.

Group.	Unit.	Location.	Wagon Lines. Rear	Forward.
	R.A.H.Q.	L.33.b.3.7.	L.33.b.3.7.	
ADVANCED GUARD ARTILLERY.	307 Bde HQ.	G.13.b.6.4.	L.10.d.9.6.	
	A/307 (2 guns)	G.33.d.45.55.	L.17.d.2.7.	G.20.a.05.95.
	(2 guns)	G.32.d.65.60.		
	(2 guns)	G.32.d.10.55.		
	B/307 (4 guns)	G.12.c.00.15.	SELSEY FARM)	G.8.d.1.9.
	(2 guns)	G.17.c.4.6.	L.11.c.)	
	C/307 (4 guns)	G.28.a.8.4.	L.23.b.4.8.	G.19.b.6.5
	(2 guns)	G.29.a.0.5.		
	D/307 (4 Hows)	G.15.b.3.8.	L.10.d.4.3.	
	(2 Hows)	G.22.b.8.5.		
	B/306 (4 guns)	G.10.a.35.75.	L.11.a.05.15.	
	(2 guns)	G.11.d.1.8.		
Brigade in READINESS	306 Bde HQ.	L.11.d.25.75.)	L.10.a.60.95.	
	A/306 (6 guns)	G.19.d.15.50.)	to	
	C/306 (6 guns)	G.14.a.70.00.)	L.11.c.30.90.	
	D/306 (6 Hows)	G.14.d.25.10.	L.11.a.6.8.	
	61st. D.A.C. HQ	L.20.c.7.0.	L.20.c.7.0.	
	61st T.M.H.Q.	L.17.b.75.10.		
	X/61 T.M.B.	L.17.b.75.10.		
		H.25.a.8.2. (1 - 4" Newton)		
	Y/61 T.M.B.	L.17.b.75.10.		
	61st. D.A.G.O.	L.17.b.75.10.		

Spencer Batchelor.
Lieutenant,
R.O.R.A., 61st. Division.

12.9.18.

SECRET   Copy No. 33

                                                 13.9.1918.

61st DIVISIONAL ARTILLERY ORDER No.153.

1. The 306th Brigade R.F.A. less 1 18-pdr Battery will relieve 307th Brigade R.F.A. less 1 18-pdr Battery as follows :-
    One section per Battery on 15th inst.
    Brigade H.Q. and remaining sections of Batteries 16th inst.

2. Units of 307th Brigade R.F.A. will take over positions from 306th Brigade R.F.A. but will not occupy same.

3. On completion of relief 306 Brigade R.F.A. plus 1 18-pdr Battery will form Advanced Guard Artillery.
    307th Brigade R.F.A. less 1 18-pdr Battery will be located in Wagon lines and will remain "in readiness" (vide para. 5(b) 61st D.A. Instructions No.12)

4. 306th Brigade R.F.A. will arrange to clear all ammunition from the positions which they hand over.

5. Receipts for all ammunition handed over, and taken over, will be forwarded to this office on completion of relief

6. Rear Wagon Lines will not be exchanged.

7. Details of relief to be arranged by Brigade Commanders.

                                              Captain R.A.
                                              Bde. Major, 61 Div. Artillery.

                        DISTRIBUTION

            Copy No. 1 - 5   306th Brigade R.F.A.
                      6 -10   307th Brigade R.F.A.
                     11 -14   61st D.A.C.
                     14 -17   61st D.T.M.O.
                         18   61st Division 'G'
                         19   61st Division 'Q'
                         20   R.A. XI Corps.
                         21   R.A. 59th Division.
                         22   R.A. 66th Division.
                         23   H.A. XI Corps.
                         24   C.B.S.O. XI Corps.
                         25   28th Brigade R.G.A.
                         26   182nd Infantry Brigade.
                         27   183rd Infantry Brigade.
                         28   184th Infantry Brigade.
                         29   No. 1 Coy. 61st Div. Train.
                         30   42 Squadron R.A.F.
                         31   A.L.O. 42 Squadron R.A.F.
                         32   XI Balloon Coy R.A.F.
                     33 -34   War Diary
                         35   File.

SECRET.   Copy No. 17

61st. DIVISIONAL ARTILLERY INSTRUCTIONS No. 16.

Corps Battle Line. 1. The 61st. Divisional Sector of the Corps Battle Line (at present the line MUDDY LANE POST (exclusive) - NOUVEAU MONDE - thence line of LYS to G.16.b.8.7. and line of ETILBECQUE to G.10.b.6.0.) will be known as the Left Divisional Sector.

   The Divisional Sector will be sub-divided into Sections as follows :-

   Right Brigade - NOUVEAU MONDE Section.
   Left Brigade - SAILLY Section.

   The inter-brigade boundary remains as follows -
The grid line between L.13. and L.19. Eastward to
L.17.d.0.0. thence in a straight line to G.22. central.

Nucleus Garrison Posts 2. Posts with nucleus garrisons to cover the undermentioned important points and main lines of approach are now established.

Nau MONDE Section.
   (i) MUDDY LANE POST (G.33.c.1.5. and G.33.c.1.7.) - Road Mixed platoon of 61st and 59th. Divisions.
   (ii) NOUVEAU MONDE (G.27.c.7.2.) - 2 roads.
   (iii) G.27.c.4.5. - Road Bridge.
   (iv) On high ground immediately East of Canal at G.21.d.7.0. - this post to be responsible for footbridge at G.27.c.9.3. and road bridge at G.21.d.5.2. (PONT DE LA JUSTICE).
   (v) G.21.d.8.8. - 2 road bridges. Post also to be responsible for foot-bridges at G.21.d.7.6. and G.21.b.95.60. respectively.
        Mixed platoon of Right and Left Brigades.
   (vi) G.16.c.8.6. (Pt. TOURNANT) - road bridge.
   (vii) G.16.b.6.6. - road bridge. Post also to be responsible for footbridge at G.16.b.35.35. and for road bridge at G.16.b.85.85.
   (viii) G.10.d.75.45. - road bridge. Post also to be responsible for footbridge at G.10.d.80.15.
   (ix) House G.10.b.0.1. Mixed platoons of 61st. and 40th Divisions

ACKNOWLEDGE.

                                    F.P.Lye.
14.9.18.   Captain, R.A.,
                            Bde. Major, 61st. Div. Artillery.

Distribution.

Copy No. 1 306 Bde. RFA   11 38 Bde R.G.A.
        2 307 Bde. RFA   12 H.A. XI Corps
        3 150 Army Bde RFA   13 C.V.S.O. XI Corps
        4 61st D.A.C.   14 182 Inf. Bde.
        5 61 D.T.M.O.   15 183 Inf. Bde.
        6 61st Div 'G'   16 184 Inf. Bde.
        7 C.R.E. 61 Div   17)
        8 R.A. XI Corps   18) War Diary
        9 R.A. 06th Div
       10 R.A. 59th Div   19 File.

SECRET.   Copy No: 28

61st. DIVISIONAL ARTILLERY INSTRUCTIONS NO: 17.

DEFENCE AGAINST GAS.

1.   The general instructions regarding defence against gas are contained in S.S.534 - "Standing Orders for defence against Gas". Attention is also called to the instructions contained in 61st. Divn. G.C.17/3 of 23.8.18, paras. 4 & 5.
     The following instructions are supplementary to, or in amplification of, above instructions.

2.   The ALERT ZONE will be the area forward (Eastward) of a line running approximately 6,000 yards West of the most advanced troops.
     The location of this zone will be determined by the positions of the advanced troops, and any alteration of its western boundary will be notified from time to time.
     The present western boundary is as follows :-

          G.25.d.8.8. - G.19.b.7.7. - G.8.d.8.5.

     (The Divisional Gas Officer arranges that the western limit of the ALERT ZONE is marked by notice boards when crossed by roads.)

3.   The READY ZONE will consist of the area between the Western edge of the ALERT ZONE and a line about 10,000 yards West of that Zone.
     Its location will move automatically with the movement of the ALERT ZONE.
     The Western limits, which are marked by notice boards, will be notified from time to time.
     The present Western limit of the READY ZONE is :-

          The general line RIEZ DU VINAGE - RUE DES VACHES - CALONNE CHURCH - PT. TOURNANT (K.15.d.) - ARREWAGE - CAUDESCURE (all inclusive).

4.   Box respirators will always be worn in the "ALERT" position by everyone in the ALERT ZONE.
     Box respirators will be carried by everyone when in the READY ZONE.

5.   Attention is drawn to S.S.212, which deals with YELLOW CROSS GAS and measures to be taken to counteract its effect.

6.   A large percentage of casualties from gas shelling are due to either carelessness or ignorance, and are preventable.
     Casualties can be reduced to a minimum by :-

     (a)   Rigid gas discipline.

     (b)   Giving all ranks a thorough knowledge of the properties of the various gasses, their effect, and the measures which must be taken to counteract them, with special reference to the persistency of YELLOW CROSS GAS, and its habit of reappearing after dawn under the influence of the sun. The imparting of this knowledge should be the duty of all officers.

7.   In order to reduce casualties to a minimum, all Commanders will ensure that the responsibilities of all concerned for successful anti-gas measures are fully realised and acted upon.
     All gas casualties will be investigated by C.Os. as soon as possible after they occur, in order to ascertain that all reasonable precautions were taken by officers, N.C.Os., or men, either for their own protection or for that of the men under their charge. Neglect of these precautions will be severely dealt with.

(P.T.O.)

Results of these investigations, together with any suggestions, will be forwarded to R.A.H.Q. through the usual channels, in order that as much information as possible may be available on the subject to assist the troops in the Division.

Units will make such arrangements that will ensure that all who become "gas casualties" are not evacuated before their cases are investigated; and that evidence be taken on oath at the Dressing Stations or Field Ambulances, from men whose condition permits.

8. (a) Every Unit must have a scheme ready for the evacuation of a gassed area should the tactical situation permit. These evacuations will not take place down wind.

(b) Supplies of anti-gas clothing and stocks of chloride of lime, also bi-carbonate of soda, will be held by all Batteries at their gun positions if possible.

Any spare S.D. clothing on charge will be kept at Battery Wagon Lines.

(c) Brigade Commanders will, in consultation with M.O. attached to their H.Q., issue necessary orders to their units with regard to the arrangements to be made whereby any personnel who may become splashed with the liquid of YELLOW CROSS GAS may be enabled to immediately wash with soap and water or bathe the affected parts with a solution of bi-carbonate of soda.

(d) Orders will be issued to prevent dugouts, or other protected places, from becoming contaminated during bombardments by anyone who has been in contact with gas entering and bringing in gas on their clothing, etc.

This especially refers to YELLOW CROSS GAS, as the presence of dangerous quantities of GREEN or BLUE Cross can be noticed.

9. Action to be taken at the commencement of a bombardment :-
The alarm will be spread as laid down in S.S.534.

(a) All instances of gas shelling will be reported to the Divisional Artillery Gas Officer immediately, giving location and approximate number of rounds fired.

(b) Should the bombardment exceed approximately 500 rounds, all units within 2,000 yards of the affected area will be warned by the unit in whose area the shelling occurs, giving area affected. The next higher formation or unit will be informed by wire, stating area affected, nature of gas, and approximate number of rounds.

The affected area will be picqueted in order to prevent other troops entering the gassed area.

When informing R.A.H.Q., the wire will be repeated to the Divisional Artillery Gas Officer, who will proceed, or cause a representative of the Gas Services to proceed, to the scene of the bombardment, and advise units as to the protective measures to be adopted, and if possible to diagnose the gas or gasses.

(c) Plans for evacuating affected areas will be put into practice if necessary and possible.

(d) Divisional Artillery will notify Counter-Battery Officer, in order that Heavy Artillery may deal with offending enemy batteries.

10. Formations and units, in whose area gas shells have fallen, are responsible that the contaminated area is plainly marked with notices and picqueted to prevent other troops entering it until free of gas, and that the very earliest opportunity is taken to fill in all gas shell holes.

11. The Divisional Artillery Gas Officer is responsible that a sufficient supply of material for neutralising gassed areas is located at convenient points and known to all concerned.
    He will visit R.A.H.Q. and Units periodically, and ensure that their arrangements for gas defence are in order, and report results to R.A.H.Q.

12. Definite orders will be issued that Brigade and Battery Gas N.C.Os. are not to be detailed for any other than Anti-gas duties when their Unit is in the ALERT ZONE.

13. CLOUD GAS ATTACK.
    Attention is directed to S.S.534, Appendix IV, Section 5, the provision of which will be strictly adhered to.
    Formations or units will arrange to warn :-
    (a) all troops in their area,
    (b) troops on their flanks,
    (c) Div. Art. H.Q. repeating to Divl. Art. Gas Officer.

14. The "Cloud Gas" warning message will be kept ready made out in Signal Offices of Units, and will be in the following form :-

    (a) G.A.S. (Name of part of the front from which the message originates.)

    (b) It will only be sent by order of an officer, and will be signed by him.

    (c) It will be timed.

    (d) It will be sent without preamble, or address "to" or "from".

    (e) It will take precedence over all messages except S.O.S., and will interrupt messages in course of transmission.

    (f) It will be sent by all available means.

    (g) It will be sent to the next station in rear and to each flank.

                                    Wye.
                                    Capt. R.A.,
                                    Bde.Maj., 61 Div. Artillery.

16.9.18.

DISTRIBUTION.

Copy No.			
1 - 5.	306 Bde. R.F.A.	23.	183 Inf. Bde.
6 - 10.	307 Bde. R.F.A.	24.	184 Inf. Bde.
11 - 14.	61 D.A.C.	25.	R.A. XI Corps.
15 - 17.	61 D.T.M.O.	26.	59TH. Div. Art.
18.	61 Div. 'G'.	27.	66th. Div. Art.
19.	" " 'Q'	28-29.	War Diary.
20.	61 D.A. Gas Officer.	30.	File.
21.	O.i/c R.A. Signals.	31 - 40.	Spars.
22.	182 Inf. Bde.		

"A" Form.
MESSAGES AND SIGNALS.

Army Form C. 2121.
(In pads of 100.)
No. of Message..........

Prefix .... Code .... m.	Words.	Charge.	This message is on a/c of:	Recd. at .... m.
Office of Origin and Service Instructions.	Sent		.... Service.	Date..........
....	At.......... m.			From..........
....	To..........			
....	By..........		(Signature of "Franking Officer.")	By..........

TO { McNi[ll] ...... }

Sender's Number.	Day of Month.	In reply to Number.	A A A
* BM160	17		

[illegible handwritten message]

By Tullather(?)

From
Place
Time

The above may be forwarded as now corrected. (Z)

Censor. Signature of Addressee or person authorised to telegraph in his name.

* This line should be erased if not required.

War Diary

SECRET.

R.A.G.1/5.

To all recipients of
61 D.A. Order No.153.

    Reference 61st. Divisional Artillery Order No.153 of 13th. instant, para.2.

    The positions taken over from C and D Batteries 306th. Brigade, R.F.A., are not likely to be again required and need not therefore be maintained fit for immediate re-occupation.

F.P.Wye.
Capt. R.A.,
Bde.Maj., 61 Div. Artillery.

17.9.1918.

SECRET.   R.A.G. 1.

61st DIVISIONAL ARTILLERY
GENERAL ARTILLERY INSTRUCTIONS
XI CORPS AREA.

DISPOSITIONS.

1.   The Field Artillery Batteries covering the Front of 61st
Division are grouped in accordance with the tactical situation,
one group being affiliated to each Infantry Brigade in the
Line.
        The actual dispositions and locations of Units are shown
in the LOCATION STATEMENT, issued weekly.

LIAISON

2.   Each Groups provides a Senior Liaison Officer with the
Infantry Brigade to which it is affiliated, and also a Liaison
Officer with each Battalion in the Line.
        In cases where the Group and Infantry Brigade H.Q. are
close together, the senior Liaison Officer will not normally
be required.

S.O.S. ARRANGEMENTS
(a) Field Batteries.

        The 18 pdr. Barrage will be put down as close as possible
to our Front line. Fire will not be evenly distributed,
but will be thickest at vulnerable points and dangerous
approaches, the gaps being filled by M.G. Fire, and Stokes
T.Mortars.
        4.5" Howitzers will fire on selected points, not less than
400 yards from our Front line, which are not being engaged
by 6" Newton Trench Mortars and 6" Howitzers.
        Group Commanders are responsible for arranging the S.O.S.
Lines of their Batteries in consultation with B.G.
Commanding the Infantry Brigade which they are supporting
                                                and with

(1)

O.C. Divisional M.G. Battalion.

The S.O.S. arrangements will then be submitted to C.R.A. for approval.

(i) Rates of Fire :

	Rounds per gun per minute.	
	First 5 mins.	Five to Fifteen minutes.
18 prs.	4	2
4.5" How.	3	1½

During the last five minutes, Batteries will search backwards and forwards for 200 yards.

(ii) Fire will be kept up for 15 minutes unless the Brigade or Battery Commanders have reason to suppose that it is wanted for a longer period or have ascertained from the Infantry that it is no longer required.

(b) 6" NEWTON T.Ms.

The 6" NEWTON T.Ms will fire on selected points (not less than 300 yards from out front line) arranged by D.T.M.O. in consultation with B.Gs. Commanding Infantry Brigades in the line and Field Artillery Group Commander, which will be submitted to C.R.A. for approval.

Rates of Fire.	Rounds per gun per minute.
First five minutes	4
Five to Fifteen minutes	2

S.O.S POINTERS & BOARDS.

4. (a) A Board with pointer will be erected in each Battery Position and O.P. on which will be marked the limits of Battalion and Infantry Brigade Sectors and the Divisional Front, so that the S.O.S. sentry or observer on duty, can at once ascertain the portion of the front from which the S.O.S. signals have been sent up

(b) Each gun will have an S.O.S. Board on which will be recorded the Angle, Range, Rates of Fire, etc. for S.O.S.

REPETITION OF S.O.S.
LIGHT SIGNAL. 5.

The S.O.S. Light Signal will always be repeated from O.Ps

O.C. Divisional M.G. Battalion.

The S.O.S. arrangements will then be submitted to C.R.A. for approval.

(i) Rates of Fire :

	Rounds per gun per minute.	
	First 5 mins.	Five to Fifteen minutes.
18 prs.	4	2
4.5" How.	3	1½

During the last five minutes, Batteries will search backwards and forwards for 200 yards.

(ii) Fire will be kept up for 15 minutes unless the Brigade or Battery Commanders have reason to suppose that it is wanted for a longer period or have ascertained from the Infantry that it is no longer required.

(b) 6" NEWTON T.Ms.

The 6" NEWTON T.Ms will fire on selected points (not less than 300 yards from out front line) arranged by D.T.M.O. in consultation with B.Gs. Commanding Infantry Brigades in the line and Field Artillery Group Commander, which will be submitted to C.R.A. for approval.

Rates of Fire.	Rounds per gun per minute.
First five minutes	4
Five to Fifteen minutes	2

S.O.S POINTERS & BOARDS.

4. (a) A Board with pointer will be erected in each Battery Position and O.P. on which will be marked the limits of Battalion and Infantry Brigade Sectors and the Divisional Front, so that the S.O.S. sentry or observer on duty, can at once ascertain the portion of the front from which the S.O.S. signals have been sent up

(b) Each gun will have an S.O.S. Board on which will be recorded the Angle, Range, Rates of Fire, etc. for S.O.S.

REPETITION OF S.O.S.
LIGHT SIGNAL. 5.

The S.O.S Light Signal will always be repeated from O.Ps

on the front affected.

**REPETITION OF S.O.S.
CALL BY TELEPHONE.** 6.

6. The S.O.S. will be repeated by telephone as follows :-

    From O.Ps to Batteries

      "   "   to Flank O.Ps.

      "   Batteries to Batteries on their Flanks

      "   "   to Group H.Q.

      "   Group H.Q. to H.Qs of Groups on each Flank

      "   "   to R.A.H.Q.

      "   R.A.H.Q. to Affiliated Brigade R.G.A.

      "   "   to C.B.S.O.

      "   "   to Division "G"

**DUTIES OF LIAISON
OFFICERS DURING S.O.S.** 7.

7. Their primary duty is to ensure that the guns have got the signal and open fire. They will then make every effort to find out if any portion of the front is NOT affected so as to localise where the trouble lies.

   NOTE. It is frequently easier to get negative information especially in case of small hostile attacks or raids, as those who are fighting are too busy to do more than put up the S.O.S. Signal).

Finally they will keep Group H.Q. informed of all details as regards the requirements and action of our Infantry

**ARTILLERY ACTION
WHEN HOSTILE ATTACK
IS ANTICIPATED.** 8

8. In the event of a hostile attack appearing likely the action of artillery will be divided into four phases :

(a) Harassing Fire.

This will be increased by order of the Corps when information is received that the enemy are concentrating opposite the Corps Front. Its object will be to kill Germans moving

moving the back areas, damage their morale, destroy ammunition and hinder its accumulation.

During Harassing fire all guns and howitzers will search hostile communications, approaches, distant assembly places, and billets, areas being allotted beforehand by Div. Arty and Group Commanders. The rate of fire during this period will be laid down in rounds per hour by Corps when giving the order for harassing fire to commence. Fire will be carried out in irregular bursts

(b) Counter Mortar Bombardment.

This will open when the enemy opens a heavy bombardment on our Front.

All Field Howitzers and 18 pounders firing H.E. and 6" T.Ms. will engage the hostile trench mortars which may normally be expected to be in action in an area 300 to 800 yards from the hostile front line.

A scheme for counter mortar bombardment prepared by Group Commanders and approved by C.R.A. will be put into execution on the order for counter battery bombardment being sent out. The average rate of fire during this period will be the same as for counter preparation.

(c) Counter Preparation.

It is impossible to fix beforehand the time at which (b) will change to (c). It will depend on the intensity of the bombardment and information available. If no information is available and in the absence of orders to the contrary, the counter preparation will commence one hour after phase (b) has opened

On receipt of the Order "COUNTER", all batteries will commence counter-preparation. Guns and Howitzers will open fire on their S.O.S. points and search forward 800 yards along the line of fire of their S.O.S. points; at the same time each piece will sweep sufficiently to cover the ground between its own S.O.S. Point and that of the guns or

howitzs

howitzers covering the points on its flanks.

Rates of fire for both guns and howitzers, for first 10 minutes will be 2 rounds per piece per minute, and fire must be continued until the hostile bombardment ceases or an attack follows.

After the first 10 minutes the 18 pounders and 4.5" Hows. will fire bursts of fire at frequent intervals.

The above rates of fire will be normally employed, but Group and Battery Commanders must understand that the underlying principle is : "The heavier the hostile fire, the heavier our fire should be", though they will not depart from the normal rate without reference to their immediate superiors unless signal communication has broken down.

Ammunition.

18 pounders will use 50 % of shrapnel and 50 % of H.E., but they must retain sufficient shrapnel to deal with the Infantry attack if it ensues.

Howitzers will fire 50 % at least of 106 fuzes.

4.5"s may use gas shell if the wind is suitable, in which case the fire must be concentrated on selected places and not distributed thinly along the front

(d) S.O.S.

On the commencement of the hostile attack, which will be notified by signal from the front line, all guns and Howitzers will at once open fire on their S.O.S. lines.

ARTILLERY ACTION
in case of heavy local
bombardment by the enemy 9.

9. In the event of a heavy hostile bombardment of a portion of our front line defences, which may prelude a local hostile attack, batteries covering the front affected will on their own initiative or on orders from their Group Commanders open fire on their S.O.S. lines for 5 minutes. Rate of Fire INTENSE.

(5)

MUTUAL SUPPORT 10. Group Commanders will arrange schemes for Inter-Group Mutual Support, in case of a local hostile attack developing on their own front or on that of neighbouring groups.

These schemes will be submitted to C.R.A. for approval.

When called upon for Mutual Support and the Scheme involves the fire of their Batteries being switched off their own immediate front, Group Commanders will if possible consult the B.G. Commanding Infantry Brigade to which they are affiliated before ordering their Batteries to comply. In any case the Group Commanders will notify the B.G. Commanding Infantry Brigade of action taken.

Action is case of CLOUD GAS ATTACK. 11.

(a) 18 pounder batteries will sweep the hostile front line with H.E. for 2 minutes.

4.5" Howitzers will engage trench junctions and communications trenches (not less than 400 yards distant from OUR Front Line) with H.E. for 2 minutes.

Rate of Fire INTENSE.

(b) After 2 minutes batteries will carry out COUNTER PREPARATION.

NORMAL HARASSING FIRE 12. Normally Group Commanders will arrange details for harassing in consultation with B.Gs Commanding Infantry Brigades in the Front line. The amount of ammunition to be expended for this purpose is notified to all concerned from time to time.

BATTERY POSITIONS. 13. Each Battery in action will have a main position, which will be kept as silent as possible, and in addition will have a detached section or single gun which will do all normal shooting

harassing

harassing fire etc.

ALTERNATIVE
POSITIONS. 14. Each Battery will have an alternative position with platforms ready prepared for occupation.

ANTI-TANK GUN
POSITIONS. 15. Anti-tank guns are placed in action to cover, with fire over open sights, the main avenues of approach to the CORPS BATTLE LINE available to enemy tanks.

At each Anti-Tank gun a board in the form of a "fighting map" will be kept on which will be shewn the range to all prominent objects.

Anti-tank detachments will be frequently practised in their duties, and every member of the detachment must know the range to all prominent landmarks.

OBSERVATION
POSTS. 16.
(a) Each Battery will man an O.P. from dawn to dusk.
(b) Group Commanders will select the best points from which Batteries will observe, so as to ensure that as much of the Group Front as possible is under direct observation during hours of daylight.

The number of O.Ps. to be manned by night will be ordered by Group Commanders.
(c) Each Battery or Section will have an O.P. close to the gun position from which as much ground as possible can be seen between the guns and our front or outpost line.

AMMUNITION. 17. The amounts and natures of ammunition to be kept with guns in action are laid down in 61 D.A. Instructions from time to time.

RATES OF FIRE 18. These are laid down by G.H.Q. in rounds per gun

(7)   per

per minute as follows :-

TERM	18 pounders	4.5" Howitzers.
GUN FIRE	As fast as aimed rounds can be fired.	
INTENSE	4	3
RAPID	3	2
NORMAL	2	1
SLOW	1	½
VERY SLOW	½	¼

COUNTER-BATTERY WORK & CO-OPERATION WITH AIRCRAFT.

COUNTER-BATTERY WORK.

19. Counter-Battery work is carried out by all Batteries R.G.A. but Batteries, R.F.A. will assist in neutralization and in destructive shoots when possible.

The Corps Counter-battery area is divided into an inner and outer zone for Field Artillery and Heavy Artillery respectively.

The INNER zone is the area bounded by a line drawn at 2000 yards from our Front trenches or outpost line, within the Divisional boundaries. The inner zone is sub-divided into Group or Brigade Zones by C.R.A.

The objects of Counter-Battery work are set forth in S.S. 131, page et seq.

Neutralization of active Hostile Batteries.

Field Artillery will assist in neutralising hostile batteries within their range. Any Battery knowing that a hostile battery is active should engage it and report doing so to Group H.Q. who will inform C.B.S.O. at once. Field Batteries will, as a rule fire 20 to 30 rounds unless direct observation on the hostile battery is possible when fire will be continued until the hostile battery is silenced.

Neutralising fire will be brought to bear as rapidly as possible and ground or balloon observation employed.

It is

harassing fire etc.

ALTERNATIVE POSITIONS. 14. Each Battery will have an alternative position with platforms ready prepared for occupation.

ANTI-TANK GUN POSITIONS. 15. Anti-tank guns are placed in action to cover, with fire over open sights, the main avenues of approach to the CORPS BATTLE LINE available to enemy tanks.

At each Anti-Tank gun a board in the form of a "fighting map" will be kept on which will be shewn the range to all prominent objects.

Anti-tank detachments will be frequently practised in their duties, and every member of the detachment must know the range to all prominent landmarks.

OBSERVATION POSTS. 16.

(a) Each Battery will man an O.P. from dawn to dusk.

(b) Group Commanders will select the best points from which Batteries will observe, so as to ensure that as much of the Group Front as possible is under direct observation during hours of daylight.

The number of O.Ps. to be manned by night will be ordered by Group Commanders.

(c) Each Battery or Section will have an O.P. close to the gun position from which as much ground as possible can be seen between the guns and our front or outpost line.

AMMUNITION. 17. The amounts and natures of ammunition to be kept with guns in action are laid down in 61 D.A. Instructions from time to time.

RATES OF FIRE 18. These are laid down by G.H.Q. in rounds per gun per

It is essential that the number of rounds fired should be continually altered and that salvoes or single rounds should be fired at irregular intervals.

ZONE CALLS.   20.

(a) **For Counter-Battery Targets.**

If the Field Artillery are engaged on barrage work, the Divisional Artillery will inform C.B.S.O. beforehand so that the C.H.A. can engage their zone temporarily.

Zone calls must always be answered promptly.

If the wireless set is attached to a Battery, an alarm gong, bell or whistle will be kept at the ground station.

N.F.Calls.

Each Brigade or Group will detail one Battery daily to answer these calls within the Brigade or Group C.B. Zone.

One section only of the Battery will be employed and about 10 to 12 rounds 4.5" Howitzer or double that amount for 18 pounders will be fired on each call received. If observations are received an additional 6 rounds per Howitzer Section or 12 rounds per 18 pdr. Section will be fired after any necessary correction has been applied.

Guns will open with a salvo of shrapnel and continue with H.E. Howitzers will fire a salvo with 106 fuze, then continue with 50% direct action and 50 % delay action fuzes.

Balloons on receiving the N.F. call on their wireless will, if possible, observe the firing on the hostile battery and will call up the Battery (through Brigade or Group H.Q.) which has taken up the N.F. call and give observations. The responsible battery will however open fire at once and will not wait to get into communication with the balloon before doing so.

All Batteries dealing with these calls must know which hostile batteries can be seen from O.Ps. In case a hostile battery is not visible from O.Ps. a good reference point should be selected as a datum point but if possible direct observation

from

from a balloon or O.P. should be obtained.

On completion of the shoot B.C. will report to his Brigade or Group H.Q.

W.P. N.F. Calls.

The C.B. S.O. will at once inform Groups which hostile Batteries they are to engage in the square indicated, but to prevent loss of time, batteries detailed for N.F. duty will at once open fire on one of the hostile batteries in the square.

N.F. A.A. Calls.

Calls are used when an observer desires to bring fire to bear on active anti-craft gun or guns. Action to be taken is similar to that taken in the case of a G.F. call (see para b). Field Artillery will open fire if the target lies within the zones allotted to them for N.F. Calls.

(b) FOR FLEETING OPPORTUNITY TARGETS.

The following instructions with regard to the replies to be given by the Artillery of the XI Corps to L.L. and G.F. Calls are based on the principle that the power of the artillery should be developed when remunerative targets are seen, in accordance with the tactical situation. When indications exist of the near approach of an attack and when the attack is in progress, the number of guns detailed to reply to these Calls must be reduced in order to avoid thinning out the density of fire at the decisive points.

G.F. & L.L. Calls.

These are combined with and follow the zone call, e.g.

    W A G F W A G F W A G F
    W A G F 50 FAN W 6 a 26 51
or W A L L W A L L W A L L
    W A L L 2000 FAN W 6 a 26 51

Reply to G.F. Calls.

(1) Under normal conditions.

All Field Artillery Batteries will reply, which can be brought to bear, except those engaged on shoots with aeroplane observation.

(ii) During Counter Preparation.

All superimposed batteries covering the zone in which the Target lies, will reply.

(iii) During S.O.S.

One superimposed 18 pounder battery will be detailed by R.A.H.Q. to reply.

REPLY TO L.L. CALLS.

(i) Under normal conditions.

All batteries which can bear except those engaged on fire for destruction with aerial observation, whether on hostile batteries or other objectives will reply.

(ii) During Counter Preparation.

All Batteries engaged on counter-battery work and one section of all other batteries will reply, which can be brought to bear.

(iii) During S.O.S.

One superimposed 18 pounder battery to be detailed by R.A.H.Q. will reply.

In all the above cases the rate of and duration of fire will be INTENSE for 3 minutes.

XX Calls.

In order to test the rapidity with which batteries can open fire in response to LL Calls, arrangements have been made with No. 42 Squadron, R.A.F. to send test calls from time to time.

These Test Calls will take the form:-

XX 1000 FAN N.32.c.5.5.

and will be answered by a single salvo from every Field Battery that can bring fire to bear.

Note. The Prefix LL will on no, account be used when sending the test calls.

R.A.

R.A.H.Q. to be informed of the time of receipt of call and the time at which each Battery replied, and will investigate all cases of unnecessary delay.

MOVING WARFARE. 21. Co-operation between Artillery and Aeroplane in a moving Battle.

In the event of operations which necessitate batteries constantly taking up fresh positions and probable disorganization of communications, the co-operation between aeroplane and artillery requires that special measures should be taken to ensure getting the best value from air observation.

When a Field Artillery Brigade or Battery occupies a new position and is ready to fire, with wireless mast installed, it will put out its "aeroplane call to F.A. Brigade or Battery", in force on that date as a ground signal to notify:-

(a). The identity of the unit and consequently its call.

(b) That a battery is in action with sufficient ammunition to respond to aeroplane calls without delay.

(c) That the wireless mast is adjacent to where the ground signal is placed and that it is in action.

Unless the above conditions are met the Brigade or Battery will not exhibit its call, except as mentioned below.

If the Brigade having put out its ground signal has had no call in response, and it is desired to call the attention of an aeroplane to its position, a white Very Light will be fired.

The sites for displaying ground signals must be very carefully selected as observers will be working over a strange country and on a wide area.

The above arrangements are also extended so as to assist in:-

(a) Locating the positions to which Brigades and Batteries of artillery have moved, and

(b) transmitting orders to them.

As soon as it is apparent that batteries have moved, low flying aeroplanes will be detailed to make a special reconnaissance usually at a height of about 500 feet, of the areas in which it is assumed the artillery will be situated for the purpose of pin-pointing the exact location and informing Corps R.A. with the least possible delay.

The aeroplane engaged on this special reconnaissance will send wireless call as follows :-

Squadron Call, pilots personal number, signal for " are you receiving my signals", and a special call for batteries' code letters, e.g.

    W.S.B.G.S. P.Captain JONES of 42nd Squadron is calling for code letters from batteries of XI Corps.

All the Batteries or Brigade Headquarters concerned whose wireless installations take in this call and those units whose wireless installations are, from some cause or other, not functioning, but who desire to communicate their whereabouts to the reconnoitring machine will display their code letters by white ground strips in the manner described :- .hereunder.

Example.

    Code Call - Field Artillery Brigade with their wireless station in working order.

    X
    Code Call - The same, with their wireless station deficient or out of order.

    Code Call - Battery H.A. with wireless station working and three guns in action (One strip under Code Call for each gun in action.

    X
    Code Call - The same, with their wireless station deficient or out of order but having three guns in action.

Batteries which have lost their wireless installations will place a sentry to watch for this special reconnoitring machine.

Their ground strips will be displayed during the whole flight of this patrol over the battery area.

The code call used by each Battery will be the "aeroplane to Battery" call issued and altered periodically by the 42nd Squadron R.A.F.

A Field Battery will use the figures I, II, III and IV after its Brigade Call to indicate whether it is A. B.C. or D Battery.

Batteries

Batteries which are in urgent need of ammunition and which are out of touch with their echelons will exhibit the letter "A" under their code call. This call will however be regarded somewhat in the nature of an "S.O.S." and will only be used in case of urgent necessity.

A spark transmitting set is being provided adjacent to the Corps Counter Battery Office, so that in the last resort (but only when all other means of communication fail), short orders can be transmitted to such batteries as have their wireless stations working.

A place in the firing battery will be definitely allotted for the carriage of the wireless operator, wireless installation and ground strips, or for ground strips only in the case of batteries not provided with wireless.

Furthermore, a N.C.O. and gunner will be detailed in each unit provided with a wireless installation, to assist the wireless operator in dismantling, packing up and re-erecting the wireless mast.

It is impressed on Battery Commanders that the wireless installation is as much a part of the battery equipment as any other store, and that they are therefore personally responsible that the best possible arrangements are made for it in every way.

All units will take steps to provide themselves with the necessary ground strips as early as possible.

Further co-operation of aeroplanes with Artillery Brigades or batteries will be carried out as laid down in S.S. 131.

- SECRET -   Copy No: 17

61st. DIVISIONAL ARTILLERY DEFENCE INSTRUCTIONS NO: 1.

(To be read in conjunction with
61st. D.A. Instructions No. 12.)

1. **OCCUPATION OF "CORPS BATTLE LINE" POSITIONS.** In the event of a strong hostile attack developing, or information of an impending attack in force being received, the order "MAN BATTLE STATIONS" for the defence of the Corps Battle Line will be sent to 61 D.A. Brigade "in readiness" and the D.T.M.O., also to the Army Field Artillery Brigade in Corps Reserve, if placed under orders of this Divisional Artillery by Corps.

2. **LOCATIONS OF FIELD ARTY. and 6" NEWTON TMs.** Positions and H.Q. for Field Artillery and 6" NEWTON T.M. positions are shewn in Appendices A & B respectively.

3. **ANTI-TANK GUNS.** Anti-tank guns are in action as follows:-

    No.1 at G.33.a.6.9.
    No.2 at G.27.d.9.8. with alternative position at
                                     G.33.a.55.80.

    The Advanced Guard Artillery will provide a guard of 1 man over each gun, and find necessary detachments in case of attack.
    In the event of the withdrawal of the Advanced Guard, No.2 gun, if circumstances permit, will be moved to its alternative position.

    Ammunition:-

    76 rounds H.E. 101 delay fuze (for use against tanks),
    76 rounds shrapnel (for engaging advancing Infantry),
        will be maintained with each gun.

4. **UNITS RESPONSIBLE FOR COVERING C.B.L. and PROVIDING LIAISON OFFICERS.** The Brigade in readiness will be responsible for covering the Corps Battle Line, and will provide Liaison Officers with Infantry Brigades and Battalions covering this line, until the arrival of the A.F.A. Brigade from Corps Reserve, or the withdrawal of the Advanced Guard Artillery, when two Artillery Groups will be formed - one being affiliated to each Infantry Brigade - which will provide necessary liaison officers.

5. **S.O.S. LINES.** S.O.S. lines for the CORPS BATTLE LINE, when one, two or three Artillery Brigades are in action, are shewn on tracing, APPENDIX 'C'.

6. **INSTRUCTIONS RE OPENING FIRE.** Until the withdrawal of the Advanced Guard is complete, Units will only open fire:

    1. To bring observed fire to bear on advancing Germans.

    2. Under orders from their Brigade or Group Commander, acting on a request from the Advanced Guard Artillery or from the Infantry.

7.	MUTUAL SUPPORT WITH FLANK DIVISIONS.	Arrangements for MUTUAL SUPPORT are shewn in APPENDIX 'D'.
8.	ARTILLERY ACTION WHEN HOSTILE ATTACK IS ANTICIPATED.	The arrangements for artillery action to be put into force when a hostile attack is anticipated, will be made in accordance with para. 8, 61st. D.A. General Artillery Instructions, XI Corps Area.
9.	LOCATIONS OF WAGON LINES, D.A.C. & A.R.P.	Locations of Wagon Lines, D.A.C. and A.R.P. are shewn in APPENDIX 'E'.
10.	AMMUNITION.	The following amounts of ammunition will be dumped on the order "MAN BATTLE STATIONS" being received :-

Per gun.

```
18-prs.    250 rounds  A.
           200    "     AX (106 fuzes as far as possible.)
            50    "     A Smoke.

4.5" Hows. 275    "     BX (106 as far as possible.)
            25    "     B Smoke.
           200    "     GAS (per Battery.)
```

6" NEWTON Trench Mortars - 50 rounds per gun.

11.	S.O.S. LIGHT SIGNALS.	20 S.O.S. Rifle Grenades, for each O.P. to be manned by night, will be drawn by Brigades on authority from S.C.R.A. on order "MAN BATTLE STATIONS" being sent out.
12.	ANTI-GAS STORES.	The Divisional Artillery Gas Officer will arrange for necessary supply of chloride of lime and bi-carbonate of soda, etc., for Battery Positions.
13.	CAMOUFLAGE MATERIAL.	Camouflage for Battery Positions, etc., will be issued to Batteries from RING DUMP, NEUF BERQUIN, on authority from Staff Captain, R.A.
14.	TELEPHONE WIRE.	The Officer i/c R.A. Signals will arrange for supply of telephone wire to Units, as required.
15.		ACKNOWLEDGE.

F.P. Wye.
Capt. R.A.,
Bde.Maj., 61 Div. Artillery.

19.9.1918.

DISTRIBUTION.

```
Copy.No. 1 - 306 Bde. RFA.        Cop No. 10 - 59th. Div. Art.
         2 - 307 Bde. RFA.                11 - 28 Bde. R.G.A.
         3 - 150 A Bde. RFA.               12 - XI Corps H.A.
         4 - 61st. D.A.C.                  13 - XI Corps C.B.S.O.
         5 - 61 D.T.M.O.                   14 - 182 Inf. Bde.
         6 - 61st. Divn. 'G'.              15 - 183 Inf. Bde.
         7 - C.R.E. 61 Div.                16 - 184 Inf. Bde.
         8 - R.A. XI Corps.             17-18. War Diary.
         9 - 28 A Bde. RFA.                19 - File.
```

SECRET.

R.O.1.

61st. DIVISIONAL ARTILLERY,

LOCATION STATEMENT - 19.9.1918.

Group.	Unit.	Location.	Wagon Lines Rear.	Forward.
ADVANCED GUARD ARTILLERY.	306 Bde. H.Q.	G.13.b.60.30.	L.10.a 60.95.	
	A/306. (2 guns) (2 ") (2 ")	G.33.d.20.60. G.32.d.50.55. G.32.c.98.60.	to L.11.c.30.90.	G.20.a.05.95.
	B/306. (4 ") (2 ")	G.10.a.2.2. G.11.d.1.7.		G.8.d.1.9.
	C/306. (2 ") (2 ") (2 ")	G.28.b.15.70. G.26.a.90.55. G.28.c.07.32.		G.19.b.6.5.
	D/306. (1 How.) (2 ") (2 ")	M.5.b.35.80. G.11.a.65.05. G.11.b.08.22.	L.11.a.6.8.	
	B/307. (3 guns) (3 ")	G.18.a.60.60. G.10.b.95.35.	L.11.c.	
BRIGADE IN READINESS.	307 Bde. H.Q.	L.10.d.7.3.	L.10.d.9.6.	
	A/307. (6 guns)	G.19.d.15.50.	L.17.d.2.7.	
	C/307. (6 ")	G.14.a.70.00.	L.23.b.4.8.	
	D/307. (6 Hows.)	G.14.d.25.10.	L.10.d.4.3.	
	61 D.A.C. H.Q.	L.20.c.7.0.	L.20.c.7.0.	
	D.T.M.O. H.Q.	L.17.b.75.10.		
	X/61. H.Q. (1 6" NEWTON) (1 ")	L.17.b.75.10. H.8.b.35.97. H.8.c.90.25.		
	Y/61. H.Q. (1 6" NEWTON)	L.17.b.75.10. H.25.c.88.20.		
	61st. D.A.C.O.	L.17.b.75.10.		

19.9.1918.

Spencer Batchelor.
Lieut.
R.O., R.A., 61st. Division.

APPENDIX 'A'.

61st. DIVISIONAL ARTILLERY DEFENCE INSTRUCTIONS No. 1.

LOCATIONS OF POSITIONS to cover
THE CORPS BATTLE LINE.

'A' Brigade.   (Brigade in Readiness.)

  H.Q.   L.10.d.8.2.

  1 18-pr.Bty.   (4 guns)   L.24.c.95.45.
                    (2 ")   G.19.d.15.50.

  1   do.   (6 ")   G.7.b.8.2.

  1   do.   (6 ")   G.8.b.1.7.

  1 4.5"How.Bty.   (6 Hows.) L.18.a.3.5.

'B' Brigade.   (Reinforcing Brigade.)

  H.Q.   L.26.b.75.35.

  1 18-pr.Bty.   (2 guns)   L.26.b.0.6.
                    (4 ")   L.27.b.2.4.

  1   do.   (6 guns)   L.16.d.1.6.

  1   do.   (6 ")   L.11.b.2.2.

  1 4.5"How.Bty.   (6 Hows.) L.22.d.30.75.

'C' Brigade.   (Advanced Guard Artillery.)

  H.Q.   L.20.c.7.0.

  1 18-pr.Bty.   (6 guns)   L.11.a.2.0.

  1   do.   (2 ")   L.21.c.94.70.
                    (4 ")   L.27.a.20.75.

  1   do.   (6 ")   L.22.a.7.6.

  1 4.5"How.Bty.   (6 Hows.) L.15.d.95.10.

NOTE.   On the Advanced Guard Artillery being ordered to withdraw, any portions of the "Brigade in readiness" attached to the Advanced Guard Artillery, will automatically come under orders of the Brigade to which they belong.

APPENDIX 'B'.

61st. DIVISIONAL ARTILLERY DEFENCE INSTRUCTIONS NO: 1.

6" NEWTON TRENCH MORTAR POSITIONS.

(1)   2 T.Ms.   at   G.26.d.6.9.

(2)   1 "   "   G.27.a.10.75.

(3)   1 "   "   G.21.c.80.90.

(4)   1 "   "   G.15.d.80.80.

(5)   1 "   "   G.16.a.60.80.

(6)   2 "   "   G.10.c.90.50.

APPENDIX "C"
S.O.S LINES FOR 1 BRIGADE R.F.A.
AND 8 6" NEWTON TRENCH MORTARS

LEGEND

18 Pdrs ⭕
4.5" Hows △
6" Newtons ■

Northern Divisional Boundary

1 How
4 Guns
1-18 Pdr
1-18 Pdr

Inter Brigade Boundary

CORPS BATTLE LINE

6 Guns
6 Guns

Southern Divisional Boundary

APPENDIX "C"

S.O.S LINES FOR 2 BRIGADES R.F.A.
AND 8-6" NEWTON TRENCH MORTARS

LEGEND
18 Pdrs ⬭   4.5 Hows △
6" Newtons ■

APPENDIX
GUN LINES FOR 3 BRIGADES R.F.A.
AND 3 C" NEWTON TRENCH MORTARS.
LEGEND
18 Pounders :-
4.5 Howitzers :-
6" Newtons :-

APPENDICES 'C' & 'D' will be forwarded later.

APPENDIX 'E'.

61st. DIVISIONAL ARTILLERY DEFENCE INSTRUCTIONS NO: 1.

WAGON LINES for Brigades & D.A.C. covering CORPS BATTLE LINE.

'A' BRIGADE.	1 Battery.	K.11.b.6.5.
	1 "	K.12.a.2.2.
	1 "	K.11.a. L'EPINETTE.
	1 "	K.11.a. L'EPINETTE.
'B' BRIGADE.	1 Battery.	K.24.d. ROBERMETZ.
	1 "	K.24.d. "
	1 "	K.23.a.1.5. SACHET FARM.
	1 "	K.23.c. central.
'C' BRIGADE.	1 Battery.	K.10.d. cent. ITCHIN FARM.
	1 "	K.16.a.8.8. BONAR FARM.
	1 "	K.16.a.5.8.
	1 "	K.9.d.1.5. TAXI FARM.
D.A.C.	No.1 Section.	K.14.b. central.
	No.2 "	K.3.c.7.1.
B.A.C.		K.1.c.3.0.
A.R.P.	ANSELL DUMP. E.7.c.	

S E C R E T.   R.G.1.

AMENDMENT NO:1
to
61st. DIV. ARTILLERY LOCATION STATEMENT of 19.9.18.

& B/307.
Delete all reference to D/306 and substitute the
following :-

D/306. (2 Hows.)   M.5 b 35.80.
        (3   ")   G.22 b.75.50.
        (1 How.)   G.23 c.50.65.

B/307. (2 guns)   G.15 a.60.60.
        (3   ")   G.16 a.75.80.
        (1 gun)   G.12.c.00.15.

Spencer Batchelor
Lieut.
R.O., R.A., 61 Divn.

21.9.1918.

War Diary

S E C R E T.

R.A.G. 4/6.

AMENDMENT NO: 1
to
61st. DIVISIONAL ARTILLERY ORDER NO. 154.

1. Reference 61st. Divisional Artillery Order No.154 of to-day's date, para.3:-
   For "A, C & D batteries" read "A & C batteries"

2. Advanced Guard Artillery and 307th. Bde. R.F.A. to acknowledge.

F.P. Nye.
Capt. R.A.,
Bde.Maj., 61 Div. Artillery.

22.9.1918.

S E C R E T.

Copy No: 34

61st. DIVISIONAL ARTILLERY ORDER NO: 154.

22nd. Sept. 1918.

1. 'A', 'C' & 'D' batteries, 307th. Brigade, R.F.A., will proceed from Wagon Lines to action on night 23rd/24th. inst., under orders to be issued by O.C. Advanced Guard Artillery.

2. These batteries will come under orders of O.C. Advanced Guard Artillery, at 6 p.m. on 23rd. inst.

3. O.C. Advanced Guard Artillery will notify arrival of these units in action to this office, by code word "COWGATE".

4. ACKNOWLEDGE - (Advanced Guard Artillery and 307 Bde. R.F.A. only.)

F.P.Wye.

Capt. R.A.,
Bde.Maj., 61 Div.Artillery,

Issued at 6 p.m.

DISTRIBUTION.

Copy No:		
1 - 6.	Advanced Guard Artillery.
7 - 10.	307th. Bde. R.F.A.
11 - 14.	61st. D.A.C.
15 - 17.	61st. D.T.M.O.
18.	61 Divn. 'G'
19.	61 Divn. 'Q'
20.	R.A. XI Corps.
21.	59th Div. Art.
22.	66th Div. Art.
23.	H.A. XI Corps.
24.	C.B.S.O., XI Corps.
25.	28th Bde. R.G.A.
26.	182 Inf. Bde.
27.	183 Inf. Bde.
28.	184 Inf. Bde.
29.	No.1 Coy, 61 Div.Train.
30.	42 Squadron, R.A.F.
31.	A.L.O., 42 Sqdn. R.A.F.
32.	XI Balloon Coy. R.A.F.
33 - 34.	War Diary.
35.	File.

War Diary
13

S E C R E T.

Copy No: ....

61st. DIVISIONAL ARTILLERY ORDER NO. 155.

22nd. Sept. 1918.

1. In order to be prepared to assist in a minor operation which may be undertaken by XV Corps at an early date,

(a) D/307 will proceed into action in the neighbourhood of WATERLANDS (B.26.b.) and will be in position by the morning of 24th. September. The battery will remain silent until the Zero hour on the day of the operation.

(b) Task for operation will be to prevent observation towards the North West, from buildings in ARMENTIERES in C.26. and C.27, by formation of a smoke screen.
1,000 rounds smoke shells will be allotted.
Rate of fire - 1 round per gun per minute from Zero to Zero plus 2 hours and again for 2 more hours after a pause, length of which will be notified.

(c) Date and time of operation will be notified direct by XV Corps through H.A. XI Corps and this office.

2. S.C.R.A. 66th. Division, will arrange supply of ammunition to battery.

3. Officer i/c R.A. Signals will arrange telephone communications

4. ACKNOWLEDGE.

Capt. R.A.,
Bde.Maj., 61 Div. Artillery.

Issued at 11:30 p.m.

DISTRIBUTION.

Copy No. 1 - 2. 307th. Bde. R.F.A.
3. 306th. Bde. R.F.A.
4. 61 D.A.C.
5. 61 Divn. 'G'.
6. 61 Divn. 'Q'.
7 - 8. R.A. XI Corps.
9. 66 Div. Art.
10. 59th. Div. Art.
11. 11th. Corps H.A.
12. R.A. Signals.
13 - 14. War Diary.
15. File.

War Diary

S E C R E T.

R.A.C.1/6.

To all recipients of
61 D.A. Order No.154.

Amendment No.1 to -
1. 61st Divisional Artillery Order No.154 dated 22/9/18, is cancelled.
2. Advanced Guard Artillery and 307 Bde. R.F.A. to acknowledge.

F. P. Wye

23.9.1918.

Capt. R.A.,
Bde. Maj., 61 Div. Artillery.

War Diary

S E C R E T.

R.A.G.1/6/1.

AMENDMENT NO: 1
- to -
61st. DIVISIONAL ARTILLERY ORDER NO.155 of 22.9.18.

1. Para. 1(a) for "24th." read "27th."
2. Cancel para. 2.
3. ACKNOWLEDGE.

F.P. WYE.

23.9.1918.

Capt. R.A.,
Bde.Maj., 61 Div. Artillery.

War Diary

S E C R E T.

R.A.G.1/3.

AMENDMENT NO: 2
to
61st. DIVISIONAL ARTILLERY ORDER NO: 155 of 22.9.18.

1. Cancel para. 1 of Amendment No.1 dated 23.9.18, and substitute :-

   Para.1 (a) - For "24th." read "6 a.m. on 28th."

2. 306 and 307 Bdes. to acknowledge.

F.T. Wye

Capt. R.A.,
25.9.18.   Bde.Maj., 61 Div. Artillery.

To all recipients of 61 D.A. Order No.155.

S E C R E T.

Copy No: ......

61st. DIVISIONAL ARTILLERY INSTRUCTIONS NO: 18.

23rd. September, 1918

1. On night 23rd/24th. September, the Advanced Guard Artillery and 28th. Brigade, R.G.A., will carry out the following area shoots :-

    Between 12 midnight   (a) On BARTLETTE FARM and vicinity,
    and 1 a.m.   (paying particular attention to
                                     hedge H.26.a.35.35. - H.26.a.2.5.-
                                      H.26.a.30.65.)

                            (b) On JUNCTION POST (H.32.a.85.25. -
                                H.32.a.8.3. - H.32.a.95.45. -
                                H.32.b.00.35.)

    Between 1 a.m. and   On Buildings and enclosures in H.21.a.
    1.30 a.m.   and Trench in H.20.b.

2. On 24th. instant :-

(a) <u>Trench Mortars.</u>
    6" NEWTON Trench Mortars will continue to cut wire in front of BARTLETTE FARM and JUNCTION POST, also at H.14.d.6.4. and in H.9.b.

(b) <u>Field Artillery.</u>
    4.5" Hows. in action at M.5.b.35.80. will co-operate with 6" T.Ms.

(c) <u>Heavy Artillery.</u>
    8" Hows. will bombard BARTLETTE FARM (H.26.a.) and JUNCTION POST (H.32.a.)
    6" Hows. will fire on trench in H.14.d. paying particular attention to the portions close to the road and the building about this point.

3. Night 24th/25th. instant :-

(a)   If the wind is favourable (i.e. N. through W to SSW) there will be a GAS PROJECTOR discharge against the following targets :-

        (1) BARTLETTE FARM area - H.26.a.4.4.
        (2) JUNCTION POST area - H.32.a.8.3.

    The night of the discharge will be known as "Y" night.
    The following codes will be used in connection with the discharge of gas :-

        "OPERATION WILL TAKE PLACE ......" - RHODE.

        "OPERATION POSTPONED" - - - - ISLAND.

        "OPERATION COMPLETED" - - - - RED.

        "OPERATION CANCELLED" - - - - EGG BOUND.

P.T.O.

Zero hour for the discharge of projectors will be
communicated by giving the hour in figures as follows:-

    10.15 p.m. will be 1015.
    12.00 (midnight) will be 1200.
    1.45 a.m.   "   " 145.

If the discharge is to take place at 1.45 a.m., message will read, "145 RHODE".

(b)   Field Artillery.
       O.C. Advanced Guard Artillery will arrange the Field Artillery Barrage in connection with the above.

(c)   Heavy Artillery.
       From Zero to plus 15 minutes.
       GAS shell will be fired on Trenches and enclosures about CROIX BLANCHE in H.33.a. & c. and H.26.d. also tracks in H.26.b.

4.   On 25th. instant, and subsequent days if required by Infantry, Trench Mortars and 4.5" Hows. will continue programme vide. paras 2(a) and (b).

5.   Y plus 1 night:

(a)   There will be a projector discharge of smoke and innocuous Gas on BARTLETTE FARM and JUNCTION POST, which places will be stormed and consolidated by our Infantry.

(b)   Field Artillery.
       Will carry out barrages under orders to be issued by O.C. Advanced Guard Artillery.

(c)   6" NEWTON T.Ms.
       Will fire in accordance with arrangements made by D.T.M.O. direct with G.O.C. Advanced Guard and O.C. Advanced Guard Artillery.

(d)   Heavy Artillery.
       From Zero to Zero plus 5, bombard BARTLETTE and JUNCTION POST.
       Plus 5 mins. to Plus 35. Trenches and enclosures about CROIX BLANCHE in H.33.a. & c. and H.26.d., also tracks in H.26.b. and FLEURBAIX.

(e)   Counter-Battery Programme.
       C.B.S.O. XI Corps will arrange for neutralisation of hostile batteries.

(f)   59th. Divisional Artillery will co-operate:
       From Zero to plus 15 minutes a creeping barrage will be put down in the vicinity of TWO TREE FARM (M.2.c.) to simulate an attack on that place.

6. Local protective barrage.

(a)   The O.C. Advanced Guard Artillery will arrange for a protective barrage to come down in the form of a Box Barrage round JUNCTION POST and BARTLETTE FARM, if called for by the Garrisons.
       The signal for this Barrage will be a Rifle Grenade bursting in "RED over GREEN over YELLOW".

       (The S.O.S. Signals for the remainder of the front remains the same.)

(b)   S.O.S. Lines. The O.C. Advanced Guard Artillery will arrange new S.O.S. lines to come into force on completion of the attack.

7. Zero hour for Y plus 1 night will be notified by D.R. to all concerned.

8. Watches will be synchronised on Y and Y plus 1 night at 183rd. Inf. Brigade H.Q. at 8 p.m., except that 59th. Divisional Artillery will synchronise with 61 Div. Artillery by telephone at 9 p.m. under arrangements of O.i/c R.A. Signals.

9. ACKNOWLEDGE.

F.P.Hye

Capt. R.A.,
Bde.Maj., 61 Div. Artillery.

Issued at 3.15 p.m.

```
Copy No. 1 - 306th. Bde. R.F.A.
         2 - 307th. Bde. R.F.A.
         3.  D.T.M.O.
         4.  D.A.C.
         5.  183rd. Inf. Brigade.
         6.  28th. Bde. R.G.A.
         7.  XI Corps H.A. (for C.B.S.O.)
         8.  59th. Div. Art.
         9.  66th. Div. Art.
        10.  61 Divn. 'G'.
        11.  R.A. XI Corps.
        12.  O.i/c R.A. Signals.
     13-14.  War Diary.
        15.  File.
```

War Diary

S E C R E T.

Copy No: 13

61st. DIVISIONAL ARTILLERY INSTRUCTIONS NO: 19.

25th. Septr. 1916.

1. D/307 will withdraw from action to Wagon Lines at dawn 26th. instant, preparatory to carrying out 61st. Divisional Artillery Order No.155.

2. ACKNOWLEDGE.
(306 & 309 Bdes. only.)

F.P. WYE

Capt. R.A.,
Bde.Maj., 61 Div. Artillery.

Issued at 12 noon

DISTRIBUTION.

Copy No.1 - 2.	307 Bde.RFA.	Copy No.9.	56th. Div. Art.
3.	306 Bde.RFA.	10.	59th. Div. Art.
4.	61 D.A.C.	11.	XI Corps H.A.
5.	61 Divn. 'G'.	12.	R.A. Sigs.
6.	61 Divn. 'Q'	13-14.	War Diary.
7 - 8.	R.A. XI Corps.	15.	File.

War Diary

S E C R E T.

R.A.G. 1.

AMENDMENT NO: 1
to
61st. DIVISIONAL ARTILLERY INSTRUCTIONS NO: 18 of 23.9.18.

1. Para. 5 (d) :
   2nd. line - After "BARTLETTE" insert "FARM".

   4th. line - For "Plus 5 mins. to plus 35" read "plus 5 mins. to plus 45."

2. ACKNOWLEDGE.

F.P.Wye.
Capt. R.A.,
Bde.Maj., 61 Div. Artillery.

25.9.1918.

To all recipients of 61st. D.A.
Instructions No.18 - 23.9.1918.

SECRET. R.G.1.

61st. DIVISIONAL ARTILLERY.

LOCATION STATEMENT - 26.9.18.

Ref: Map Sheets 36A & 36.

Group.	Unit.		Location.	Wagon Lines.
ADVANCED GUARD ARTILLERY.	306 Bde.RFA. H.Q.		G.13.b.60.30.	L.11.d.25.75.
	A/306.	(2 guns) (2 ") (2 ")	G.33.d.20.60. G.32.d.50.55. G.32.c.98.60.	L.10.a.60.95.
	B/306.	(4 ") (2 ")	G.10.c.25.45. G.17.a.59.71.	to
	C/306.	(2 ") (2 ") (2 ")	G.28.b.15.70. G.28.a.90.55. G.28.c.07.32.	L.11.c.30.80.
	D/306.	(2 Hows.) (3 ") (1 ")	M.5.b.35.80. G.22.b.75.50. G.23.c.50.65.	L.11.a.5.7.
	A/307.	(2 guns) (2 ")	G.21.a.65.80. G.21.a.30.75.	L.17.d.2.7.
	B/307.	(2 ") (3 ") (1 ")	G.18.a.60.60. G.16.a.75.80. G.12.c.00.15.	L.11.c.
	C/308	(6 ")	G.27.a.1.4.	L.23.b.4.8.
	D/307.	(6 Hows.)	Withdraws to Wagon Lines 27.9.18. L.10.d.4.3.	
ANTI-TANK GUNS.	1 - 18-pr. 1 - "		G.33.a.6.9. G.27.d.9.8.	
	D.T.M.O. HQ.		L.17.b.75.10.	
	X/61.	(1 6"NEWTON) (1 ") (1 ") (1 ")	H.25.c.82.15. H.25.c.8.2. H.8.c.90.30. H.8.b.35.97.	
	61st. D.A.C. HQ.		L.20.c.7.0.	
	61st. D.A.G.O.		L.17.b.75.10.	

Spencer Batchelor
Lieut.
R.O., R.A., 61 Division.

26.9.1918.

SECRET War Diary

Copy No: 29

61st. DIVISIONAL ARTILLERY ORDER NO: 156.

26 Sept. 1918.

1. H.Q. 307th. Bde. R.F.A. will relieve H.Q. 306th. Bde. R.F.A. on 27th. instant, command of Advanced Guard Artillery to pass to O.C. 307th. Bde. R.F.A. at 6 p.m.

2. On relief, H.Q. 306th. Bde. R.F.A. will withdraw to Wagon Lines.
   Completion of relief to be wired to this office by code word "BRUSSELS".

3. (a) B/306 Bde. R.F.A. and B/307 Bde. R.F.A. will be withdrawn from action to Wagon Lines on Night 27/28th. instant, under arrangements to be made by Brigade Commanders.

   (b) These Units will come under command of O.C. 306 Bde. R.F.A. as soon as they have withdrawn from action.

   (c) Their arrival in Wagon Lines to be wired to this office by code word "OSTEND".

4. On completion of reliefs mentioned in paras. 1, 2 & 3, Advanced Guard Artillery will consist of :-

   H.Q. 307th. Bde. R.F.A.
   A, C & D/306.
   A & C/307.

   Brigade in readiness :-

   H.Q. 306th. Bde. R.F.A.
   B/306.
   B/307.
   D/307. (temporarily in action under 66 Div. Art.)

5. O.C. 307th. Bde. R.F.A. will arrange any redistribution of Batteries which he may consider necessary on night 27/28th., and will notify this office of his proposals forthwith.

6. O.C. 307th. Bde. R.F.A. will arrange S.O.S. lines for Advanced Guard Artillery for night 27/28th. inst. in consultation with B.G. Comdg. Advanced Guard and O.C. 306th. Bde. R.F.A., and will notify R.A.H.Q. of arrangements made by evening D.R. 27th. instant.

7. All ammunition in positions to be vacated will be handed over to Units remaining in action, under arrangements to be made by O.C. 307 Bde. R.F.A.

8. ACKNOWLEDGE.

F.P. Wye
Capt. R.A.,
Bde. Maj., 61 Div. Artillery.

Issued at 6 p.m.

DISTRIBUTION.

Copy No.		
1 - 5.	306th. Bde.	
6 -10.	307th. Bde.	
11.	D.T.M.O.	18. 61 Bn. M.G.C.
12.	D.A.C.	19. 28 Bde. R.G.A.
13.	61 Divn. 'G'.	20. R.A. XI Corps.
14.	61 Divn. 'Q'.	21. R.A. 59th. Divn.
15.	182 Inf. Bde.	22. R.A. 66th. Divn.
16.	183 Inf. Bde.	23. H.A. XI Corps.
17.	184 Inf. Bde.	24. C.B.S.O. XI Corps.
		25. 42nd. Squad. R.A.F.
		26. A.L.O. 42 Sqn. RAF.
		28-29 War Diary

18 PDR BARRAGE MAP
to accompany
61ST R.A. ORDER No 156

LEGEND
18 Pdr: Start Line — Red
Lifts — Blue
Protective barrage — Green
Dividing Line between Brigades — Brown

Sheet No 36 N.W. refers
1:20.000

R.A.H.Q. 29.9.18

25

+26' to +28'
+22' to +26'
+19' to +22'
+16' to +19'
+13' to +16'
+10' to +13'
+7' to +10'
+4' to +7'
Zero to +4'

307 Brigade
+28' to +58'
306 Brigade
+25' to +58'
+22' to +58'
+19' to +58'

31

33

34

H

Tracing taken from Sheet _____

of the 1: _____ map of _____

Signature _____ Date _____

War Diary

SECRET.

R.A.C.10.

AMENDMENT NO: 1
to
61st. DIVISIONAL ARTILLERY ORDER NO: 156.

1. Paras. 1 and 2 are cancelled.

    Para. 3 (b) - for "306" read "307".

    Paras. 5 and 7 - for "307" read "306".

    para. 4, line 3: - for "307" read "306".

    " " line 7: - for "306" read "307".

2. 306 and 307th. Bdes. to ACKNOWLEDGE.

F. Hyé.

Capt. R.A.,
Bde. Maj., 61 Div. Artillery.

27.9.18.

To all recipients of 61 D.A. Order No. 156.

SECRET.

Copy No: 23

61st. DIVISIONAL ARTILLERY INSTRUCTIONS NO: 20.

OPERATIONS.

26 Sept. 1918.

Information. 1. There are still indications of a possible further withdrawal of the enemy on the XI Corps front.

In order to ascertain at short notice whether the enemy is withdrawing, the Advanced Guard Commander is prepared to carry out a reconnaissance in force on a selected portion of the enemy front at 48 hours notice. For the purposes of this operation two Brigade R.F.A. will probably be placed at the disposal of the O.C. Advanced Guard Artillery.

Intention. 2. Information as to the actual withdrawal of the enemy as a result of the above operation, or from other sources, will be immediately followed by a vigorous renewal of our advance.

Objectives. 3. The objectives to be reached will be :-

1st Objective: CROIX BLANCHE - FLEURBAIX - ERQUINGHEM.
2nd Objective: LA BOUTILLERIE (exclusive) - BOIS GRENIER - RUE MARLE (exclusive).

Dispositions for an Advance. 4. In order to ensure greater vigour to our advance, the Division will be prepared to operate on a front of two Infantry Brigades, with H.Q. and a portion of one Brigade R.F.A. co-operating with each Infantry Brigade.

H.Q. and Units of 306th. Brigade R.F.A. with Right Infantry Brigade and H.Q. and units of 307th. Brigade R.F.A. with Left Infantry Brigade

Units not in the line will remain in their Wagon Lines in readiness to reinforce or to cover the CORPS BATTLE LINE on receipt of orders from this office.

24 hours notice of such a change will, however, be given.

The inter-brigade boundary will be the grid line running East and West through H.19.central.

Position of Brigade HQ. 5. Headquarters of Brigades in the line, and of the Artillery Brigades supporting them, will be located in close proximity to one another, the Artillery and Infantry Brigade Headquarters being situated at the same spot in each case.

The bounds forward of these Headquarters will be laid down by Division.

Accommodation in area vacated by enemy. 6. There is every reason to expect that the enemy has elaborated his system of mining dugouts, buildings, and cross roads in the area over which the advance will take place. It is, therefore, important that the troops are warned beforehand to avoid any places likely to be mined. Headquarters of Brigades, Battalions, Companies, and Units of Divisional Troops will not occupy dugouts or buildings in the area vacated by the enemy. Accommodation must be taken forward or improvised, and arrangements made accordingly beforehand.

Intelligence. 7. Intelligence Officers of Infantry Brigades have been instructed to keep the Artillery Brigade Commanders and Liaison Officers at Brigade H.Q. constantly informed as to the line to which our Infantry have advanced in order to assist the Artillery in keeping the closest possible touch with the situation at all times, and to supplement the information obtained by the Artillery through their Observing Officers and Liaison Officers.

P.T.O

<u>Communication.</u> 8. Emphasis is again laid upon the importance of fully
utilizing every alternative means of communication
possible.

LUCAS lamps must be more extensively used than has
formerly been the case. There is no restriction to
the use of the lamp in a forward direction.

9. Lateral communication and liaison between Artillery
Brigades and between Batteries is essential to mutual
co-operation, and will receive special consideration.

10. ACKNOWLEDGE.

F. P. Wye

Capt. R.A.,
Bde.Maj., 61 Div. Artillery.

26.9.1918.

DISTRIBUTION.

Copy No:	
1 - 5.	306th. Bde. R.F.A.
6 -10.	307th. Bde. R.F.A.
11.	D.T.M.O.
12.	D.A.C
13.	28th Bde R.G.A.
14.	61st Divn 'G'
15.	182 Inf. Brigade.
16.	183 Inf. Brigade.
17.	184 Inf. Brigade.
18.	61 M.G. Bn.
19.	C.R.E.
20.	R.A. XI Corps.
21.	R.A. 59th. Divn.
22.	R.A. 66th. Divn.
23 -24.	War Diary.
25.	File.

- 2 -

SECRET.

R.A.G. 1/4.

ADDENDUM
to
61st. DIVISIONAL ARTILLERY INSTRUCTIONS NO:20.

Reference 61 D.A. Instructions No.20 dated 26.9.18.

After para. 6 add :

"Grenades, bombs, or boxes of perdite are placed under the floors of Nissen Huts, dug-outs, etc., and the striker mechanism attached by means of a wire to old clothes, rubbish, or odd articles on the floor. Any attempt to clear out the floors of these huts without careful inspection results in the wire being pulled and the explosive fired."

F.P. Nye
Capt. R.A.,
Bde. Maj., 61 Div. Artillery.

29.9.1918.

To all recipients of 61 D.A. Instructions No. 20.

SECRET.   War Diary

Copy No: 30

61st. DIVISIONAL ARTILLERY ORDER NO:157.

28th. Sept, 1918

1. (a) The Divisional front will be re-organized on a two Brigade front during night 28th/29th. instant, in accordance with 61st. Divisional Artillery Instructions No.20 of 26th. instant.

   (b) Headquarters 307th. Brigade, R.F.A. will move to G.8.b.1.7. and will take command of its Units, which will cover Left (182nd.) Infantry Brigade on completion of Infantry relief, when 306th. Brigade, R.F.A. will cover Right (184th.) Infantry Brigade. Completion of relief to be wired by code word "CAPORAL" to this Office.

2. In accordance with orders already issued by wire, the undermentioned batteries will go into action to-night :-

   B/306 Brigade, R.F.A. to G.27.a.1.4.
   B/307 Brigade, R.F.A. to G.21.a.65.60.)
                          G.21.a.30.75.)

   These Units will come under orders of O.C. 306 Brigade R.F.A. until completion of Infantry relief, when they will come under Orders of their respective Brigade Commanders. Orders for D/307 Bde.R.F.A. will be issued later.

3. On completion of relief, 306 Bde.R.F.A. will provide Guards over Anti-tank guns and will be responsible for providing the necessary detachments in case of attack. The attention of Units detailed to provide these detachments will be drawn to 61st. Divisional Artillery General Artillery Instructions, para.15.

4. 306th. and 307th. Brigade, R.F.A. will render ammunition Returns for their Units from 29th. inst. onwards.

5. All further details to be arranged by Bde. Commanders.
6. ACKNOWLEDGE.

J.P.Rye.
Capt. R.A.,
Bde.Maj., 61 Div. Artillery.

Issued at 12 noon.

DISTRIBUTION.

Copy No.				
1 - 5.	306th. Bde.	20.	R.A. XI Corps.
6 - 10.	307th. Bde.	21.	59th. Div. Art.
11.	D.T.M.O.	22.	66th. Div. Art.
12.	D.A.C.	23.	H.A. XI Corps.
13.	61 Divn. 'G'.	24.	C.B.S.O. XI Corps.
14.	61 Divn. 'Q'	25.	42nd. Squadron, RAF.
15.	182 Inf. Bde.	26.	A.L.O. 42 Sqn. RAF.
16.	183 Inf. Bde.	27.	XI Balloon Coy. RAF.
17.	184 Inf. Bde.	28.	C.R.E. 61 Divn.
18.	61 Bn.M.G.C.	29-30.	War Diary.
19.	28 Bde. R.G.A.	31.	File.

SECRET.

Copy No: 25

61st. DIVISIONAL ARTILLERY ORDER NO: 158.

29th. Sept. 1918.

1. 184 Infantry Brigade will carry out an attack on the enemy's positions near JUNCTION POST on Monday, 30th. September, and will consolidate and hold the line from the Cross Roads at H.26.d.05.15. along the road running thence to CROIX BLANCHE cross roads as far as H.32.b.65.70 and thence S.W. along trench to H.32.a.70.00.
    Both flanks will be joined back to our old line by means of posts.

2. (a) Barrages for 18-pdrs. and 4.5 inch Hows., and Tasks for 6" Hows. are shown on attached tracings.

   (b) When the Protective Barrage Line is reached, Batteries will search and sweep outwards 200 yards by lifts of 100 yards and back again, & so on till end of the operation.

3. 6" NEWTON Trench Mortars (3 guns) will fire on BARTLETTE FARM (H.26.a.) and immediate vicinity, throughout the operation: i.e. from Zero to plus 58 minutes.

4. Ammunition.
    18-pdrs.
        75% A.   10% graze,
        25% AX.   106 Fuze.

    4.5" Hows.
        All BX, 106, except that Hows. firing on trenches will fire 25% BX 101 Fuze.

5. Rates of Fire.
   (a) 18-pdrs. and 4.5" Hows.
        Zero to Zero plus 4   -   INTENSE.
        Zero plus 4 to Zero plus 28.   RAPID.
        "   " 28 "   "   "   40.   NORMAL.
        "   " 40 "   "   "   50.   SLOW.
        "   " 50 "   "   "   54.   RAPID.
        "   " 54 "   "   "   58.   SLOW.

   (b) 6" NEWTON T.Ms.
        Zero to Zero plus 4.   INTENSE.
        "   plus 4 to Zero plus 28.   NORMAL.
        "   "   28 "   "   "   58. SLOW.

6. O.C. 306th. Brigade, R.F.A. will detail an Officer to be with Battalion H.Q. at H.31.d.0.8. with necessary signal communication.

7. In order to call for the Protective Barrage to be continued or re-opened, the following signals will be fired by the Infantry :-

   (a) Between 6 a.m. and 6 p.m., a Rifle grenade signal bursting into RED and BLUE smoke.
       Between 6 p.m. and 6 a.m., a Rifle grenade light signal, RED over GREEN over YELLOW.

   (b) On this signal being sent up, Batteries will open fire on their Protective Barrage Lines for 15 minutes.
        Rate of Fire.
            4 minutes INTENSE;
            8   "   NORMAL;
            3   "   SLOW.

- 1 -

8. The normal/

8.   The normal S.O.S. Signal remains the same.

9.   ZERO HOUR will be notified in minutes plus or minus of 3 a.m., thus :

        5.45 a.m. will be plus 165
        6.20 a.m. "   "   " 200.

10.   Arrangements for synchronising watches will be notified later.

11.   ACKNOWLEDGE.

                                        F.G. Kye
                                        Capt. R.A.,
                                        Bde.Maj., 61 Div. Artillery.

Issued at 3 pm.

                    DISTRIBUTION.

        Copy No. 1 - 5.   306th. Bde. R.F.A.   ¤
                 6 - 10.   307th. Bde. R.F.A.   ¤
                11.   D.T.M.O.   ¤
                12.   61 D.A.C.
                13 - 16.   184 Infantry Bde.   ¤
                17.   182   "   "
                18.   28th. Bde. R.G.A.   ¤
                19.   XI Corps (for C.B.SO.)
                20.   61 Divn. 'B'   ¤
                21.   61 Divn. 'Q'
                22.   R.A. XI Corps.   ¤
                23.   R.A. 59th. Divn.   ¤
                24.   R.A. 66th. Divn.
                25 - 26.   War Diary.
                27.   File.   ¤

        ¤   Tracings attached.

4.5" HOWITZER TASKS
to accompany
61 R.A. ORDER No. 168

Sheet No 36 N.W. refers.
1:20,000.

R.A.H.Q.   29.9.18

LEGEND.
D.307. Start Line —
Lifts |
Protective barrage ○

D.306. Start Area ▭
Lifts △
Protective barrage ▲

25

+25' to +58'
+22' to +25'
+19' to +22'
+16' to +19'
+13' to +16'
+10' to +13'
+7' to +10'
+4' to +7'
Zero to +4'

○ 2 Hows
○ 2 Hows
○ 1 How
○ 1 How

← 18 Pdr Protective Barrage

31

Zero to +6'
+6' to +10' →
+10' to +14'
+14' to +58'

34

H

6" HOW: TASKS (1 How on each point)

to accompany

61ST D.A. ORDER No 158

LEGEND
From Zero to +58"
From Zero to +15"
+15" to +58"

Sheet No 36 N.W. refers
1:20.000

R.A.H.Q 29.9.18

SECRET.

61st. DIVISIONAL ARTILLERY.

LOCATION STATEMENT - 30.9.1918.

Sheets 36A & 36.

Unit.	Location.		Wagon Lines.
61st. R.A. Hdqrs.		L. 33. b. 3. 7.	
306 Brigade R.F.A.	H.Q.	G. 13. b. 60. 30.	L. 11. d. 25. 75.
A/306.	(2 guns)	G. 33. d. 20. 60.	L. 10. a. 60. 95.
	(2 ")	G. 32. d. 50. 55.	
	(2 ")	G. 32. c. 98. 60.	
B/306.	(6 ")	G. 27. a. 1. 4.	to
C/306.	(2 ")	G. 28. b. 15. 70.	L. 11. c. 30. 80.
	(2 ")	G. 28. a. 90. 55.	
	(2 ")	G. 28. c. 07. 32.	
D/306.	(2 Hows.)	M. 5. b. 35. 80.	L. 11. a. 5. 7.
	(3 ")	G. 22. b. 75. 50.	
	(1 ")	G. 23. c. 50. 65.	
ANTI-TANK GUNS.	(1 - 18pdr)	G. 33. a. 6. 9.	
	(1 - ")	G. 27. d. 9. 8.	
307 Brigade R.F.A.	H.Q.	G. 8. b. 1. 7.	L. 10. d. 9. 6.
A/307.	(2 guns)	G. 16. b. 70. 95.	L. 17. d. 2. 7.
	(4 ")	G. 16. a. 75. 75.	
B/307.	(2 ")	G. 21. a. 65. 80.	L. 11. c.
	(4 ")	G. 21. a. 30. 75.	
C/307.	(2 ")	G. 10. c. 30. 45.	L. 23. b. 4. 8.
	(4 ")	G. 10. b. 6. 8.	
D/307.	(6 Hows.)	G. 21. c. 89. 89.	L. 10. d. 4. 3.
61st. D.T.M.O. X/61.	H.Q.	L. 17. b. 75. 10.	
	1 - 6" TM	H. 25. c. 80. 25.	
	1 - 6" "	H. 25. c. 82. 15.	
	1 - 6" "	H. 25. c. 8. 2.	
	1 - 6" "	H. 8. c. 90. 30.	
	1 - 6" "	H. 8. b. 35. 97.	
61st. D.A.C. H.Q.		L. 20. c. 7. 0.	
No. 1 Sect.		L. 21. d. 8. 8.	
2 "		L. 7. c. 7. 8.	
S.A.A. "		L. 14. c. 8. 7.	
61st. D.A.G.O.		L. 17. b. 75. 10.	

30.9.18.

Lieut.
R.O., R.A., 61 Division.

War Diary

S E C R E T.

R.A.G.10.

AMENDMENT NO: 1
- to -
61st. DIVISIONAL ARTILLERY ORDER NO:158 -29.9.18.

Delete para 5(a) and substitute :-

18 pdrs. and 4.5" Hows.

Zero to Zero plus 4	- -	INTENSE.
Plus 4 to plus 28	- -	Normal.
" 28 " " 50	- -	Slow.
" 50 " " 54	- -	Normal.
" 54 " " 58	- -	Slow.

J.T.KYE

Capt. R.A.,
Bde.Maj., 61 Div.Artillery.

29.9.1918.

To all recipients of above Order.

(6392) Wt. W6192/P875 1,500,000 4/18 McA & W Ltd (E 2815) Forms W3091/4.   Army Form W.3091.

Cover for Documents.

Nature of Enclosures.

61ˢᵗ Divisional Artillery

War Diary

— for —

October 1918.

VOL: 30

Notes, or Letters written.

WAR DIARY or INTELLIGENCE SUMMARY

Army Form C. 2118.

Place	Date	Hour	Summary of Events and Information	Remarks and references to Appendices
HILL WORKS. (N OF LA GORGUE) 36 A.M.E 1/20,000 Ref Map L32 b Square	1st Oct. 1918		Artist harassing fire throughout the period. Bands of [men?] were put up to the ERQUINHEM SWITCH during the evening by Goth. brigade as it was reported by L.F. Plane to be strongly occupied by the enemy. Noying by BAILLEUL FM was constantly fired on. There was a very noticeable decrease in hostile artillery fire. JB	JM
	2nd Oct.		Support was given to the operation by the Infantry & their objectives were gained & they pushed on their line about 300 yds East. Divisional Artillery less F's battery of each Brigade followed the Infantry & open fire wherever opportunity arose. Located SECTRAUD. 61st DA Order No 159. & Amm Instr No 15 & DA Defence JM Instructions No 1 were issued. CRA & BM conferred with Infantry Brigade Commanders during the day. There was very little hostile artillery fire. The day was wet & rainy but cleared later. BM with 59 RA with reference to relief by them of our artillery.	JM
	3rd Oct.		A first day. The advance was continued & our artillery moved forward in support. The going was very difficult owing to craters in the roads. BM & CRA 59 visited Bat H.Qrs with reference to the relief. 61st DA Order No 160 & 161 issued. During the afternoon and night the relief was commenced in accordance with Serial No 1 of Instruction No 150 March Table.	JM
FONTES	4th Oct.		Relief continued until completed. 61st DA moved to new area on completion of relief. CRA 59 Divn assumed command of Artillery covering line from & at 1000 hrs at which time RA HQ to new area.	JM
	5th Oct.		BM proceeded to DOULIEU to reconnoitre harness areas accompanied by S.C.R.A. who arranged accommodation in new area for Divisional Artillery & Nor Cay Br. D/v Train. Divisional Artillery arranged in rest until the necessary arrangements commenced in accordance with Administrative Instruction to 61st DA Order No 161 a/15total JB	JM

Army Form C. 2118.

WAR DIARY
or
INTELLIGENCE SUMMARY.
(Erase heading not required.)

Instructions regarding War Diaries and Intelligence Summaries are contained in F. S. Regs., Part II. and the Staff Manual respectively. Title pages will be prepared in manuscript.

Place	Date	Hour	Summary of Events and Information	Remarks and references to Appendices
FONTES	6		Entraining of Div Arty continued throughout the day. The arrangements at THIEVRES Station were poor causing much delay. CRA proceeded to DOULLENS by road	
DOULLENS area	6/7	night	Trains arrived by train throughout the night in DOULLENS area and proceeded to billets 307 Bde RFA at SARTON, 309 Bde RFA-BRYVILLE, D.A.C.-AMPLIER — Hd Div Train MEZEROLES-BRYVILLE Hd Coy Hd Div Train SARTON.	
AMPLIER	7		R.A.H.Q. opened at AMPLIER during the afternoon. Limited combined detraining — trains very late facilities at THIEVEL very bad — trench ramps only available for detraining the horses and mules. D.A Order No 162 for march of Div Arty to XVII Corps Area issued.	
AMPLIER	8		Units commenced march according to table move with 61 D.A.Arty HUMBERCAMP (LENS 1:100,000) arrived at SARTON about 0800 hours and marched again at 14 hours to HUMBERCAMP. (4690.25)	
LAGNICOURT	9		Units continued march. R.A.H.Q. moved via ISAPOLUME and VAUX VRAUCOURT to LAGNICOURT	
LAGNICOURT	10		61. D.A Order Nos. 163 - 164 - 165 and 61 D.A Instruction No 22 issued hours completed march.	
do	11		61 D.A Order No 166 for relief of 40 "Div Arty on leaving Group Artillery XTh Corps issued C.R.A. reconnoitred new front.	
do	12		Both General Battery Commanders visited new front to arrange to details of relief.	
HYESNES-LEZ. HUBERT	13		61 D.A Instruction Nos 23 and 24 Relief carried out of 40 Div Arty by day. C.R.A 61 Div assumed command of artillery (consisting of 61 Div Arty, 5 Div Arty and 93 Army Bde RFA.) covering 24th Division at 6pm 61 S.R.Order No 167 and Location Statement No1 issued.	
do	14		Quiet day on K.front.	
	15		Quiet day on K.front. Arrangements made during the day for an attack on THIUSSY at 0570 hours on 15 inst. Order No 168 was issued.	

WAR DIARY or INTELLIGENCE SUMMARY

Army Form C. 2118.

Place	Date	Hour	Summary of Events and Information	Remarks and references to Appendices
AVESNES-LEZ-AUBERT	16		The 72nd Inf Bde 24th Division carried out an operation under a barrage at 05.10 hours and captured the village of HAUSSY and area ground 15 N + N.W. with some 400 prisoners. The enemy shelled the village very heavily during the afternoon and then counter attacked from S.E compelling our troops in NOIRHAM from the village, but a fresh posn. maintained about K.11 d. 3. 9. Our Batteries expended 3 times the S.O.S. rate.	C.F.
do	16/17		There was considerable shelling of the battery areas during the day particularly about Y.10. a. Y.16. & and 61 DA section No 109 (a section of S2 Div Arty) was heavily shelled and ammunition and Battn detachment to Battn. detachment to the high ground. During the night the enemy succeeded in forcing our defending troops back to the high ground Y. 16 - Y.15 - MONTRÉCOURT WOOD. with forward posts at Y.17.b.13. near MONTRÉCOURT MILL centre Y.17.a.2. Batteries carried out normal night harassing fire. There were no S.O.S.	
do	17		Arrangements are being pushed forward for an attack by the 19 Division (in conjunction with attack by formations of 1st and 3rd Armies) to capture the high ground west of the river HARPIES. A conference was held by G.O.C. 19 Div at RIEUX during the late afternoon which was attended by CRA's and A.M.S. 19 Div Arty and by Div M.G at which the details for the attack were arranged. Our Batteries were less active during the day, moves having been issued to conserve ammunition for coming operation. There were also returns exercises in hostile Artillery activity. Batts of 52 Div Arty was relieved by 72 and 315 Army (?) RFA. Arriving Batteries by day. The 16 Fd Battalion after dark. Arty Y/24th Division supporting and HQ by 19 Division were completed. 61 Div Arty included No 1 & 5 Army Brigade. No 1 & 61 DA under No 1, 169 and 168 army (Gowers) Brigades remained in usual.	C.F.
do	17/18		Enemy Artillery activity on battery areas with C.A's and H.E. shell. Command of the artillery covering the 19 Division passed to CRA. 19 Div at 17.00 hours. CRA 61 Div took over command of Support Group Artillery XVII Corps with HQ at bullet Nº.9. AVESNES by - AUBERTS. AVESNES HQ Wd HQ at 1400 hours. Conference held at Wd HQ at 1400 hours to arrange details of covering operation.	C.F.

Army Form C. 2118.

WAR DIARY
or
INTELLIGENCE SUMMARY.
(Erase heading not required.)

Instructions regarding War Diaries and Intelligence Summaries are contained in F. S. Regs., Part II. and the Staff Manual respectively. Title pages will be prepared in manuscript.

Place	Date	Hour	Summary of Events and Information	Remarks and references to Appendices
St. AUBERT	Sept. 19.		C.R.A. 62nd Div. took over command of Rt. Group Artillery covering 19th Div. at 1300 hours with HQ at St AUBERT. Very quiet day on the front. Arrangements for made during day for attack.	
"	20.15		The 57th & 58th (?) Inf. Bdes attacked under a barrage at 0500 hours & captured HAUSSY & high ground to E of it. Attack was successful. Enemy retaliation was slight. Our forward guns + Bdes moved forward. 1. CRA moved forward to HAUSSY at 1400 hours. Normal harassing fire no. S.O.S. D.A.O. 170. & 171 issued.	
HAUSSY.	21st		Lt. Col. R.W.S. Brooke took over command of Rt. Group Artillery at 1700 hours. CRA returned to former HQ at ST. AUBERT. CRA attended conference at 62 Div HQ - for arrangements for attack by 51. Div. Intended shelling during day on Battalion outpost of HAUSSY - HAUSSY leaving shelled.	
ST. AUBERT	22nd /31		C.R.A. attended conferences at 62 Div H.Q. at 1200 hours to arrange for new attack. Quiet day on the front. Localise Retaliation harass fire.	

WAR DIARY or INTELLIGENCE SUMMARY

Army Form C. 2118.

Place	Date	Hour	Summary of Events and Information	Remarks and references to Appendices
ST. AUBERT	23rd		Bdes co-operated in operation by Division on right. RSCARMAIN captured. RAHQ moved to new HQ in ST AUBERT. 61st Div. Infantry relieved 19th Div. CRA 61st Div took over command of artillery covering 61st Div Front at 12 noon. 1400 hours from CRA 19th Div. DAQ 172 & location statement issued. Relieved & intermittent shelling of forward systems during day.	
do.	24th		The 182 & 183 Inf Bdes attacked at once the line of village SOMMAING — BERMERAIN supported by Artillery barrage. Infantry held up at VENDEGIES. RAHQ moved forward & opened at MONARS COURT at 1200. DAQ 173 issued.	
MONTRECOURT	25th		Infantry took VENDEGIES. Headquarters line of railway. RAHQ moved forward to VENDEGIES opened at 1700 hours. DAQ 174 issued.	
VENDEGIES	26th		Shelled shelling during day on battery positions forward area. Artillery regrouped as per DAQ 174. Location statement & DRI 26 issued. 307 Bde fired in support of local operation by 184 Bde.	
do.	27th		Situation unchanged. Artillery co-operated during morning on MA 183 & CH 83 with hivouac. Enemy in force Enemy found in strength — reconnoitring patrols successfully dealt with by our Inf. Enemy counter attacked over position W. of above at 1250 hours. Conference at DHQ at 1500 hours. CRA attended. Location Statement issued.	

Army Form C. 2118.

WAR DIARY
or
INTELLIGENCE SUMMARY.
(Erase heading not required.)

Instructions regarding War Diaries and Intelligence Summaries are contained in F. S. Regs., Part II. and the Staff Manual respectively. Title pages will be prepared in manuscript.

Place	Date	Hour	Summary of Events and Information	Remarks and references to Appendices
VENDEGIES	28th	—	Situation unchanged. Artillery engaged much movement. Fairly quiet day. Large number of N.F. calls.	D.A.O. 176 & 177 issued.
do	29th	—	Hostile Artillery very active on back areas with N.Y. fire. VENDEGIES heavily shelled with gas and H.E. Arrangements made for attack on MAPRSCOURS. Barrage map. issued. Also Corps Instructions No.1 for operation.	
do	30th	—	Situation unchanged. Other artillery carried out usual harassing fire & engaged movement on high ground N. of MAPRSCOURS. Intermittent hostile shelling. D.A.O. 176 & location statement issued. Also addendum No.1 to addendum 16.	D.A.O. 178.
do	31st	—	Situation unchanged. Quiet night. Arrangements made for attack. Much harassing fire on MAPRSCOURS area during day. General calm. D.A.O. No. 179 issued.	

War Diary

S E C R E T.

Copy No: 15

61st. DIVISIONAL ARTILLERY ORDER NO: 159.

2nd. Oct. 1918.

1. B/306 and B/307 will be withdrawn from action to Wagon Lines and come into reserve under their respective Brigades as soon as they are out of range.

2. (a) As soon as the Trench Mortars at present emplaced are out of range, these pieces will be withdrawn from action.

   (b) D.T.M.O. will arrange for one mobile trench mortar to be at the disposal of each Infantry Brigade Commander in the line. These mobile trench mortars will be moved forward to some central position on their respective Brigade fronts, from which they can be quickly taken forward into action.

3. ACKNOWLEDGE.

J.P.Pye

Capt. R.A.,
Bde.Maj., 61 Div. Artillery.

Issued at 1200

DISTRIBUTION.

Copy No.	
1 - 2.	306th. Bde. R.F.A.
3 - 4.	307th. Bde. R.F.A.
5.	61 D.T.M.O.
6.	61 D.A.C.
7.	61 Div. 'G'
8.	R.A. XI Corps.
9.	59th. Div. Art.
10.	66th. Div. Art.
11.	182 Inf. Brigade.
12.	183 Inf. Brigade.
13.	184 Inf. Brigade.
14.	61 Bn. M.G.C.
15 -16.	War Diary.
17.	File.
18.	XI Corps H.A.
19.	28 Bde. R.G.A.

SECRET.

61st. DIVISIONAL ARTILLERY.

DISPOSITIONS as at 10 p.m. on 2.10.1918.

306th. Bde. R.F.A.

    H.Q.   G. 29. a. 95. 65.

    A/306. (2 guns)   G. 35. a. 8. 8.
            (2 ")   H. 31. a. 4. 8.

    C/306 (2 ")   G. 30. c. 6. 8.
          (2 ")   H. 20. d. 2. 1.

    D/306. (2 Hows.)   M. 4. b. 4. 8.
           (4 ")   H. 25. c. 8. 2.

    B/306. Withdrawn to Wagon Lines L. 10. a. 60. 95.

307th. Bde. R.F.A.

    H.Q.   G. 23. c. 0. 9.

    A/307. (6 guns)   G. 24. c. 6. 8.

    C/307. (4 ")   H. 7. a. 5. 2.

    D/307. (6 Hows.)   G. 24. d. 9. 8.

    B/307. Withdrawn to Wagon Lines L. 23. b. 4. 8.

                                    Spencer Betchley.

2.10.1918.   Lieut.
                              R.O., R.A., 61 Division.

SECRET.   Copy No: 16

                                      R.A.G. 1/4/2.

              AMENDMENT NO: 1
                    to
61st. DIVISIONAL ARTILLERY INSTRUCTIONS NO:1 of 19.9.18.
                  - DEFENCE -

1.   Line 4, after "Instructions No.12" add "and 20."

2.   Cancel para. 1 and insert :-

   "1.   In the event of a strong hostile attack developing,
    or information of an impending attack being received, the
    Order "MAN BATTLE STATIONS" for the defence of the Corps
    Battle Line will be sent to Field Artillery units in reserve,
    to D.T.M.O., also to any Units which may be placed under
    orders of this Divisional Artillery by Corps."

3.   APPENDIX 'A' is cancelled and revised APPENDIX 'A' attached
will be substituted.

4.   Cancel para. 3 and insert :-

   "Positions are prepared for Anti-tank guns at :-
         No.1 - G.33.a.6.9.
         No.2 - G.33.a.55.80.
         No.3 - G.27.d.9.8."

   Note: At present there are no Anti-tanks guns on charge of
   this Divisional Artillery.

5.   Cancel para. 4 and insert :-

       "Units in reserve will be responsible for covering the
   Corps Battle Line until the withdrawal of the units operating
   with Advanced Infantry Brigades and, or the arrival of
   Artillery reinforcements.
       306 and 307 Brigade and D.T.M.O. will detail which
   positions their Units in reserve would occupy."

6.   Para. 6, line 1, cancel "Guard" and insert "Infantry Brigades."

     Para. 6, cancel sub-para. 2 and insert :-
     "2.   At the request of their Brigade Commanders or of
      the Infantry."

7.   Cancel para. 7 and insert :-

   "7.   The following arrangements for Mutual Support have been
    made with Flank Divisions :-

Code Call.	To whom sent.	Action taken.
HELP 61 Div.Art.	59 Div.Arty. 66 Div.Arty.	2 flank 18-pr. batteries barrage on their S.O.S. lines.
HELP 59 Div.Art.	61 Div.Arty.	2 Right 18-pr. batteries barrage on S.O.S. lines.
HELP 66 Div.Art.	61 Div.Arty.	2 left 18-pr. batteries barrage on S.O.S. lines.

                                                    P.T.O.

8. Add new para.:-

"16. The following O.Ps. are suitable for the Corps Battle Line:-

(1) G.20.d.25.40.
(2) L.24.b.99.45.
(3) G.28.a.60.30."

9. ACKNOWLEDGE.

F.R. WYE
Capt. R.A.,
Bde.Maj., 61 Div.Artillery.

2nd. October, 1918.

DISTRIBUTION.

Copy No.	
1	306th. Bde. R.F.A.
2	307th. Bde. R.F.A.
3	61st. D.A.C.
4	61st. D.T.M.O.
5	61st. Divn. 'G'
6	C.R.E.
7	R.A. XI Corps.
8	59th. Div. Art.
9	28th. Bde. R.G.A.
10	XI Corps H.A.
11	XI Corps C.B.S.O.
12	182nd. Infantry Bde.
13	183rd. Infantry Bde.
14	184th. Infantry Bde.
15-16	War Diary.
17	File.

S E C R E T.

APPENDIX 'A'.

61st. DIVISIONAL ARTILLERY DEFENCE INSTRUCTIONS NO:1.

LOCATIONS of POSITIONS to cover the CORPS BATTLE LINE.

'A' BRIGADE. (307th. Brigade, R.F.A.)

    H.Q.   L.10.d.8.2.

    1 18-pr.Bty. (6 guns) L.11.b.2.2.

    1   do.   (6 ") G.7.b.8.2.

    1   do.   (6 ") G.8.b.1.7.

    1 4.5" How. (6 Hows) L.18.a.3.5.
      Bty.

'B' BRIGADE. (306th. Brigade, R.F.A.)

    H.Q.   L.26.b.75.35.

    1 18-pr.Bty. (2 guns) L.28.b.0.6.
               (4 ") L.27.b.2.4.

    1   do.   (4 guns) L.24.c.95.45.
               (2 ") G.19.d.15.50.

    1   do.   (6 ") L.11.b.2.2.

    1 4.5" How. (6 Hows) L.22.d.30.75.
      Bty.

'C' BRIGADE. (Reinforcing Brigade.)

    H.Q.   L.20.c.7.0.

    1 18-pr.Bty. (6 guns) L.11.a.2.0.

    1   do.   (2 ") L.21.c.94.70.
               (4 ") L.27.a.20.75.

    1   do.   (6 ") L.22.a.7.6.

    1 4.5"How. (6 Hows) L.15.d.95.10.
      Bty.

War Diary

SECRET.   Copy No: 22

61st. DIVISIONAL ARTILLERY ORDER NO: 160.

Ref: Map Sheets HAZEBROUCK   3. Oct. 1918.
     5a. 1:100,000.

1. The 61st. Division will be relieved by the 59th. Division between the 2nd. and 5th. instant, and will withdraw to an area East of AIRE. The movement of the Divisional Artillery will be in accordance with attached Table.
   After relief, the Division will be in G.H.Q. Reserve at 24 hours notice.

2. The following distances will be maintained between Units on the line of march :-
   (a) Between Batteries and Sections D.A.C.   100 yards.
   (b) Between Artillery Brigades.   500 yards.
   (c) Between groups of 6 vehicles.   25 yards.

3. All documents relating to the area, 1/10,000 and 1/20,000 maps, defence Orders and Instructions, aeroplane photographs and current Intelligence Summaries, will be handed over to relieving Units and receipts taken.

4. In every case command will pass on completion of relief which will be wired to R.A.H.Q. by code as follows :-
   306th. Bde. R.F.A.   "SUPERIOR INK".
   307th. Bde. R.F.A.   "NEW YORK".
   D.T.M.O.   "WATERMAN".
   D.A.C.   "SKILLED WORK".

5. All Units of 59th. Div. Artillery arriving in the area before 10.00 4th. instant, will come under Orders of C.R.A. 61 Division.
   Command of the Artillery covering the Left Divisional Sector will pass to C.R.A. 59th. Division at 1000 on 4th. inst.

6. In order to give assistance and local information to incoming Units, the undermentioned personnel will be left in the line with Units of 59th. Div. Artillery (if required by them) for a period of 24 hours :-
   With each B.H.Q.   1 Officer.
   "   "   Bty.   1 Officer & 2 Signallers.

7. All Units will retain their own guns or howitzers.

8. All further details of reliefs and moves will be arranged by Os.C. Units concerned.

9. R.A.H.Q. will close at RILL WORKS and open at FONTES (Billet No.58) at 1000 on 4th. instant.

10. Administration Orders attached.

11. Arrival of Units in the new area will be notified with locations to R.A.H.Q. as soon as possible.

12. ACKNOWLEDGE.

                                          Capt. R.A.,
Issued at 0015.   Bde. Maj., 61 Div. Artillery.

DISTRIBUTION.

Copy No.1-5. 306 Bde.	No.14. 61 Div. 'Q'	No.19. 59th. Div. Art.
6-10. 307 Bde.	15. 61 D.A.P.M.	20. 66th. Div. Art.
11. D.A.C.	16. No.1 Coy. Train.	21. - 22. War Diary.
12. D.T.M.O.	17. R.A. XI Corps.	23. File.
13. 61 Div. 'G'	18. H.A. XI Corps.	

MARCH TABLE Issued with 61st. Divisional Artillery Order No.160.

Serial No.	Date.	Unit or Formation.	From	To.	Route.	Relieved by.	Remarks.
1.	Octr. Night 3/4th.	1 Section of Batteries, 61 M.A. (less B/306 & B/307.)	Action.	Wagon Lines.	Any.	1 Section per Bty. 59 Div. Arty. less B/295 & B/296.	Completion of relief to be wired to B.S.D.A. by code: "TRALEE" 305 Bde. "MANIN" 307 Bde.
2.	4th.	No.1 Coy. 61 Div. Train.	Les BEFORDS EN LABERES.	ST.VENANT GUARBEQUE.		No.1 Coy. 59th. Div.Train.	To commence march at 8.30 a.m.
3.	4th.	R.A.H.Q. 61 Divn.	RILL WORKS.	FONTES.	ST.VENANT GUARBEQUE.	R.A.H.Q. 59th.Div.	
4.	4th.	61 D.A.C.	Wagon Lines.	MAZINGHEM.	"	59 D.A.C.	To commence march at 1000 at which hour 59 M.A.C. will assume responsibility for supply of all ammunition.
5.	4th.	61 Div.Trench Mortars.	Billets.	FONTES.	"	59 Div.Trench Mortars.	March to commence on completion of relief of mobile T.Ms. in action.
6.	4/5th.	306 Bde. R.F.A.	Action. & "B" W.L.	FONTES.	"	Remainder 295 Bde. R.F.A.	To march under Brigade arrangements.
7.	4/5th.	307 Bde. R.F.A.	Action. & "B" W.L.	LAMBRES.	"	Remainder 295 Bde.R.F.A.	To march under Brigade arrangements.

R.A.Q. 545/1.

61st DIVISIONAL ARTILLERY ADMINISTRATIVE INSTRUCTIONS
issued in connection with 61st Div. Art Order 160.
----------------oOo----------------

Headquarters, R.A.
3.10.1918.

1. **BILLETS.**
   All units will send a representative to report at 1600 on the 3rd instant as follows :-

   306th Brigade to AREA COMMANDANT, NORRENT FONTES.
   307th Brigade) to Sub-Area Commandant, LAMBRES.
   61st D.A.C.   )
   No.1 Co. ASC)

   from whom numbers of billets and positions of wagon lines will be obtained. Following billets allotted in FONTES, RAHQ - 58, 64, 65. DTMO. 75, 76, 77, 78, 81, 83, 84, 85, 86.

2. **AMMUNITION.**
   All ammunition in positions and dumps will be handed over to incoming units. Receipts obtained, will be forwarded as soon as possible. Amounts, by natures, will be telephoned to this office on completion of handing over. Bdes. will be responsible for notifying relieving Brigades of any ammunition in evacuated or A.T. gun positions.
   Units will march out with full echelons. 59th D.A. will be responsible for accounting for all ammn as & from 1000 (4th instant

3. **TRANSPORT.**
   Baggage wagons will report to units on the evening of the 3rd instant. Lorries will report on the 4th instant as follows :-

   3 to R.A.H.Q. at   0830
   2 to 306th Bde H.Q. W.L. at 1400
   2 to 307th Bde H.Q. W.L. at 1400
   1 to D.A.C. H.Q. at   0900
   6 to T.M. H.Q. at a time to be notified later.

4. **SUPPLIES.**
   All units will send guides to LAMBRES CHURCH at 1400 on the 4th instant to guide supply wagons to new wagon lines.
   Railhead changes to AIRE on the 4th instant.

5. **TRENCH & AREA STORES.**
   All Trench and Area Stores, including Pack Saddles surplus to establishment, tents, trench shelters, Armstrong huts, petrol tins, hot food containers, and anti-gas clothing will be handed over and receipts forwarded to R.A.H.Q. as soon as possible after relief.

6. **DIVISIONAL CANTEEN.**
   Arrangements for drawing this week will be notified later.

Captain,
a/S.C.R.A., 61st Division.

War Diary

SECRET.

Copy No: 33

61st. DIVISIONAL ARTILLERY ORDER NO: 161.

3rd. Octr. 1918.

1. **Move.** The Division complete with all transport, will move by rail on the 5th. and 6th. instant.
   The Artillery and No.1 Coy. 61 Divisional Train, will entrain in accordance with attached Table. The actual times of departure and Detraining Stations will be notified later.

2. The journey will take approximately 5 hours.

3. Attention is drawn to Chap:5, Section 30 of F.S.P.B.1914.

4. (a) Lieut. E.W.TUNBRIDGE, R.F.A. will act as Liaison Officer between the R.O.D. Staff and Units entraining at BERGUETTE.
   306 and 307 Brigades, R.F.A., will provide a Captain or Senior Subaltern for this duty; 306th. Brigade at THIENNES and 307th. Brigade at STEENBECQUE, respectively.
   These Officers will be at their respective Stations 4 hours before the first train is due to leave, and will travel by the last train.

   (b) Orders as regards Officers to perform the above duty at detraining stations will be issued later.

5. All Units will arrive at their entraining Stations 3 hours before the train is timed to depart.

6. Lorries to take stores and blankets to Entraining Stations and from Detraining Stations will be provided. Arrangements will be notified later.

7. ACKNOWLEDGE.

                                    [signature]
                                    Capt. R.A.
                                    Bde.Maj., 61 Div. Artillery.

Issued at 17.

DISTRIBUTION.

Copy No. 1 - 7.   306th. Bde. R.F.A.
         8 - 14. 307th. Bde. R.F.A.
        15 - 19. 61 D.A.C.
        20 - 22. 61 D.T.M.O.
        23.   No.1 Coy. 61 Div. Train.
        24.   Lt. E.W. TUNBRIDGE, R.F.A.
        25.   61 Div. 'G'.
        26.   61 Div. 'Q'.
        27.   61 D.A.P.M.
        28.   Traffic Officer, AIRE Station.
        29.   R.T.O. BERGUETTE.
        30.   R.T.O. THIENNES.
        31.   R.T.O. STEENBECQUE.
        32.   R.A. XI Corps.
        33. - 34. War Diary.
        35.   File.

ENTRAINING TABLE.

Train No.	Entraining BERGUETTE.	Train No.	Entraining THIENNES.	Train No.	Entraining STEENBECQUE.
25	No.1 Brigade H.Q.(Arty.) No.1 Section, D.A.C. less 4 G.S.Wagons and 16 Limbered Amun.Wagons & Teams "Y" T.M.Battery.	20.	½ S.A.A. Section D.A.C. and (1 Coy.complete with Cooker and Team) C Battalion,184 Inf.Bde.	21	½ S.A.A. Section D.A.C. and (1 Coy.complete with Cooker and Team) "C" Battalion 183 Infantry Bde.
28	No.2 Brigade H.Q.(Arty.) No.2 Section,D.A.C.(less 4 G.S.Wagons and 16 Limbered Amun.Wagons & Teams "Y" T.M. Battery.	23.	"A" Battery,No.1 Brigade (Arty.) 1 G.S.Wagon, 4 Limbered Amun. Wagons & Teams of No.1 Section, D.A.C.	24	"A" Battery, No.2 Brigade(Art.) 1 G.S.Wagon, 4 Limbered Amun. Wagons & Teams of No.2 Sect. D.A.C.
31.	H.Q., R.A. H.Q., D.A.C. No.1 Coy. Div. Train.	26.	"B" Battery, No.1 Brigade (Arty.) 1 G.S.Wagon, 4 Limbered Amun. Wagons & Teams of No.1 Section, D.A.C.	27	"B" Battery, No.2 Brigade(Art.) 1 G.S.Wagon, 4 Limbered Amun. Wagons & Teams of No.2 Sect. D.A.C.
		29	"C" Battery, No.1 Brigade (Arty.) 1 G.S.Wagon and 4 Limbered Amun. Wagons & Teams of No.1 Section, D.A.C.	30	"C" Battery, No.2 Brigade(Art.) 1 G.S.Wagon & 4 Limbered Amun. Wagons & Teams of No.2 Sect. D.A.C.
		32	"D" Battery, No.1 Brigade (Arty.) 1 G.S.Wagon, 4 Limbered Amun. Wagons & Teams of No.1 Section, D.A.C.	33	"D" Battery, No.2 Brigade(Art.) 1 G.S.Wagon, 4 Limbered Amun. Wagons & Teams of No.2 Sect.

War Diary

SECRET.

R.A.Q.545/2.

61st. DIVISIONAL ARTILLERY ADMINISTRATIVE INSTRUCTIONS.

4th. Oct. 1918.

1. Reference para.1 of 61 Div. Artillery Order No.161 dated 3rd. instant.

    (a) 306th. Brigade R.F.A. will travel by trains shown for No.1 Brigade (Arty.)
    307th. Brigade R.F.A. will travel by trains shown for No.2 Brigade (Art.)

    2.(b) Detraining Stations.
    Units entraining at BERGUETTE and STEENBECQUE detrain at DOULLENS.
    Units entraining at THIENNES detain at ROSEL.

    (c) Times of departure of trains.

Train No.	Date.	Departs.	Train No.	Date.	Departs.	Train No.	Date	Departs
7	6	0330 hours.	20	6	1617 hours	21	6	1710 hours
			23	6	1917 hours	24	6	2010 hours
25	6	2130 hours	26	6	2217 hours	27	6	2310 hours
28	7	0030 hours	29	7	0117 hours	30	7	0210 hours
31	7	0330 hours	32	7	0417 hours	33	7	0510 hours

2. O.C. D.A.C. will detail an Officer at each detraining Station to act as liaison officer between R.O.D. Staff and Units detraining. These officers will travel by trains Nos. 20 & 21 and will remain at detraining stations until the last trains are cleared.

3. Lorries for conveying surplus stores and kit to the entraining stations will report to Units as follows :-

    1 each to R.A.H.Q., 306th. Bde; 307th. Bde. & D.A.C. at 16.30 on the 6th. instant. All stores and kit will be taken to entraining stations as follows :-

    R.A.H.Q., D.A.C., D.T.M.O. to BERGUETTE.
    306th. Brigade   to THIENNES.
    307th. Brigade   to STEENBECQUE.

    The lorry reporting to the D.A.C. will also move stores for D.T.M.O. by mutual arrangement between O.C.D.A.C. and D.T.M.O.
    All drivers must be given written instructions and will be returned to their Park as soon as possible as they are urgently required for other work.

4. **Supplies.** Refilling Point on 5th. instant will be at LA BEFORE FARM, LAMBRES.

Supply wagons with rations and forage for consumption on the 7th. will report after refilling on the fifth and will travel with Units.

In the case of wagons being detached as for D.A.C., rations and forage should be split, and distributed on the G.S. Wagons travelling with batteries.

All supply wagons must be returned to No.1 Coy. A.S.C. immediately on arrival in the new lines as they will be required to refill on the 7th.

5. **Surplus Kit.**
Immediately on arrival in the new area all Units will at once overhaul all stores and personal kit with a view to dumping everything that is not actually required for active operations.

Units will probably only be able to rely on their Baggage wagons, and it is essential that all stores and kit be reduced to a minimum.

A surplus kit store will be established at DOULLENS.

Units will be notified later exact location and arrangements for dumping.

6. ACKNOWLEDGE.

Captain,
Staff Captain, R.A.,
61st Division.

DISTRIBUTION.

No.1 - 5.	306th. Brigade, R.F.A.
6 -10.	307th. Brigade, R.F.A.
11 -16.	61st. D.A.C.
17 -19.	61st. D.T.M.O.
20.	No.1 Coy. 61 Div.Train.
21.	Lieut. E.W.TUNBRIDGE.
22.	61st. Div. 'G'.
23.	61 Div. 'Q'.
24.	61 D.A.P.M.
25.	Traffic Officer, AIRE Station.
26.	R.T.O. BERGUETTE.
27.	R.T.O. THIENNES.
28.	R.T.O. STEENBECQUE.
29.	R.A. XI Corps.
30-31.	War Diary.
32.	File.

SECRET.   Copy No: 25

61st. DIVISIONAL ARTILLERY ORDER NO: 162.

7th. Octr. 1918.

Ref: Maps - LENS & VALENCIENNES 1/100,000.

1. The 61st. Divisional Artillery and No.1 Coy. 61 Div. Train will move by march route to an area about MOEUVRES - GRAINCOURT (Area 'D'), commencing on 8.10.18, in accordance with attached March Table.

2. The following distances will be maintained between Units on the line of march :-
   (a) Between Batteries and Sections D.A.C.   100 yards.
   (b) Between Artillery Brigades.   500 yards.
   (c) Between groups of 6 vehicles.   25 yards.

3. Os.C. Brigades, D.A.C. and No.1 Coy. 61 Div. Train, will send forward daily, parties to reconnoitre positions to halt for the night within the areas shown in the March Table.

4. Roads as shown on the maps do not always exist.
   On 8th. instant, 307 Brigade, R.F.A. will send forward an Officer to reconnoitre the road for the march on 9th. instant.
   On 9th. instant, 306 Brigade, R.F.A. will send forward an Officer to reconnoitre the road for the march on 10th. instant.
   These Officers will notify O.C. No.1 Coy. 61 Div. Train the best route to take, and will march at the head of the leading Brigade, R.F.A.

5. R.A.H.Q. transport and personnel, and 61 Div. Trench Mortars are attached to 61st. D.A.C. during the march.

6. Administrative instructions to follow.

7. R.A.H.Q. will close at AMPLIER on 9th. and re-open in Area 'D' at a time to be notified later.

8. The G.O.C. wishes strict attention to be paid to March Discipline, packing of vehicles and cleanliness of harness and equipment.

9. ACKNOWLEDGE.

                                              Capt. R.A.,
                                              Bde. Maj., 61 Div. Artillery.
Issued at 5.45 p.m.

DISTRIBUTION.

```
Copy No. 1 - 5.   306th. Bde. R.F.A.
         6 - 10.  307th. Bde. R.F.A.
        11 - 14.  61 D.A.C.
        15.       61 D.T.M.O.
        16.       No.1 Coy. 61 Div. Train.
        17.       61st. Divn. 'G'
        18.       61st. Divn. 'Q'
        19.       61st. D.A.P.M.
        20.       61st. A.D.V.S.
        21.       61st. A.D.M.S.
        22.       R.A. XVII Corps.
        23.       R.T.O. DOULLENS.
     24-25.       War Diary.
        26.       File.
```

MARCH TABLE issued with 61 D.A. Order No.162.

Serial No.	Dets.	Unit.	From.	To.	Starting Point.	Time.	Route.	Remarks.
1	8	307 Bde.RFA	ORVILLE.	BRETENCOURT.	Cross Roads N of M in MONDICOURT.	8.15 am.	MONDICOURT - LA BELLEVUE - X rds. SE of BEAUMETZ.	To be clear of starting point by 0930 hrs
2	8	61 D.A.C.	AMPLIER.	do.	do.	8.45 am.	do.	
3	8	No.1 Coy.ASC	SARTON.	do.	Rd.junction 200 yds.IW of M in SARTON.	8.45 am.	THIEVRES - PAS - GAUDIEMPRE - POMMIER - BERLES au BOIS.	
4	8	306 Bde.RFA	SARTON.	do.	do.	10 a.m.	do.	
5	9	No.1 Coy.	BRETENCOURT.	BOYELLES.	Rd.junction 200 yds. N of BLAIRVILLE Church.	7.15 am.	BLAIRVILLE - FICHEUX-BOISLEUX.	
6	9	306 Bde.	do.	do.	do.	8 a.m.	do.	
7	9	307 Bde.	do.	do.	do.	8.30 am.	do.	
8	9	61 D.A.C.	do.	do.	do.	9 a.m.	do.	To be clear of FICHEUX by 1000 hours
9	10	No.1 Coy.	BOYELLES	MOEUVRES-GRAINCOURT Area.	Further details later.			
10	10	306"Bde.	"	"				
11	10	307 Bde.	"	"				
12	10	61 D.A.C.	"	"				

SECRET.

R.A.G.10/1.

ADDENDUM to
MARCH TABLE issued with 61 D.A. Order No.162.

Serial Nos. 5 to 8 inclusive, column 5, for "BOYELLES" read "CROISILLES".

Serial Nos. 9 to 12 inclusive, cancel table and substitute new Table as follows :-

Serial No.	Date	Unit.	From.	To.	Route.	Remarks.
9	10	306 Bde RFA	CROISILLES	MOEUVRES - GRAINCOURT Area.	LAGNICOURT-X Roads ½ mile N.W. of DOIGNIES.	To be clear of CROISILLES by 0730 hours.
10	10	307 Bde. RFA	do.	do.	do.	To be clear of CROISILLES by 0800 hours.
11	10	61 D.A.C.	do.	do.	do.	To be clear of CROISILLES by 0830 hours.
12	10	No.1 Coy., 61 Div. Train.	do.	do.	do.	To be clear of CROISILLES by 0845 hours.

ACKNOWLEDGE.

H.P. Nye.
Capt. R.A.,
Bde. Maj., 61 Div. Artillery.

8.10.18.

To all recipients of 61st. Div. Artillery
Order No. 162 of 7.10.1918.

War Diary

SECRET.

AMENDMENT NO: 1
to
61st. Div. Artillery Order No.162 of 7.10.1918.

Para.1

for "Area about MOEUVRES - GRAINCOURT (Area D)"

read "Area South West of MOEUVRES."

Capt. R.A.,
A/Adjt., 61 Div. Artillery.

8.10.1918.

To all recipients of 61 D.A. Order No.162.

War Diary

23

SECRET.   Copy No: 23
                                                     10.10.1918.

61st. DIVISIONAL ARTILLERY ORDER NO: 163.

1. From all information to hand, the enemy is carrying out a retirement on a large scale. A vigorous pursuit has been ordered along the whole Army front.

2. The pursuit by the XVII Corps is to be carried out with the utmost determination. The hostile rearguards are to be attacked as soon as located. The one aim and object of all ranks will be to get at the enemy's main forces and bring them to battle.

3. The attached map shows the Corps boundaries for the advance.

4. The organisation for the advance will be, for the present, as follows:-
   (a) Leading Group.
        24th. Division.
        Corps Mounted Troops.
        5 Brigades Field Artillery - Brig.-Gen. PALMER (Acting C.R.A.)
        1 Bde. H.A.
   (b) Support Group.
        19th. Division.
        4 Brigades of Field Artillery - Brig.-Gen. RUDKIN (Acting C.R.A.)
   (c) Reserve Group.
        61st. Division.
        61st. Divisional Artillery.
   (d) Corps Group.
        3 Brigades of Heavy Artillery.

   The grouping of Artillery will be adjusted by the Corps from time to time to conform to the relief of Divisions, but the principle will remain the same as regards the amount of artillery allotted to each Group
   The position of the Artillery of the Support and Reserve Groups will always be well forward in these formations, in order that it can move up to supplement the artillery of the leading Group when required.

5. One Section of Tunnellers is allotted by Corps to accompany the leading Group for the purpose of searching for and removing mines and "booby traps" in the villages, and to report when the latter are safe for occupation. Attention is called to 61st. Div. Art. R.A.G. 2/1/13 publishing the various markings to be made on all buildings, dugouts, etc., after examination.

6. In accordance with the above detail, the Division will be prepared to move forward at short notice. In the meantime, every advantage will be taken, by all units in the Division while in Reserve Group, of the excellent facilities and ground in their neighbourhood for training purposes.

7. The strictest march discipline of all arms will be enforced. Troops will move off the roads to halt whenever possible.

8. The main cable route through Corps area will be as follows :-
   MT. SUR L'OEUVRE - the railway to A.18. central - main road to B.20.b. - CAUROIR - AVESNES by the CAMBRAI - SOLESMES road - ST. AUBERT.
   Divisional and Brigade H.Q. will always be situated in or near this route.

9. In the event of the Division being ordered to advance through the Leading and Support Groups, the following troops will form the Advanced guard of the Division :-
        Commander - Brig.-Gen. B.D.L.G. ANLEY, C.M.G., D.S.O.
        183 Inf. Bde.
        306 F.A. Bde.
        1 Coy. 61 Bn. M.G.C.
        478 Field Coy. R.E.
   Officers commanding the above Units will get into touch with B.G.C. 183 Inf. Bde.

P.T.O.

10. ACKNOWLEDGE.

J.P. WYE
Capt. R.A.
Bde.Maj., 61 Div. Artillery.

Issued at 17.00

DISTRIBUTION.

Copy No. 1 - 5.   306th. Bde. R.F.A.
        6 - 10.   307th. Bde. R.F.A.
        11.   61 D.T.M.O.
        12. 15.   61 D.A.C.
        13. 16.   61 Div. 'G'.
        14. 17.   O.i/c R.A. Signals.
        15. 18.   R.A. XVII Corps.
        16. 19.   19th. Div. Art.
        17. 20.   24th. Div. Art.
        18. 21.   Bde.Maj., XVII Corps H.A.
            22-23. War Diary.
            24.   File.

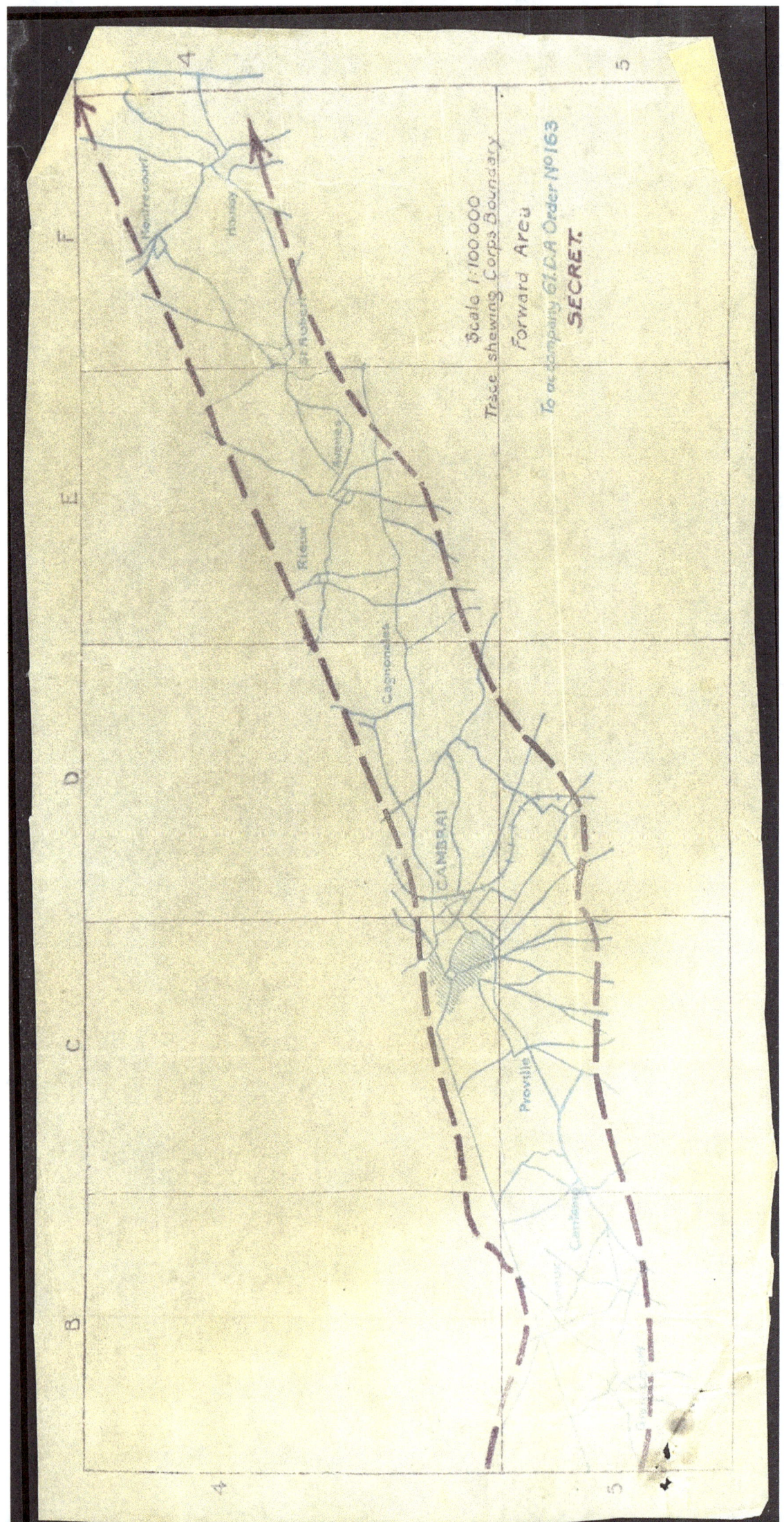

SECRET.　　　　　　　　　　　　Copy No: 25

61st. DIVISIONAL ARTILLERY ORDER NO: 164.

10.10.1918.

Reference Map 57C. 1/40,000.

WARNING ORDER.

1. In order to conform to the rapid advance this morning the Division will be prepared to move tomorrow to areas as shown below.

    (a) **Advanced Guard Brigade Group.**
    Consisting of 183rd. Brigade Group, plus 306 Bde. R.F.A. 2 Mobile 6" NEWTON T.Ms. and one Company 61st. Bn. M.G. Corps, to an area in squares L.2, 3 and 4.

    (b) **Support Brigade Group.**
    Consisting of 182nd. Bde. Group, plus 307 Bde. R.F.A., and one Company 61st. Bn. M.G. Corps, to an area in squares F.25. and 26.

    (c) **Reserve Brigade Group.**
    Consisting of 184th. Bde. Group, plus D.A.C., 61st. Bn. M.G. Corps (less two companies) No.1 Coy. 61 Div. Train, to an area in squares E.22, 28 and 29 and K.4. and 5.

2. R.A. Headquarters will remain at LAGNICOURT for the present.

3. ACKNOWLEDGE.

　　　　　　　　　　　　　　　　　　　[signature]

　　　　　　　　　　　　　　　　　　　Capt. R.A.,
　　　　　　　　　　　　　　　　Bde. Maj., 61 Div. Artillery.

Issued at 18.00

DISTRIBUTION.

Copy No.	
1 - 5.	306th. Bde. R.F.A.
6 - 10.	307th. Bde. R.F.A.
11.	D T M.O.
12 - 15.	61st. D.A.C.
16.	61 Divn. 'G'.
17.	O.i/c. R.A. Signals.
18.	R.A. XVII Corps.
19.	19th. Div. Art.
20.	24th. Div. Art.
21.	Bde. Major, XVII Corps H.A.
22.	182 Inf. Bde.
23.	183 Inf. Bde.
24.	184 Inf. Bde.
25 - 26.	War Diary.
27.	File.

War Diary 17

~~61st Divisional Artillery Instructions No...~~

1. The advance of the Field Artillery and its dispositions through~~out the pursuit~~ will be based on the following principles :-

   (a). Five Brigades with leading Division, of which one Brigade will be the ADVANCED GUARD Brigade. The remaining Brigades will advance by leapfrogging in couples, taking up "positions of observation" in rotation from the rear. Immediately the enemy's rearguard is located holding a defensive line, all brigades will be advanced to effective range of this line, with batteries specially detailed for close support of the Infantry.

   (b). Three Brigades will move in support and will march with the Division in support. They will similarly advance by leapfrogging, taking up "positions of observation" or "positions of readiness" according to whether the pace of the advance is slow or rapid. They will be prepared to immediately reinforce the leading Divisional Artillery, and the C.R.A. supporting group will keep in close touch with C.R.A. leading Division.

   (c). The Brigades in reserve will march with the Reserve Division. The advance will be made clear of main roads wherever the state of the going permits.
   All brigades except those in reserve will have mounted officers' patrols constantly out.

2. HEAVY ARTILLERY.

   (a). The R.G.A. Brigade affiliated to the leading Division will advance by batteries leapfrogging similarly to the Field Artillery. The two 6" howitzer batteries and the two 60 pounder batteries working in couples. All four batteries will advance to effective range immediately it is ascertained that the enemy is holding a defensive line.

   (b). The remaining brigades will march under the orders of B.G. Corps Heavy Artillery, who will keep in close touch with the movements of the support and reserve divisions to enable him to select the best time and routes for advancing batteries.

3. Strictest march discipline will be maintained. Troops will move off the roads to halt whenever possible. If it is necessary to halt on a road the officer in command of a column of vehicles must warn his drivers in ample time previous to giving the signal to halt so as to enable all vehicles and mounted men to move to the edge of the road and to ensure that intervals of 25 yards between every 6 vehicles are maintained as passing places for traffic.
   All Commanding Officers will pay particular attention to march discipline for the next few days to ensure that their officers N.C.O's and O.Rs are adopting the correct procedure. Seizing the right time to water horses requires judgment and forethought.

4. Every artillery unit is responsible for its own protection from surprise, and patrols must always be employed on the flanks.

ACKNOWLEDGE.

10.10.1918.

Captain, R.A.,
Bde-Major, 61st Div. Artillery.

DISTRIBUTION.

Copy No. 1 - 5   306 Bde   17 - 18 War Diary.
         6 - 10 307 Bde   19   File
         11- 14 61 D.A.C.
         15   61 D.T.M.O.
         16   61 Div 'G'

S E C R E T.   Copy No: ......

61st. DIVISIONAL ARTILLERY ORDER NO: 165.

10.10.18.

Ref: Map 57C, 1/40,000.

1. Units of 61st. Divisional Artillery and No.1 Company, 61st. Div. Train, will move into the areas laid down in 61 Div. Artillery Order No.164 on 11th. instant as follows :-

    306th. Bde. R.F.A. will be clear of present lines by 0800 hour
    307th. Bde. R.F.A.   "   "   "   "   " 0830   "
    61st. D.A.C.   "   "   "   "   " 0900   "
    No.1 Coy. 61 Div. Train "   "   "   "   " 0930   "

2. (a) The two mobile 6" NEWTON T.Ms. attached to Advanced Guard Brigade Group will march immediately in area of 306th. Bde. R.F.A.

   (b) 61 Div. Trench Mortars, less mobile sub-sections mentioned in para.2(a) above, will move under arrangements to be made by S.C.R.A. and will join the Reserve Brigade Group.

3. The moves in all cases will be completed by 12.00 hours.

4. Locations to be forwarded to R.A.H.Q. as soon as possible after arrival in the new area.

5. Completion of moves to be notified by code to R.A.H.Q. as under :-

    306th. Bde. R.F.A.   LANCS.
    307th. Bde. R.F.A.   YORKS.
    61st. Div. T.Ms.   NORFOLK.
    61st. D.A.C.   SUFFOLK.
    No.1 Coy. Train.   HANTS.

6. Administrative Instructions follow.

7. ACKNOWLEDGE.

                                    F.P. Wye
                                    Capt. R.A.,
                                    61st. Div. Artillery.

Issued at 18.00

DISTRIBUTION.

    No. 1 - 5   306th. Bde. R.F.A.
        6 -10   307th. Bde. R.F.A.
        11.   D T M O.
        12 -15. 61st. D.A.C.
        16.   61 Divn. 'G'.
        17.   O.i/c R.A. Sigs.
        18.   R.A. XVII Corps.
        19.   19th Div. Art.
        20.   24th. Div. Art.
        21.   Bde Maj., XVII Corps R.A.
        22.   182 Inf. Bde.
        23.   183 Inf. Bde.
        24.   184 Inf. Bde.
        25 -26. War Diary.

SECRET.   R.A.Q. 545/17.

ADMINISTRATIVE INSTRUCTIONS with reference to
61st Div. Artillery Order No. 165.

                              Headquarters, R.A. 10.10.18.

1.   The locations of units are as follows :-

        306th Bde - L.2.a. b. & c.
        307th Bde - F.25.c. & d.
        D.A.C.   - E.28.a. & b.
                (North of BAPAUME-CAMBRAI Road)
        No.1 Coy.,
        61 Div. Train.- K.3. c.8.8.

2.   Water point for horses and water carts at F.15.c.5.1.
        Water troughs are at SUGAR FACTORY E.29.a.7.9.
        There is also water at the S.W. end of ANNEUX village.

3.   Refilling Point tomorrow October 11th is at K.3.b.6.6.,
        ½ mile South of BAPAUME-CAMBRAI Road, on the road to HAVRIN-
        COURT. Guides from all units will report there at 1200.
        Coal dump is on track N. of SUGAR FACTORY at E.29.a.7.9.

4.   O.C., D.A.C. will reserve an area with a frontage to
        the main road in the area allotted to the D.A.C. by 184 Bde,
        for the accommodation of 61st T.M.Bs.
                An officer will be detailed by D.T.M.O. to ascertain exa
        location from 61st D.A.C.

5.   All tents and trench shelters will be carried into the
        new area - any which cannot be moved will be collected and
        placed in charge of a guard and R.A.H.Q. notified.

                                        Major,
R.A.H.Q.   S.C.R.A., 61st Division.

        DISTRIBUTION :- To all recipients of Order 165.

S E C R E T. *War Diary*

R.A.G.10/6.

AMENDMENT NO: 1
to
61st. DIVISIONAL ARTILLERY ORDER NO.166 -11.10.18.

Para.7 is cancelled.

Serial No.4 of Relief Table is cancelled.

Further instructions will be issued later. *in twenty martin*

F. Phyfe

12.10.1918.
Capt. R.A.,
Bde.Maj., 61 Div. Artillery.

To all recipients of above Order.

SECRET.   Copy No: ....

61st. DIVISIONAL ARTILLERY ORDER NO: 166.

11.10.18.

Ref: Maps Sheets 57B & 57C. 1/40,000.

1. The 61st. Divisional Artillery will relieve 40th. Divisional Artillery in the line in accordance with attached Table.

2. The relief will be carried out as far as possible by day on 13th. instant, and will be completed on night 13/14th. instant.

3. 1/20,000 and 1/40,000 Maps of the forward area will be taken over by relieving Units.

4. Guns will not be exchanged.

5. Further details of relief will be arranged by Unit Commanders concerned.

6. R.A.H.Q. will be notified of completion of relief and location by code as follows :-

    306th. Bde. R.F.A.   "COUNTRY LIFE" followed by coordinates.
    307th. Bde. R.F.A.   "FIELD"   "   "
    61st. D.A.C.   "TATLER"   "   "
    61st. D.T.M.O.   "BYSTANDER"

7. Two mobile 6" NEWTON Trench Mortars will be placed at the disposal of B.G.C. Advanced Infantry Brigade, 24th. Division, from 8 p.m. 13th. instant, under arrangements to be made by 61st. D.T.M.O.

8. C.R.A. 61 Division will take over command of the Artillerys covering 24th. Division on completion of relief.

9. ACKNOWLEDGE.

Phys.

Capt. R.A.,
Bde. Maj., 61 Div. Artillery.

Issued at 0859.

DISTRIBUTION.

Copy No. 1 - 5. 306th. Bde. R.F.A.
         6 -10. 307th. Bde. R.F.A.
         11 & 12. D.T.M.O.
         13 - 16. D.A.C.
         17. No.1 Coy. 61 Div. Train.
         18. 61st. Divn. 'G'.
         19. 61st. Divn. 'Q'.
         20. 61st. D.A.P.M.
         21. R.A. XVII Corps.
         22. 40th. Div. Art.
         23. 52nd. Div. Art.
         24. 57th. Div. Art.
         25. 17th. Corps H.A.
         26. C.B.S.O. 17th. Corps.
         27. 13th. Sqn. R.A.F.
         28. 16th. Balloon Coy. R.A.F.
         29. 24th. Divn. 'G'.
         30. 24th. Divn. 'Q'.
      31-32. War Diary.
         33. File.

RELIEF TABLE to accompany 61 D.A. Order No.166.

Serial No.	Date.	Formation or Unit.	From.	To.	Route.	Relieves.	Remarks.
1	13th	306 Bde. R.F.A.	Wagon Lines	178th.Bde. RFA. Wagon Lines.	Via CANTAING & CAMBRAI.	178 Bde. RFA.	To be clear of present location by 0830 hours.
2	13th	307 Bde. R.F.A.	Wagon Lines	181th.Bde. RFA. Wagon Lines.	Via FONTAINE NOTRE DAME & CAMBRAI.	181 Bde. RFA.	To be clear ANNEUX by 0900 hours.
3	13th	61 D.A.C.	Wagon Lines	40 D.A.C. Wagon Lines.	"	40 D.A.C.	To be clear of present location by 0930 hours.
4	13th	61 Div. Trench Mortars.	Wagon Lines	40 Div. T.Ms.	"	40 Div.T.Ms.	To move under arrangements of B.G.R.A. & S.M.T.O.
5	13th	No. 1 Coy. 61 Div. Train.	Wagon Lines	New area.	"	—	To be clear of present location by 1000 hours.
6	13th	H.Q.R.A. (Includes Signals)	LAGNICOURT.	New area.	"	H.Q.R.A. 40 Div.	To be clear of LAGNICOURT by 1000 hours.

SECRET.　　　　　　　　　　　　Copy No: 38

61st. DIVISIONAL ARTILLERY INSTRUCTIONS NO: 23.

OPERATIONS.

1. The immediate support by Artillery of attacking Infantry or Tanks against Machine or Anti-Tank guns is not yet always effectively carried out.

   This support may be given either by 6" Mobile Trench Mortars or field guns at point blank range, or by field guns and Howitzers firing from a distance further back.

   The value of the 6" Mobile Trench Mortar is so marked that this weapon should be used whenever practicable.

   In the absence of these Mortars, local circumstances must determine whether point blank range or fire from a distance further back is to be employed.

   Guns firing from a short distance such as 500 to 1800 yds. are more likely to be available at the critical moment than those pushed up with the Infantry in the closest support. Teams even of four horses make a conspicuous target for machine guns and are readily knocked out by a barrage through which Infantry will pass successfully.

   The moral and actual effect, however, of a gun firing at point blank range is so marked that this should be attempted when possible. Risks must in such cases be freely run. Careful previous reconnaissance will prove of its usual value. Endeavours should be made to work the gun from point to point which commands the view while avoiding machine gun fire actually on the front line. To ensure that fire shall be available when wanted, the effort should not be confined to less than two guns on a Divisional front.

   If Trench Mortars or point blank fire is adopted, the support of Artillery a short distance further back should also be invariably arranged for.

2. Whatever method is adopted, it is essential that the Artillery F.O.O. directing the fire should be with the Infantry and see with his own eyes the obstacle which is holding up the attack.

   This F.O.O. should be provided with light wire, lamp and runner. He must call on the Infantry for runners if needed, vide 'Division in Attack'. While giving his orders direct to a gun or Mortar if with him, he should be prepared to send back orders in the event of his piece being knocked out, or of his acting as F.O.O. to guns at a further distance in rear.

3. Guns when in rear must be at all risks in vocal control of their Commander - who should be preferably the Battery Commander. Junior Officers may lack the experience, knowledge and power of taking responsibility. The only post possible for the gun Commander is the one whence he can best see the fight.

   The duty of this Battery Commander is to study the fight and shoot by his own observation if he can. He should have an expert N.C.O. detailed to look for signals from the F.O.O. with the Infantry. It is the duty of this N.C.O. to 'pick up' this F.O.O.; it is the duty of the F.O.O. with the Infantry to place himself roughly in view of the gun commanders station.

P.T.O.

4. In the reconnaissance previous to the fight the line of advance of the F.O.O. with the Infantry should be settled between him and the Battery Commander. Certain unmistakeable reference points should be mutually fixed and named.

Artillery Officers responsible for this support should have the fullest information given them by the Infantry and the greatest latitude allowed them in carrying out their tasks.

5. ACKNOWLEDGE.

F.P.Pye

12.10.18.

Captain, R.A.,
Bde. Maj., 61 Div. Artillery.

DISTRIBUTION.

Copy No.	
1 - 5.	305th. Bde. R.F.A.
6 - 10.	307th. Bde. R.F.A.
11 - 13.	61st. D.T.M.O.
14 - 25.	52nd. Div. Art.
26 - 30.	93rd. A.F.A. Bde.
31.	61st. D.A.C.
32.	61 Divn. 'G'.
33.	24th. Divn. 'G'.
34.	R.A. XVII Corps.
35 - 36.	War Diary.
37.	File.

S E C R E T.

Copy No: 40

61st. DIVISIONAL ARTILLERY INSTRUCTIONS NO: 24.

12.10.1918.

AMMUNITION, FIELD ARTY.

1. (a) During the present phase in the operations, all Batteries will normally keep two Wagon loads of ammunition per gun dumped at gun positions, exclusive of smoke, gas and incendiary shell ordered to be dumped for special purposes.

   (b) In the event of hostile gas shelling prior to or during an enemy attack, rendering the setting of fuzes for time shrapnel difficult, 106 fuzes with H.E. will be used.

   (c) H.E. with 101 delay fuzes will be used against hostile tanks, should these be used by the enemy in counter-attacks.

   (d) Echelons will be kept full.

   (e) Positions which Units vacate during the advance will be cleared of all ammunition before more is drawn from D.A.Cs. or A.R.Ps.

   (f) The following amounts of smoke and incendiary shell will as far as possible, be maintained by Batteries in their Echelons:-

   18-pr. Batteries - A Smoke, 60 rounds.
   A.T.   16   "

   4.5" How.   "   - B Smoke, 36 rounds.
   B.T.   "   12   "

FORWARD WAGON LINES.

2. Any Batteries in action within 2500 yards of the enemy will have forward limber lines for gun limbers and a few outriders, where the horses should be kept with harness on. Arrangements will be made by Batteries concerned for the horses at the forward limber lines to be relieved every 6 hours.

TELEPHONE LINES.

3. (a) Salvage of derelict telephone cable is essential, but this must on no account be done before ascertaining that the lines are spare and no longer required.

   (b) All lines must be clearly labelled at least every 440 yards.

   (c) Orders will be issued to all units to this effect and disciplinary action will be taken against anyone found cutting lengths out of or reeling up working lines.

4. 61st. Divisional Artillery Instructions Nos. 7, 11 and 13 are cancelled and will be destroyed.

5. ACKNOWLEDGE.

Capt. R.A.,
Bde. Maj., 61 Div. Artillery.

DISTRIBUTION.

Copy No. 1 - 5. 306 Bde. RFA	No. 36. 24th. Divn. 'G'
6 -10. 307 Bde. RFA	37. R.A. XVII Corps.
11 -13. 61 D.A.C.	38. 57th. Div. Art.
14 -18. 93rd. A.F.A. Bde.	39. O.i/c. R.A. Signals.
19 -33. 52nd. Div. Art.	40-41. War Diary.
34. 61 D.T.M.O.	42 File.
35. 61 Divn. 'G'.	

S E C R E T.

AMENDMENT NO: 1
- to -
61st. DIV. ARTILLERY LOCATION STATEMENT of 14.10.18.

	Location.	Wagon Lines.
307 Bde.RFA. H.Q.	V.19.d.1.6.	U.28.b.1.5.
A/307.	V.20.a.8.2.	U.28.c.
B/307.	V.20.a.7.7.	U.28.c.
C/307.	V.20.c.7.7.	U.28.c.
D/307.	U.18.b.3.8.	U.23.c.
B/56 Fwd: Section.	V.14.d.90.80.	
61st.D.A.C. H.Q.	U.26.a.2.1.	
No.1 Sect.	U.25.d.9.8.	
No.2 Sect.	U.25.b.9.4.	
61st.D.T.M.O. HQ.	Billet No.1 AVESNES.	

F.P.Kye.
Capt. R.A.,
Bde.Maj., 61 Div. Artillery.

16.10.1918.
1000 hours.

War Diary

S E C R E T.

LEADING GROUP, XVII CORPS, ARTILLERY.

LOCATION STATEMENT NO: 1.   14.10.1918.

C.R.A. Brig.-Gen., R.G.OUSELEY? CB,CMG,DSO.- H.Q. U.27.b.9.6.

Unit.	Location.		Wagon Lines.
	61st. DIVISIONAL ARTILLERY.		
R.A.H.Q.	U.27.b.9.6.		
306 Bde.RFA. HQ.	U.24.a.5.7.		C.5.a.7.5.
A/306.	V.13.a.7.3.	(6 guns)	U.23.c.1.9.
B/306.	V.13.d.2.5.	(6 ")	C.4.a.9.0.
C/306.	V.13.d.1.7.	(6 ")	Moving.
D/306.	V.13.d.05.50.	(6 Hows.)	C.5.a.05.80.
307 Bde.RFA. HQ.	U.28.b.1.6.		
A,B,C & D/307.	U.23.c.		
	52nd. DIVISIONAL ARTILLERY.		
R.A.H.Q.	U.18.d.0.2.		
9th. Bde.RFA. HQ.	V.13.c.3.5.		U.12.d. Moving.
19th. Bty.	V.14.a.9.8.	(6 guns)	U.10.
20th. "	V.8.d.35.35.	(6 ")	U.10.d.
28th. "	V.8.c.70.60.	(6 ")	U.10.d.
D/69 "	V.13.b.05.10.		U.17.c.
56 Bde. RFA. HQ.	V.19.b.00.90.		V.17.d.
A/56.	V.14.c.60.40.	(6 guns)	V.17.d.
B/56.	V.14.c.85.80.	(6 ")	U.26.b.
C/56.	V.14.a.86.12.	(6 ")	U.23.b.
527 How. Bty.	V.13.d.30.10.	(6 Hows.)	U.23.b.
93 A.F.A. Bde. H.Q.	U.24.b.6.1.		-
A/93.	V.7.c.7.7.	(6 guns)	U.16.d.
B/93.	V.7.a.6.1.	(6 ")	U.16.d.
C/93.	V.12.a.1.1.	(6 ")	U.16.d.
93rd. B.A.C.	-		U.22.d.6.6.
61st. D.A.C. HQ.	-		A.6.d.0.2.
No.1 Section.	-		A.6.c.9.1.
No.2 "	-		A.6.d.2.4.
62nd. Brigade R.G.A. H.Q.	U.27.d.9.8.		

Capt. R.A.,
Bde.Maj., 61 Div. Artillery.

14.10.1918.

S E C R E T.

Copy No: ....

61st. DIVISIONAL ARTILLERY ORDER NO: 167.

14.10.18.

1. 307th. Brigade, R.F.A. will relieve 93rd. A. Brigade, R.F.A. in action, on night 14/15th. under Orders to be issued by 52nd. Divisional Artillery.

2. On completion of relief, 93rd. Army Brigade, R.F.A. will be in mobile reserve.

3. Completion of relief to be notified to this office by code word "SHROPSHIRE".

4. ACKNOWLEDGE.

for [signature]
Capt. R.A.,
Bde. Maj., 61 Div. Artillery.

Issued at 1200.

DISTRIBUTION.

Copy No. 1 R.A. 52nd. Division.
2-6.   306th. Bde. R.F.A.
7-11. 307th. Bde. R.F.A.
12-16. 93rd. Army Bde. R.F.A.
17.   61st. D.A.C.
18.   61st. D.T.M.O.
19.   24th. Div. 'G'.
20.   24th. Div. 'Q'.
21.   R.A. XVII Corps.
22-23. War Diary.
24.   File.
25.   O.i/c R.A. Signals.

S E C R E T.

Copy No:........

61st. DIVISIONAL ARTILLERY ORDER NO: 168.

15th. Oct. 1918.

1. The 24th. Division will carry out two operations (conjointly) on 16th. October, at 0510 hours.

2. (a) The Guards Divisional Artillery have been asked to co-operate by putting down a barrage to cover the attack and capture of HAUSSY by our Infantry.

   (b) Barrage Map appended.

   (c) Rates of Fire and ammunition are shewn on Barrage Map.

3. The barrage for the attack and capture of the railway and sunken road in P.34.d., V.5.a. & d. will be carried out in accordance with orders issued by C.R.A. 52nd. Division.

4. C.R.A. 52nd. Divisional Artillery will arrange S.O.S. lines to cover the whole 24th. Divisional Front, to come into force at the conclusion of the Operation.

5. ACKNOWLEDGE.

F.P.Rhye.

Capt. R.A.,
Bde. Maj., 61 Div. Artillery.

Issued at 1700 hours.

DISTRIBUTION.

Copy No. 1 - 2. 32nd. Div. Art.
        3 - 5. 72nd. Infantry Bde.
        6 - 19. Guards Div. Art.
        20.   24th. Div. 'G'.
        21.   R.A. XVII Corps.
        22.   XVII Corps H.A.
        23.   62nd. Bde. R.G.A.
      24 - 25. War Diary.
      26 - 28. File.

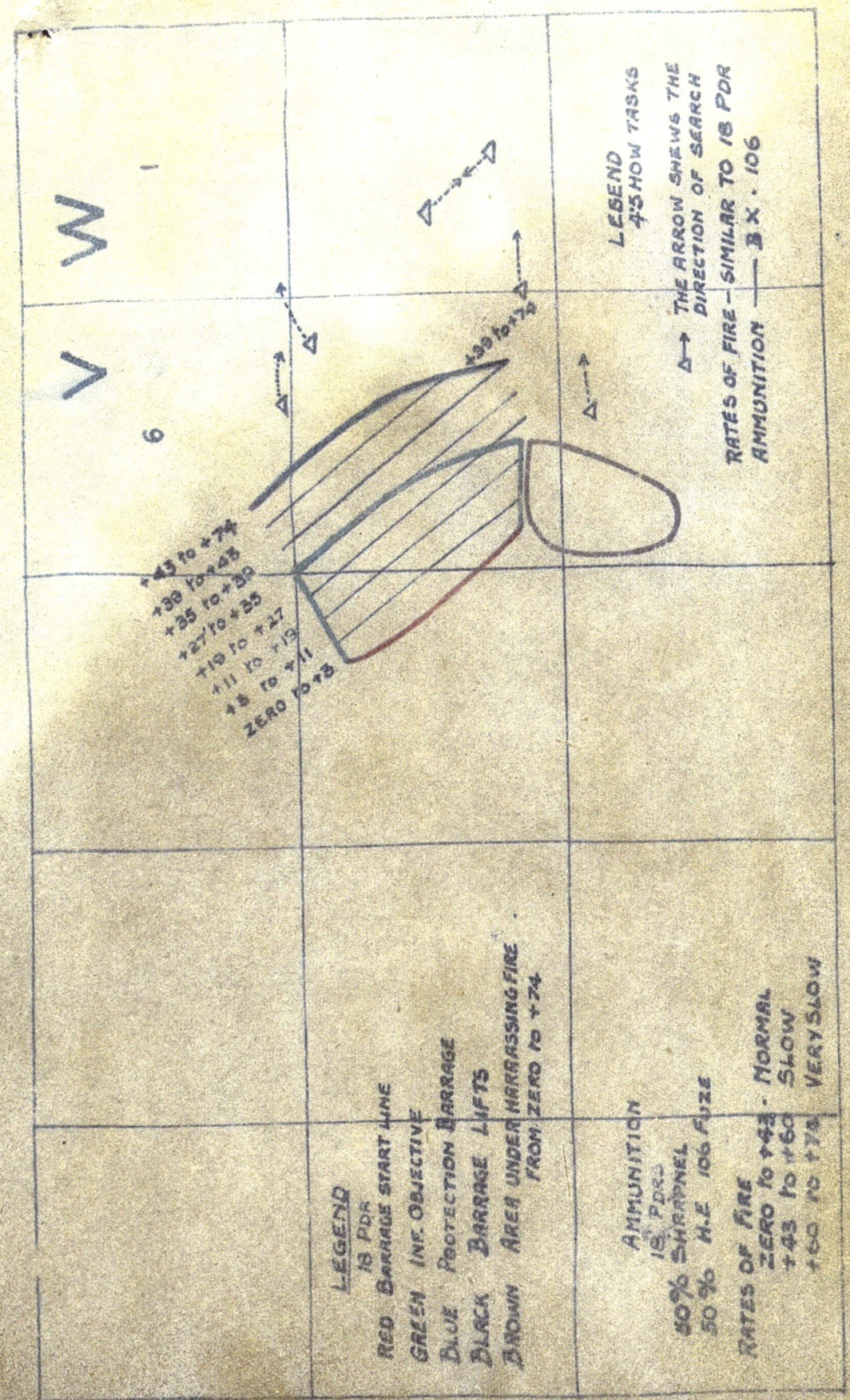

S E C R E T.

War Diary

Copy No: 14

61st. DIVISIONAL ARTILLERY ORDER NO: 169.

16/10/1918.

1. The 52nd. Divisional Artillery will be relieved in action by 72nd. and 315th. Army Brigades R.F.A. on night 17/18th. instant.

    The 72nd. Army Brigade will relieve the 9th. Bde. R.F.A.

    315th. Army Brigade will relieve the 56th. Bde. R.F.A.

2. All details of relief will be arranged by C.R.A. 52nd. Div. Artillery and Army Brigade Commanders concerned.

3. On completion of relief mentioned in para.1, O.C. 306 Brigade R.F.A. (Lt.-Col. E.W.S. BROOKE, CMG, DSO, R.F.A.) will take over command of the Artillery covering the front from C.R.A. 52nd. Div. Artillery.

4. Completion of relief will be wired to this office by code word "CANDLES".

5. (a) The command of the Leading Artillery Group, XVII Corps, will pass from C.R.A. 61 Division to C.R.A. 19th. Division, as soon after 1000 hours, 18th. Oct. 1918, as possible.

    (b) On passing of command mentioned in para.(a) above, C.R.A. 61st. Division, will assume command of Support Group Artillery, XVII Corps.

6. ACKNOWLEDGE.

F. Wye
Capt. R.A.,
Bde. Maj., 61 Div. Artillery.

Issued at... 1700

DISTRIBUTION.

Copy No.		
1 - 2.	52nd. Div. Art.
3.	93rd. Army Bde. R.F.A.
4.	306th. Bde. R.F.A.
5.	307th. Bde. R.F.A.
6.	61st. D.A.C.
7.	61st. D.T.M.O.
8.	O.C. Support Artillery Group, (2nd. N.Z. Army F.A. Bde.)
9.	72nd. A. Bde. R.F.A.
10.	315th. A, Bde. R.F.A.
11.	24th. Divn. 'G'.
12.	19th. Div. Art.
13.	R.A. XVII Corps.
14 - 15.	War Diary.
16.	File.

SECRET.

R.A.G. 1029.

AMENDMENT NO: 1
to
61st. DIVISIONAL ARTILLERY ORDER NO: 169.

1. Para. 3 is cancelled.

2. C.R.A. 24th. Divisional Artillery will take over the command of the Artillery covering the front from C.R.A. 52nd. Divisional Artillery on 18th. instant, under arrangements to be made by Commanders concerned.

Capt. R.A.,
Bde.Maj., 61 Div. Artillery.

17.10.1918.

To all recipients of 61st. D.A. Order No. 169
and R.A. 24th. Division.

War Diary

S E C R E T.

Copy No: 32

61st. DIVISIONAL ARTILLERY INSTRUCTIONS NO: 25.

17.10.1918.

AMMUNITION. 1. (a) Para. 1 (a) of 61 Divisional Artillery Instructions No. 24 is temporarily cancelled.

(b) Until further notice the following amounts of ammunition will be dumped at gun positions :-

18-pr. Batteries. 300 rounds per gun. { 45% shrapnel
{ 45% H.E.
{ 10% Smoke.

4.5" How. " 250 " " " H.E.
30 " " " GAS (C.G.)

EXPENDITURE. 2. In order to build up a reserve of ammunition for future operations, the normal daily ammunition expenditure will be limited to an average of :

50 rounds per gun 18-pr. and 25 rounds per gun 4.5" How.,

except for defensive purposes, and will be devoted to targets of opportunity, careful registration, counter-battery work and night harassing fire.

Capt. R.A.,
Bde.Maj., 61 Div. Artillery.

DISTRIBUTION.

Copy No. 1 - 5.   306th. Bde. R.F.A.
        6 - 10. 307th. Bde. R.F.A.
        11 - 15. 72nd. A.Bde.RFA (thro' 52 D.A.)
        16 - 20. 315 A. Bde. RFA ("   ")
        21 - 25. 93rd. A.Bde.RFA ("   ")
        26 - 28. 61st. D.A.C.
        29.   19th. Div. Art.
        30.   19th. Div. 'G'.
        31.   R.A. XVII Corps.
        32 - 33. War Diary.
        34.   File.

S E C R E T.

R.A.G.2/1/17.

52nd. Div. Art.   (26 copies)
306 Bde. R.F.A.   (5   "   )
307 Bde. R.F.A.   (5   "   )
61st. D.T.M.O.
61st. D.A.C.

The Divisional forward boundaries are amended and are now :-

Southern boundary.   A line drawn between the following points :-

Fork road V.18.c.4.9. exclusive - Fork roads W.7.d.6.3. inclusive - Cross roads W.4.b.8.8. inclusive.

Northern boundary.   CHAUSSIE BRUNEHART exclusive.

Capt. R.A.,
Bde.Maj., 61 Div. Artillery.

R.A.H.Q. 61 Div.
17.10.1918.

SECRET.
XVII Corps No. G.(O) 3-1.

XVII CORPS ARTILLERY INSTRUCTIONS NO: 1.
on
XVII CORPS ORDER NO: 169.

1. The Artillery supporting the attack will be grouped as follows :-

FIELD ARTILLERY.

Right Group.
Brig.-Gen. R.G.OUSELEY, 61st. D.A.H.Q.
    306th. Bde.   ) 61st. D.A.   4 Bdes.
    307th. Bde.   )
    315th. Army Bde. R.F.A.
    2nd. N.Z. Army Bde. R.F.A.

Left Group.
Lt.-Col. D.W.L. SPILLER, 24th. D.A.H.Q.
    106th. Bde.   ) 24th. D.A.   4 Bdes.
    107th. Bde.   )
    72nd Army Bde. R.F.A.
    93rd. Army Bde. R.F.A.

Corps Reserve.   19th. Div. Art.   87th. Bde.)
    88th. Bds.)

HEAVY ARTILLERY.
Brigade affiliated to 19th. Division -
    62nd. (Mixed) Brigade R.G.A. - Lt.-Col. ILES.

CORPS GROUP.   Hd. Qrs. AVESNES - U.27.d.9.8.

    35th. (Mobile) Brigade, R.G.A.
    56th. (8") Brigade, R.G.A.
    COTTER'S Brigade, R.G.A.

2. **NATURE OF ATTACK.**

The 19th. Division will attack with two Brigades. The 57th. Bds. on the Right, the 58th. Brigade on the Left.
The FIRST PHASE of the attack will consist of crossing the River, capturing the Railway Line and village of HAUSSY.
The SECOND PHASE, the capture of the high ground from MAISON BLANC. (W.1.d.) to Northern Corps Boundary at P.23. central.

3. **GENERAL PLAN OF ARTILLERY SUPPORT.**

The barrage map shows Corps and Brigade Boundaries, the four objectives shown by the RED, BLUE, GREEN, and BROWN Lines.
Brigades will be superimposed in the barrage formed by Groups so that when certain Brigades advance automatically at definite times, the protective barrage will be left without gaps.
The general siting of Field Batteries will admit of support of four Brigades up to a general line over final objective and of four Brigades over GREEN objective, and 75% of Heavy Artillery to cover up to 500 yards East of HARPIES River.
Field Artillery support beyond these limits will be met by Brigade advancing as laid down in para. 6. The timings should be adhered to if the operation progresses as is intended.
The Corps Heavy Artillery will advance one Section 60-pounders and one Section 6" Howitzers to west of LA SELLE River at ZERO plus 3 hours. These sections will be reinforced as opportunity offers.

The remaining Heavy Artillery batteries will continue to render support from original positions up to effective range and will subsequently be advanced by the B.G. CORPS Heavy Artillery in readiness for further progress next day.

4. **18-pdr. CREEPING BARRAGE.**

This is shown on barrage map and is the guide for timing lifts of 4.5" Howitzers and special 18-pdr. and Heavy Artillery Tasks allotted by Division.

Barrage for Left Infantry Brigade.

The barrage comes down at ZERO on a line parallel to and 200 yards over the River except that where the Railway is less than 200 yards from the River, it is formed on the railway. In order to procure depth at this juncture, three Brigades of each Group will fire from ZERO to ZERO plus 12 minutes at ranges of 100, 200, and 300 yards respectively over the initial barrage line and reform on this line at ZERO plus 12 minutes.

At ZERO plus 15 minutes, the barrage will commence to creep forward at the rate of 100 yards in four minutes straightening out over the railway and halting for 9 minutes, 200 yards beyond it. It will rest on the BLUE protective barrage line until Zero plus 70 mins., when it will continue to lift at 100 yards in four minutes up to the GREEN Protective Barrage line, where it rests until ZERO plus 127 minutes.

It will rest on the Protective Barrage over BROWN Line (Final objective) for 15 minutes, when barrage fire will cease.

Barrage for Right Infantry Brigade.

The barrage comes down at ZERO on a line parallel to, and 200 yards over the River. Depth will be procured as for Left Brigade barrage. At Zero plus 15 minutes, the barrage will commence to creep forward at the rate of 100 yards in 8 minutes up to the BLUE Protective Barrage Line. It will rest on this line till plus 70 minutes, when it will continue to lift forward at the rate of 100 yards in 4 minutes, up to the barrage line plus 114 minutes. It will swing left from this line in conformity with Guards Division Barrage, advancing at plus 127 minutes in conformity with Left Infantry Brigade Barrage on to the BROWN Protective Barrage Line. It will rest for 15 minutes on this line, when barrage fire will cease.

If the dispositions of the Infantry on Zero Day necessitate an alteration in the initial barrage line, the C.R.A. 19th. Division will adjust same, but the lift off the Protective Barrage over Blue Line must agree with map, in order to coordinate fire with Flank Corps.

Protective Barrages will not remain stationary, but searching fire will be employed.

Composition of Barrage. 50% H.E. 50% Shrapnel.

Special Tasks. C.R.A. 19th. Division will detail certain sections to fire THERMITE Shell at each lift of the barrage (at an increased range of 200 yards to that of the barrage guns) to mark the flanks of each Battalion.

In addition, when the batteries of one Brigade in each Group reach their Protective Barrage Line over the RED, BLUE, GREEN and BROWN Lines they will fire a salvo of Thermite shell at an increased range of 200 yards, as a signal to the Infantry that they have reached their objective.

The Right Group will not use Thermite shell on the village of HAUSSY.

4.5" Howitzer.

- 3 -

4.5" Howitzer Tasks.

The 4.5" Howitzers will form a Standing Barrage on Special points, which will be allotted by 19th. Division. It will conform to the 18-pr. Barrage and at not less than 200 yards from it.

Smoke Shell.

A Proportion of smoke shell will be dumped at positions in readiness to deny observation from the high ground South of ST.MARTIN on the final objective. If it is dawn, prior to the Infantry gaining this line, 10% Smoke will be used in the barrage.

Rates of Fire.	18-pdr.	4.5" Howitzer.
ZERO to ZERO plus 25 minutes.	NORMAL.	Half 18-pr. rates.
ZERO plus 25 minutes. to plus 30 minutes.	INTENSE.	-do-
ZERO plus 30 minutes onwards.		From SLOW to RAPID, depending upon whether the barrage is on open ground or on trenches, Sunken roads, likely machine gun posts. This implies that whilst one battery may be firing in SLOW, the next one to it may be at rapid rate.

5. HEAVY ARTILLERY.

(a) Intense neutralisation of hostile batteries from ZERO to Zero plus 45 minutes, every available gun and howitzer that can reach being utilized. A proportion will be taken off at Zero plus 45 minutes and used to form concentrations on strong points and sweeping approaches.

The Counter Battery Programme will be drawn up by the C.B.S.O. in conjunction with C.B.S.Os. of Flank Corps.

(b) Concentration and bombardments of strong points to be allotted by B.G. Corps Heavy Artillery after consultation with G.O.C. 19th. Division, lifting in accordance with a pre-arranged plan and at not less than 400 yards from 18-pr. barrage.

Dependent on the hostile artillery fire, tasks will include:-

(1) Sandpit in V.5.a.35.40. and Sunken roads at V.5.a.40.65. and 70.70.

(2) Sunken road from P.34.a.90.15. to emplacement at P.34.b.85.00.

(3) Sunken road at V.5.d.15.10.

(4) Sunken road V.5.d.35.80. and V.5.b.40.10.

(5) Pits at V.5.d.70.60.

(6) Houses and Pits on line P.35.a.65.30. to P.35.c.30.70.

(7) BOIS POLLET, V.6.a.

(8) Sunken road P.35.c.65.00. to 80.40. and from P.35.d.00.15. to 10.30.

(9) MAISON BLANCHE W.1.d.

(10) Trenches &c.

(11) Work from W.1.a.42.28. to V.1.c.72.88.

(12) Work at Q.31.a.35.35.

(13) ERYL COPSE V.7.a.

(14) Sunken roads V.6.c.00.00. to V.6.d.50.10.

(15) MAISON BLEUE Q.31.b.

(16) Houses at Cross roads P.29.b.90.70 and work from P.29.b.80.70. to 40.90.

(17) Road from P.30.a.70.60. to 90.95.

(18) Trench at P.29.b.98.40. and P.30.a.90.40.

(19) Work at Q.19.c.05.90.

(20) Dugouts in road from Q.25.a.65.55. to Q.19.d.40.40.

(21) Emplacements at Q.23.b.15.65.

(22) Enclosure at Q.26.c.85.85.

The line of machine gun posts and rifle pits from Q.33.c. to VENDEGIES will be engaged from the hour the 18-pr. Creeping Barrage reaches the VENDEGIES - SOLESMES road.

(c) Searching fire on sunken roads and approaches by long range guns.

6. **FIELD ARTILLERY ADVANCE.**

At Zero plus 45 minutes, the 307th. Brigade, R.F.A. and 93rd. Army Brigade, R.F.A. will each advance one 18-pr. battery to close support of Infantry.

At Zero plus 90 minutes, the remaining batteries of these Brigades will be advanced to LA SELLE River valley.

At Zero plus 180 minutes, each Group will advance one Brigade by Batteries over LA SELLE RIVER.

Thereafter, Brigades will be pushed forward by Batteries according to the situation.

7. **LIAISON.**

Right and Left Group Commanders will establish their Headquarters alongside their Infantry Brigade Headquarters.

The two Brigades detailed as close supporting Brigades, will establish their Headquarters under the direction of Infantry Brigadiers.

8. **TRENCH MORTARS.**

The Mobile Trench Mortars of 61st. and 24th. Divisions will accompany the 57th. Infantry Brigade and 58th. Infantry Brigade, respectively.

9. Counter Attacks.

- 5 -

9. COUNTER-ATTACKS.

These are most likely to develop on the final objective, and hostile tanks will possibly be employed. Anti-Tank guns will be found by the Brigades in close support. These will be pushed forward close to the Infantry, one Section to each Infantry Brigade. Barrage fire on the line of defensive posts from VENDEGIES to Q.33.c. will be arranged for prior to attack by C.R.A. 19th. Division and B.G. Corps Heavy Artillery.

Gas and Heavy Artillery concentrations will be put down from time to time on the HARPIES Valley from Zero plus 3 hours onwards

10. AMMUNITION.

The moving forward of Artillery and dumping of ammunition in readiness for a further the day after Zero, will be arranged by C.R.A. 19th. Division, in consultation with B.G. Corps Heavy Artillery. 50% of guns must always be in action for protective fire.

11. ACKNOWLEDGE.

(Sd.) P.R.BUTLER. Maj.
for Brigadier-General,
General Staff.

R.A. XVII Corps.
18th. October 1918.

S E C R E T.   XVII Corps No. G.(O) 242.

AMENDMENT to
XVII Corps Artillery Instructions No.1
on
XVII Corps Order No.169.

Para. 4.

Barrage for Right Infantry Brigade.

The barrage comes down at ZERO on a line parallel to and
200 yards over the River.   Depth will be procured as for
Left Brigade barrage.   At ZERO plus 15 minutes, the barrage will
lift 100 yards and will dwell here until plus 31 minutes, when it
will commence to creep forward at the rate of 100 yards ----------
cease. (See Barrage map herewith.)

(Sd.) P.R. BUTLER. Maj.
for Brigadier-General,
General Staff.

H.Q., XVII Corps.
18th. October, 1918.

S E C R E T.

61st. DIVISIONAL ARTILLERY.

LOCATION STATEMENT - 18th. Oct.1918.

Unit.	Location.	Wagon Lines.	O.Ps.
R.A.Hdqrs. 61 Div.	Billet No.9, AVESNES-les-AUBERT.		
R.A.Hdqrs. 24 Div.	U.18.d.0.2.		
72 Army Bde.RFA. HQ	V.13.c.3.5.	U.17.d.	
A/72.	V.15.c.7.4.	U.15.a.	V.9.b.5.2.
B/72. (5 guns)	V.19.b.5.2.	U.15.c.	V.8.d.9.9.
(1 gun)	V.9.a.8.8.		
C/72.	V.19.b.05.20.	U.28.b.	V.2.d.8.8.
D/72.	V.13.b.05.10.	U.23.d.	V.13.b.05.65.
315 Army Bde.RFA.HQ	V.19.a.45.75.	U.17.d.	
A/315.	V.14.c.80.40.	U.17.d.	V.9.a.2.2.
B/315. (4 guns)	V.14.c.85.80.	U.26.b.	V.14.d.5.8.
(2 ")	V.14.d.9.8.		
C/315.	V.14.a.86.12.	U.23.b.	V.9.b.3.2.
D/315.	V.13.d.30.10.	U.23.b.	V.22.c.00.95.
93 Army Bde.RFA.HQ.	U.24.b.6.1.		
A/93.	V.7.c.7.7.	U.16.d.	V.7.b.7.5.
B/93	V.7.a.8.1.	U.16.d.	V.7.b.3.4.
C/93.	V.12.a.8.1.	U.16.d.	V.7.b.2.2.
93rd. B.A.C.		U.22.d.8.6.	
306 Bde. RFA. HQ	U.24.a.5.7.	C.5.a.7.5.	
A/306.	V.13.a.7.3.	U.23.c.1.9.	V.14.b.2.1.
B/306.	V.13.d.2.5.	C.4.a.9.0.	V.14.c. & V.9.d
C/306.	V.13.d.1.7.		V.14.d.5.5.
D/306.	V.13.d.05.50.	C.5.a.05.80.	V.14.b.2.1.
307 Bde. RFA. HQ.	U.24.d.7.7.	U.28.b.1.5.	V.22.b.3.8.
A/307.	V.20.a.65.65.	U.28.c.	
B/307.	V.20.a.80.80.	U.28.c.	V.21.b.3.3.
C/307.	V.19.d.85.45.	U.28.c.	
D/307.	U.18.b.3.8.	U.23.c.	V.1.c.5.2.
61st. D.A.C. HQ.	-	U.26.a.2.1.	
No.1 Sect.	-	U.25.d.9.8.	
No.2 "	-	U.25.b.9.4.	
61st. D.T.M.O.	Billet No.1 AVESNES.		

Capt. R.A.,
Bde.Maj., 61st. Div. Artillery.

18.10.1918.

War Diary

SECRET.

61st. Div. Art. No.
R.A.G.1/3/18.

306th. Brigade, R.F.A. (6 copies)
307th. Brigade, R.F.A. (5 ")
2nd. N.Z. Army F.A. Bde. (5 ")
315 A. Bde. R.F.A. (5 ")

Reference XVII Corps Instructions No. 1 and Amendment No. 1 forwarded herewith.

1. Page 2, para. 4.

   From ZERO to Zero plus 12 minutes, the left portion of the barrage will come down as follows :-
   From V.5.c.2.3. along road to road junction V.5.c.80.15. to V.5.d.2.2. where it will join RED barrage line, thence along RED LINE.

   In order to procure the depth referred to :-
   306th. Bde. R.F.A. will fire 100 yards beyond barrage Line.
   2nd. N.Z. Army Bde. R.F.A." 200 "   "   "   "
   307th. Bde. R.F.A. will fire 300 "   "   "   "

   At Zero plus 12 minutes, the barrage will reform on the RED Barrage Line.

   Special Tasks - Thermite Shell -
   The 315th. Army Bde. will carry out this task, and will mark the Southern Corps Boundary, Inter-battalion boundary and Inter-Infantry Brigade Boundary.
   Inter-battalion boundaries are shown on maps issued to 315th. Army Brigade, R.F.A.

   NOTE - No Thermite will be used on the village of HAUSSY.

   At Zero plus 45 minutes, 1 Battery salvo Thermite on X roads V.5.c.5.1.
   At Zero plus 70 minutes, 1 Battery salvo Thermite on BOIS POLLET V.6.a.

   4.5" How. Tasks.
   4.5" Howitzers will keep 200 yards in advance of the 18-pr. Barrage and will engage the areas shown on tracings for 4.5" Howitzer Batteries issued herewith.

2. Reference para 6.
   (a) The battery of 307th. Bde. R.F.A. detailed in close support of the Infantry will, as soon as the bridge to take Field guns is built in HAUSSY, boldly push forward Sections to take on favourable targets at close range with open sights and will keep a sharp look-out for any hostile tanks which will be engaged with H.E. 101 delay Fuze.

   (b) At Zero plus 180 minutes, 306th. Bde. R.F.A. will advance by batteries to LA SELLE River.

3. Reference para. 7.
   (a) 315th. Bde. R.F.A. will send forward a Liaison Officer with left attacking Battalion (10th. Warwick present Headquarters V.18.b.5.0.)

- 1 -   306th. Bde. R.F.A./

306th. Bde. R.F.A. will send forward a Liaison Officer with Right Attacking Battalion (8th. Glosters - present Hdqrs. opposite ST. AUBERTS Church)

These Officers will be accompanied by Signallers with telephones and LUCAS Lamps, and will report at Battalion Hdqrs. at 21 hours 19th. instant.

NOTE - these Officers will call on the Infantry for Runners, should other means of communication break down.

(b) The Infantry Brigade Headquarters will move forward about 0500 hours, 20 instant, via V.9. central to the Sandpit in V.5.a.

When the Infantry Brigade is about to move, 61st. D.A. will notify O.C. 307th. Bde. R.F.A. who will either establish his Headquarters with the Infantry Brigade or provide a Senior Liaison Officer.

4. Reference para.8
The Officers and personnel from 61st. Div. Trench Mortars - trained to fire 77mm Guns - now attached to 306th. Bde. R.F.A. will open fire on ST. MARTIN as soon as they can turn any field guns captured round, or on any favourable targets which can be engaged with open sights.

5. Reference para.9.
From plus 206 minutes, Brigades will be prepared to put down an S.O.S. barrage from FME d'RIEUX along East bank of River d'HARPIES to FME d'ORCHIVAL thence to Q.19.d.0.0.

NOTE - The S.O.S. Signal is a Rifle Grenade rocket, RED - GREEN - RED.

Aeroplanes drop a RED Smoke ball for S.O.S.

6. As the Infantry reach the final objective, they will fire three green Very lights.

7. ZERO hour will be at 0200 hours 20th. Any alteration to Zero hour will be notified by Code as ..... minutes plus or minus of 0200 hours.

Viz: 0300 hours will be plus 60
0145 hours will be minus 15.

8. All Batteries will carry 10% of Smoke shell forward when they advance.

9. The 315th. Army Bde. will detail 2 18-prs and the 4.5" How. Battery to answer Zone Calls in accordance with para.5 XVII Corps Artillery Instructions No.2 of 25.8.18.

10. ACKNOWLEDGE.

F.T.Wyc.

Capt. R.A.,
Bde.Maj., 61 Div. Artillery.

19.10.1918.
1300 hours.

Copies to: 57th. Infantry Bde. (3)
R.A. 19th. Div. (1)
R.A. 24th. Div. (1)
War Diary. (2)
File (5)

Gloucesters black yellow red
Infantry report centres

SECRET.

War Diary

R.A.G.1/3/19.

306th. Bde. (6 copies)
307th. Bde. (5 ")
315th. Bde. (5 ")
2nd. N.Z. Bde. A.F.A. (5 copies)

Reference XVII Corps Artillery Instructions NO:1 on Order 169 and 61st. Div. Art. No. R.A.G.1/3/18.

1. O.C. 315th. Bde. will arrange for 50 rounds Thermite to be fired into the SANDPIT V.5.a. from ZERO to ZERO plus 15 mins.

2. Intense concentrations of 5 minutes each will be fired on the line of defensive posts from VENDEGIES at Q.33.c. at the following hours on 20th. October :-

| 0515 | 0535 | 0555 | 0630 | 0720 | 0805 |
| 0900 | 0940. |

    4.5" How. Batteries will fire Gas in the above concentrations if the weather and situation permit. Orders as to its use will be issued by these Headquarters.

3. When Batteries have occupied new positions, they must make every endeavour to get their ammunition Dumps up to the amounts laid down in para. 1 (b) 61 D.A. Instructions No.25.

4. Orders regarding Organization of traffic over roads and bridges will be issued later.

5. Contact Aeroplanes will call for flares at -

    ZERO plus 5 hours.
    ZERO plus 6 hours.
    ZERO plus 7 hours.

Flares will be lit by the most advanced Infantry on or near the final objective.
    A Counter-attack plane will be in the air from daylight onwards.

6. Watches will be synchronized at 23 hours on 19th. October.

7. Cancel 2nd. para. of para.3 (b) R.A.G.1/3/18 of to-day and substitute :-
"B.M.R.A. 61 Division, will accompany G.O.C. Infantry Brigade when he moves forward.
    O.C. 307th. Bde. R.F.A. will send two cycles Orderlies to report to B.M.R.A. at Right Group Headquarters at midnight 19/20th."

8. 306, 307 Bdes. R.F.A. and 315 Army Bde. R.F.A. will each detail an Officers patrol in accordance with XVII Corps Instructions No.2.

9. ACKNOWLEDGE.

F.P.Nye.
Capt. R.A.,
Bde.Maj., 61 Div. Artillery.

19.10.18.
1900 hours.

Copies to: 57th. Inf. Bde. (3)   R.A. 19th. Div. (1)
          War Diary (2)   R.A. 24th. Div. (1)
          File (5)

SECRET.

R.A.G.1/3/20.

306th. Bde. R.F.A.   (6)
307th. Bde. R.F.A.   (5)
315th. Army Bde. R.F.A. (5)
2nd. N.Z. A. Bde. R.F.A. (5)

Reference R.A.G.1/3/18 of to-day.

1. A smoke barrage will be fired by Brigades of Right Group from 05.30 to 0600 hours on 20th. October on the general line, W.10.a.5.4. - W.3.b.6.4. - Q.33.a.80.80.

If the final objective has not been reached by that time, the firing of the smoke barrage will be postponed by C.R.A. Right Group, until the objective has been reported captured, when it will be fired for half an hour as above.

The smoke barrage will not be fired if in the opinion of C.R.A. Right Group, bad visibility renders it unnecessary, when Brigades will be notified.

2. Field Artillery bridges are being constructed by the C.R.E. as under, and will be available for the use of Groups as detailed:

    <u>Right Group</u>.   V.11.d.7.5.

    <u>Left Group</u>.   P.33.d.1.5.

Two bridges are also being constructed by C.E. XVII Corps to take heavy traffic. Their exact locations will be forwarded later. Right and Left Groups may use the Southern and Northern ones respectively. When these bridges are completed guns and Wagons going East will use the Corps bridges returning via Field Artillery Bridges.

3. In the event of the enemy having withdrawn before the Operation is timed to take place, the 19th. Division will advance on a two (Infantry) Brigade front. In this case 306th. Bde. R.F.A. will be attached to 58th. (Left) Infantry Brigade, and 307 Bde. R.F.A. will be attached to 57th. (Right) Infantry Brigade, to act as Advanced Guard Artillery.

4. ACKNOWLEDGE.

P. Wye.

Capt. R.A.,
Bde. Major, 61 Div. Artillery.

19.10.1918.
20.10 hrs.

Copies to: 57th. Inf. Bde.   (3)
                19th. D.A.   (1)
                24th. D.A.   (1)
                War Diary.   (2)
                File.   (5)

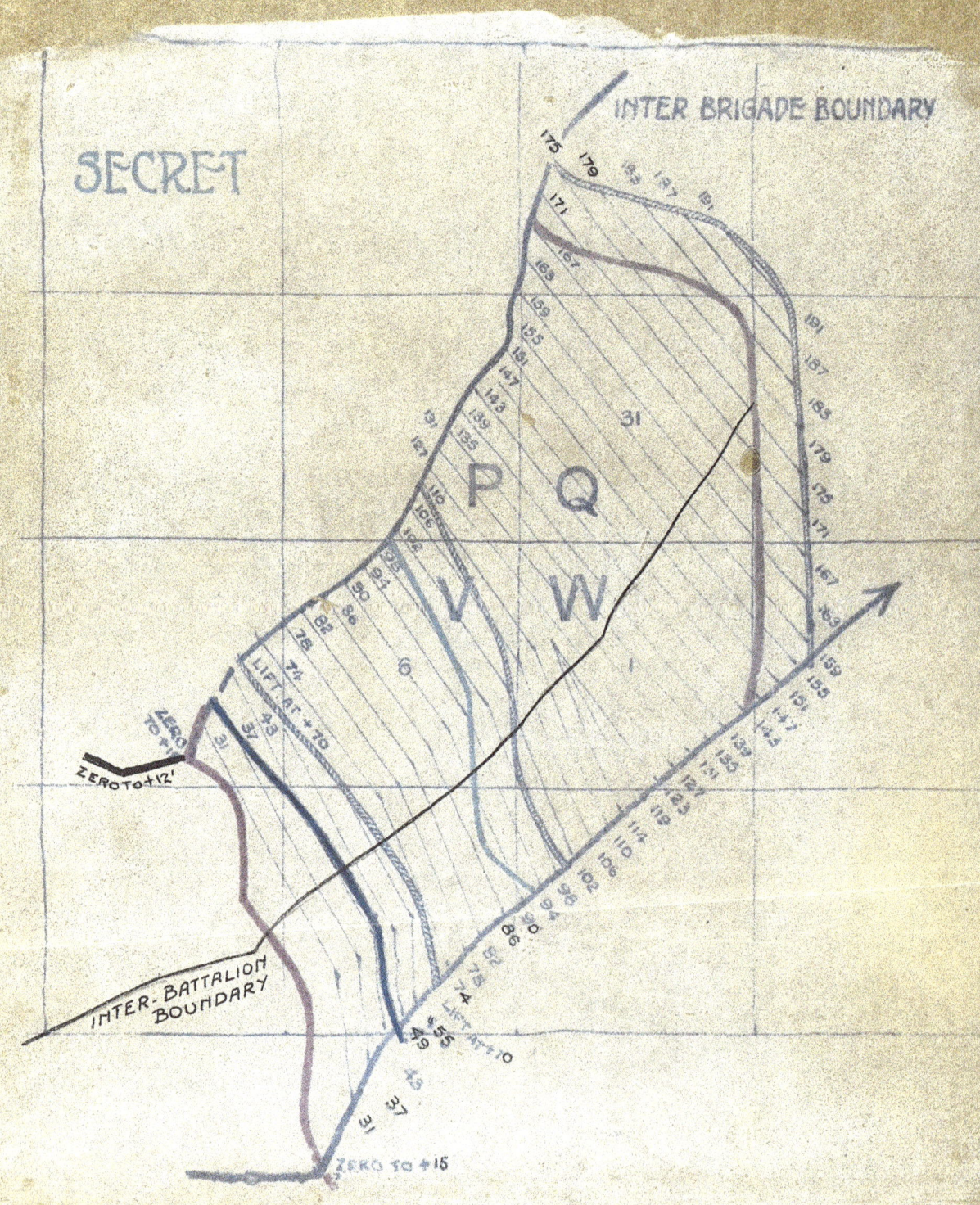

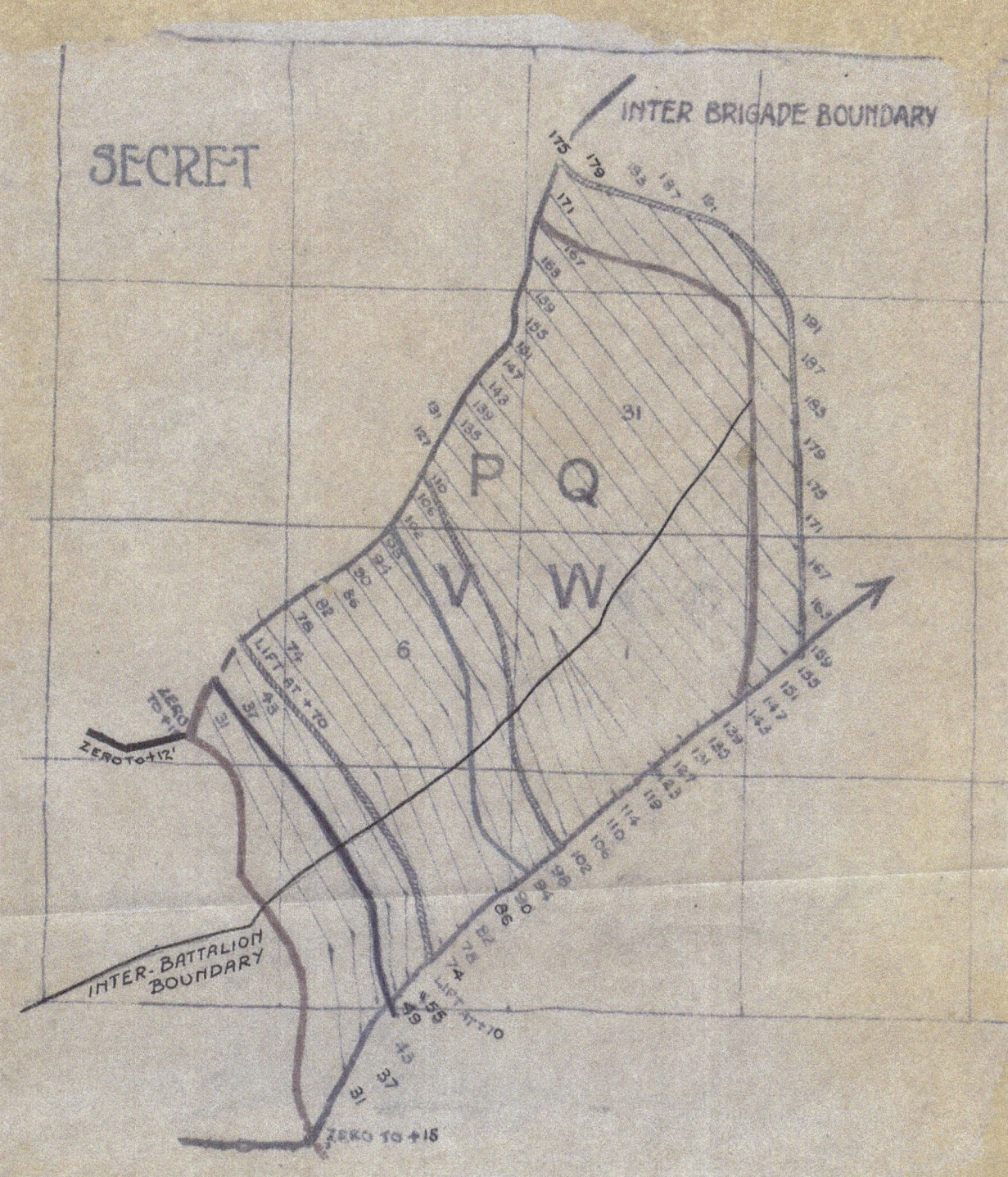

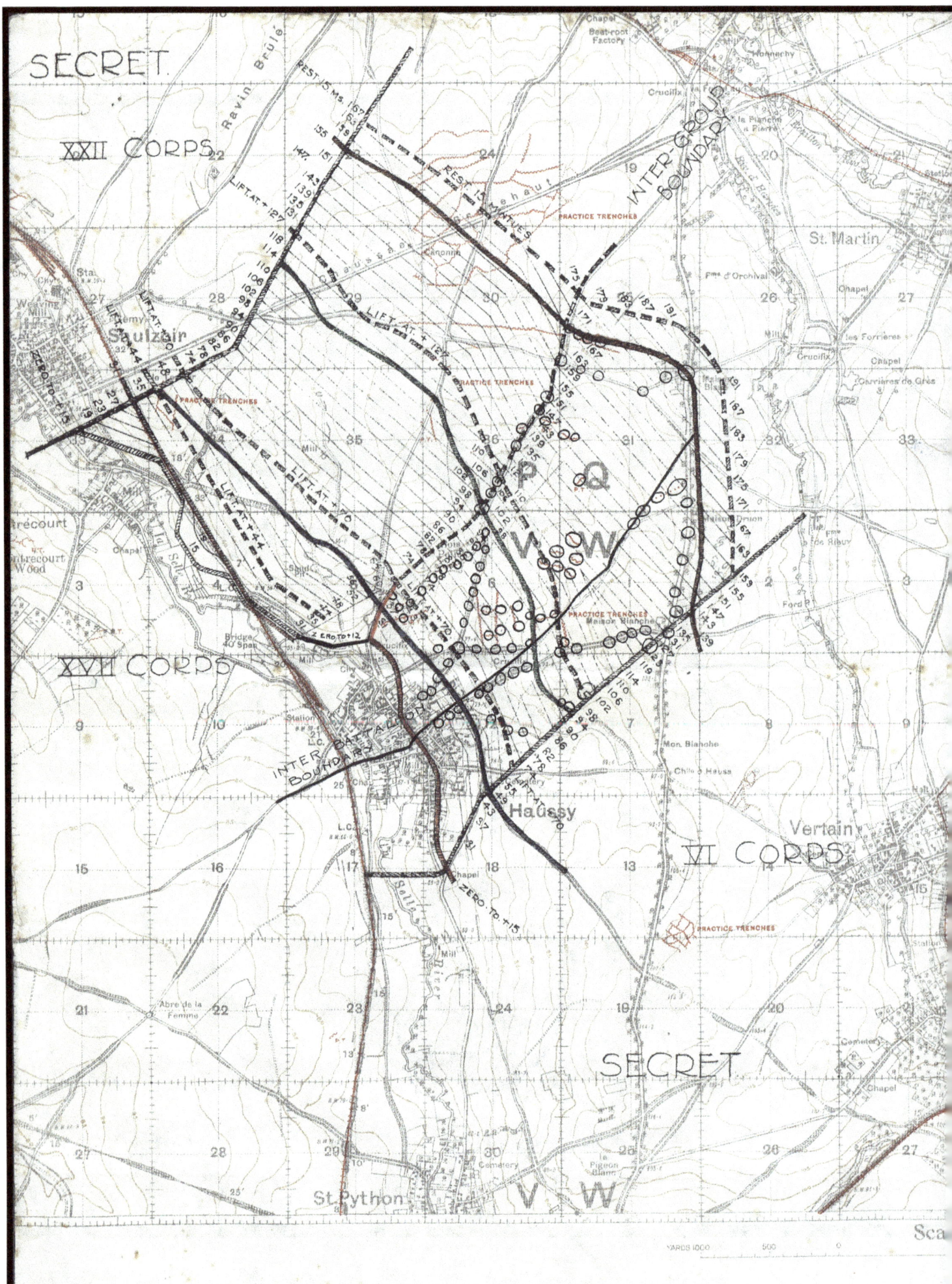

SECRET.

Copy No. 5

61st. DIVISIONAL ARTILLERY ORDER No. 172.

20. 10. 1918.

1. The 2nd. N.Z. Army Brigade R.F.A. will be withdrawn from action to its wagon lines on the 20th. October, at an hour to be notified later.
   The withdrawal will take place by batteries at three quarters of an hour interval.

2. The Brigade will march, under orders to be issued later, on the morning of the 21st. October to the VIGNLY area, where it will come under the orders of IV Corps.
   If weather permits, the march is to take place as far as possible across country and off roads.

3. The O.C. 2nd. N.Z. Army Bde, R.F.A. will report to G.R.A. 61. Division at BEAUVOIS for orders on the afternoon of 20th.. October.

4. The Brigade will be rationed for the march up to and including 23rd. October.

5. ACKNOWLEDGE.

Capt. R.A.
Bde. Maj., 61 Div. Artillery.

Issued at 0300 hours.

Copy No. 1 2nd. N.Z. Bde. R.F.A.
         2 306th. Bde. R.F.A.
         3 307th. Bde. R.F.A.
         4 315th. Army Bde. R.F.A.
       5-6 War Diary.
         7 File.
         8 19th. R.A.

SECRET.

War Diary

6

SECRET.   Copy No:......

61st. DIVISIONAL ARTILLERY ORDER NO: 171.

                                                 20th. Oct. 1918.

1.   The 2nd. N.Z. Army Brigade, A.F.A. will march to
BEAUVOIS Area on morning of 21st. October, coming under
orders of 42nd. Division on arrival in IV Corps Area.

        Route via. CAMBRAI - no restrictions as to time.

2.   Intervals of 500 yards between batteries and 25 yards
between groups of 6 vehicles will be strictly maintained.

3.   Ammunition in Echelons will be dumped at W.14.c.8.8.

        Further Instructions as to refilling will be issued.

4.   2nd. N.Z. A.Bde. to ACKNOWLEDGE.

                                    Munnay Capt
                                for Bde.Maj., 61 Div. Artillery.

Issued at 1200 hours.

                        DISTRIBUTION.

        Copy No.1 - 2nd. N.Z. Army Bde.A.F.A.
             2. 306th. Bde. R.F.A.
             3. 307th. Bde. R.F.A.
             4. 315th. A. Bde. R.F.A.
             5. 19th. Div. Art.
           6-7. War Diary.
             8. File.

SECRET.   Copy No: 68

61st. DIVISIONAL ARTILLERY ORDER No: 172.

Reference Map: Sheet 51A.SE.   23rd. Oct. 1918.
              1:20,000.

1. On the 24th. instant, the 61st. Division will carry out an attack on the high ground East of the River ECAILLON, i.e. approximately the line Q.17 - Q.10 - Q.3.

2. The Artillery supporting the attack will be grouped as follows :-

   FIELD ARTILLERY.
   RIGHT GROUP.
   Brig.-Gen. E.J.R.PEEL, CMG, DSO, R.A., 19th. D.A.H.Q.

       305th. Bde. R.F.A.)
       307th. Bde. R.F.A.)   4 Brigades.
        87th. Bde. R.F.A.)
       315th. A.Bde. R.F.A.)

   LEFT GROUP.
   Lt.-Col. D.W.L.SPILLER, DSO, R.F.A., 24th. D.A.H.Q.

        72nd. Army Bde. R.F.A.)
        28th. Bde. R.F.A.   )
        93rd. Army Bde. R.F.A.)   5 Brigades.
       106th. Bde. R.F.A.   )
       107th. Bde. R.F.A.   )

   MOBILE TRENCH MORTARS (6" NEWTON)

       Attached Right Infantry Bde. - 2 T.Ms. 24th. Div. T.Ms.
       Attached Left Infantry Bde. - 2 T.Ms. 61st. Div. T.Ms.

   HEAVY ARTILLERY.

       Brigade affiliated to 61st. Division :
       62nd. (Mixed) Bde. R.G.A. - Lt.-Col. H.V.ILES, R.G.A.

3. NATURE OF ATTACK.

   The attack will be carried out by two Infantry Brigades. The 183rd. Infantry Bde. on the Right and the 182nd. Infantry Brigade on the Left.

4. GENERAL PLAN OF ARTILLERY SUPPORT.

   (a) The barrage map shows Division and Brigade Boundaries and objectives.

   (b) The fire of Artillery Brigades will be superimposed in the barrage formed by Groups.

   (c) The general siting of Field Artillery will admit of support of four brigades (2 in each Group) up to a general line over the final objective.
       Field Artillery support beyond this limit will be met by Brigades advancing as laid down in para.10.
       The timings mentioned in para.10 must be adhered to if the Operation progresses as is intended.

5. **18-pdr. CREEPING BARRAGE.**

   (a) This is shown on barrage map, and is the guide for timing lifts of 4.5" Howitzers and special 18-pdr. and Heavy Artillery Tasks.

   (b) The barrage comes down at Zero on a line parallel to and 200 yards beyond the Infantry start line, and will advance at such a rate as will ensure it lifting at Zero plus 9 minutes from the line shown on the barrage map; this is necessary in order to co-ordinate the barrage with flank Corps.

   (c) From Zero plus 9 minutes onwards, the barrage will lift at the rate of 100 yards in 3 (three) minutes up to the BLUE (1st. Objective) Protective Barrage Line, where it will rest and at Zero plus 40 minutes will again advance, but will lift at the rate of 100 yards in 6 (six) minutes up to the BLACK (2nd. Objective) Protective Barrage Line, except that Batteries firing WEST of the road Q.7.d.3.5. to Q.2.c.3.3. will lift their fire in accordance with the times shown on the barrage map, to conform with 4th. Div. barrage.
   The barrage will lift off the BLACK protective barrage line at Zero plus 180 minutes, and will advance 100 yards in 4 (four) minutes up to the BROWN (3rd. Objective) Protective Barrage Line. Each Battery will fire on this line for 15 (fifteen) minutes after which barrage fire will cease.

   (d) Protective Barrage fire will in each case search to a depth of 500 yards and will alternate with bursts of fire.

   (e) As the Left Flank Division has its final objective through squares K.33, no Artillery fire without direct observation will come down in squares K.33 and K.34. until the final dispositions of that (the 4th.) Division are known.

6. **COMPOSITION OF THE BARRAGE.**

   (a) Right Group. 18-pdr. 45% Shrapnel, 45% H.E., 10% Smoke.
       Left Group. 18-pr. 50% Shrapnel, 50% H.E.

   (b) On Right Group front, 10% smoke shell will be employed from the BLUE Barrage Line onwards.
   Each Brigade in this Group will detail one of its Battery Commanders to observe the barrage and to report to his Brigade Commander whether the percentage of smoke is sufficient, should be increased or discontinued altogether.

7. **SPECIAL TASKS.**

   (a) Group Commanders will arrange for one round Thermite shell to be fired on the boundaries between battalions at each lift of the barrage, at an increased range of 200 yards to that of the barrage guns.
   In addition, when the batteries of one Brigade in each Group reach each Protective Barrage Line, they will fire a salvo of Thermite shell at an increased range of 200 yards as a special signal to the Infantry that the particular objective has been reached.

   NO THERMITE SHELL will be fired ON ANY VILLAGE.

   (b) **4.5" Howitzer Tasks.**
   The 4.5" Howitzers will form a Standing Barrage on special points which will be allotted by Group Commanders in consultation with B.Gs. Commanding Infantry Brigades. (Right Group will include the Rifle and Machine Gun Pits on the Spur Q.26.b. - Q.20.d. also in Q.15.c.)

From the advance from the BLUE to the BLACK Line, the gardens on the S.E. and S.W. edges of the three villages will be engaged to keep down M.G. fire that may flank the open slopes between these villages.

The 4.5" Howitzer Barrage will conform to that of the 18-pdrs. and will keep not less than 200 yards in advance thereof.

8. RATES OF FIRE.

	18-pdr.	4.5" Hows.
ZERO to ZERO plus 5 minutes.	INTENSE.	
ZERO plus 5 mins to plus 20 mins.	RAPID.	
ZERO plus 20 mins to plus 25 mins.	NORMAL.	
ZERO plus 25 mins to plus 35 mins.	SLOW.	½ rates.
ZERO plus 35 mins to plus 40 mins.	INTENSE.	
ZERO plus 40 mins to plus 70 mins.	NORMAL.	
ZERO plus 70 mins to plus 125 mins.	SLOW to RAPID according to whether barrage is passing over open ground or on sunken roads, gardens etc.	
ZERO plus 125 to ZERO plus 170 mins.	VERY SLOW.	
ZERO plus 170 mins to plus 180 mins.	RAPID.	½ rates.
ZERO plus 180 mins to final barrage line.	SLOW to NORMAL.	

Batteries will drop to slow fire immediately they get to each of their protective barrage lines.

9. S.O.S. LINES TO COVER FINAL OBJECTIVE.

S.O.S. Barrage lines over the final objective will be arranged by Group Commanders in consultation with Infantry Brigadiers concerned.

10. ARTILLERY ADVANCE.
(a) Field Artillery.
At Zero plus 90 minutes the 306th. Brigade, R.F.A. and 72nd. Army Brigade, R.F.A. will advance by batteries to close support of the Infantry. 306th. Brigade in support of 183rd. Infantry Brigade and 72nd. Army Brigade in support of 182nd. Infantry Brigade. These Brigades will each

find one/

find one Section of Anti-tank guns which will be placed in position close to the Infantry on final objectives.

At ZERO plus 200 minutes, the 315 Army Brigade, R.F.A. and 88th. Brigade R.F.A. will advance (by batteries) and take up positions in the ECAILLON Valley.

Thereafter Group Commanders will order Brigades to advance in accordance with the requirements of the tactical situation, bearing in mind the necessity of maintaining continuity of fire on their respective fronts. 50% of guns must always be in action for protective fire.

Brigade and Battery Commanders will reconnoitre and get their Units into action as quickly as possible in their new positions.

The approximate position of O.Ps. must be decided upon beforehand and every Unit will establish an O.P. from which good observation can be obtained as rapidly as possible.

All remunerative targets will be engaged irrespective of zones. Field Batteries will inform any neighbouring R.G.A. batteries of targets which they themselves cannot reach.

Thorough preparation will be made by Battery Commanders prior to the Operation to ensure visual communication being rapidly established to supplement the telephone in case of lines being cut.

The value of mounted Orderlies (horse and cycle) and runners has been overlooked in the past.

Officers patrols will be sent forward during the Operation in accordance with XVII Corps Artillery Instructions No.2 of 25.8.18.

(b) 6" Newton Trench Mortars.

The 6" NEWTON Trench Mortars accompanying the attacking Groups will advance in the general line of the Inter-battalion boundary of the Infantry Brigades with which they are working.

11. LIAISON.

(a) Right Group H.Q. will be at 183 Infantry Brigade H.Q., Hill V.5.c.2.2.
Left Group Headquarters will be at 182 Infantry Brigade H.Q. Sandpit V.5.a.

(b) Group Commanders will detail a LIAISON Officer to accompany attacking Battalions.

12. BRIDGES.

Field Artillery Bridges are to be constructed by the 61st. Div. R.E. at Q.7.c.2.3. and Q.28.a.8.8.
Subsequently Heavy Bridges are to be built under Corps arrangements at Q.14.c.4.9., Q.20.a.3.5., Q.21.d.5.5., and Q.20.a.9.8.

13. HOSTILE ARTILLERY FIRE.

Reports of Hostile artillery activity will be forwarded as quickly as possible to 61 Div. Art. Headquarters, giving the following information :-

Time shelling/

Time shelling commenced.
  Number of guns or Hows. firing.
  Calibre.
  Nature of shell.
  Approximate rate of fire.
  Target.
  Direction of fire - Grid bearing to flash or of sound.
  Position from which bearing was taken.

The importance of sending this information through as quickly as possible must be impressed on all Officers and N.C.O. Observers.

14. TANKS (BRITISH)

Should Tanks be employed, the best protection which the Artillery can afford them from hostile Artillery fire is to blind the hostile gunners with smoke.

15. ZONE CALLS.

Group Commanders will detail batteries to answer Zone Calls in accordance with para.6, XVII Corps Artillery Instructions No.2 of 23.8.18.

16. LIGHT SIGNALS.

(a) The 61st. Division Infantry indicate their positions from time to time by firing white Very Lights.

(b) RED flares will be lit by the troops on or near the final objective.

(c) The S.O.S. Signal is a Rifle Grenade Signal bursting into RED over GREEN over RED.

17. COOPERATION WITH R.A.F.

Contact Aeroplanes will call for flares at ZERO plus 3½ hours;
  ZERO plus 5 hours.
  ZERO plus 7 hours.

A Counter-attack machine will be in the air continuously from daylight.

18. REPORTS.

Advanced Divisional Headquarters will close at ST.AUBERT at ZERO hour on 24th. instant and will open at MONTRECOURT at the same hour.

19. SYNCHRONISATION OF WATCHES.

Groups will synchronise watches with R.A. 61 Div. by telephone at 1830 hours on the 23rd. instant.

20. Zero hour/

20. ZERO HOUR will be 0400 hours 24th. instant.
Any alteration to ZERO HOUR will be notified by Code
as .... minutes plus or minus of 0400 hours, viz:

   0300 hours will be minus 60.
   0515 hours will be plus 75.

21. ACKNOWLEDGE.

          F.P.Nye.

           Capt. R.A.,
         Bde.Maj., 61 Div. Artillery.

<u>Issued at 1000 hours.</u>

<u>DISTRIBUTION.</u>

Copy No.		
1 - 25.	Right Group:	21 Maps.(5 copies per Bde. & 1 for D.A.H.Q.)
26 - 55.	Left Group.	26 " (do.)
56 - 57.	24 Div.T.Ms.	1 Map.
58 - 59.	61 Div.T.Ms.	1 "
60.	182nd. Inf. Bde.	
61.	183rd. Inf. Bde.	
62.	61st. Div. 'G'.	
63.	61st. Div. 'Q'.	
64.	R.A. XVII Corps.	
65.	2nd. Div. Art.	
66.	4th. Div. Art.	
67.	12th. Batt. Tank Corps.	
68 - 69.	War Diary.	1 Map.
70.	File.	
71.	184th. Inf. Bde.	
72.	61 D.A.C.	

War Diary.

S E C R E T

61st. DIVISIONAL ARTILLERY.
LOCATION STATEMENT - 22.10.18.

Unit.	Location.	Wagon Lines.
R.A. Hdqrs. 61 LDiv.	U.24.a.5.7.	U.24.a.5.7.
306 Bde. RFA. HQ.	V.5.c.6.1.	C.5.a.7.6.
A/306.	V.6.c.2.6.	V.13.a.2.9.
B/306.	V.5.d.6.6.	V.19.b.3.5.
C/306	V.4.b.3.1.	U.18.b.5.7.
D/306.	V.5.c.2.6.	U.18.b.9.0.
307 Bde. RFA. HQ.	V.16.b.6.6.	U.24.d.7.5.
A/307.	V.16.d.7.6.	V.19.d.5.5.
Adv: Sect.	V.12.a.9.0.	
B/307.	V.16.b.3.7.	V.19.c.9.3.
1 Anti-tank gun.	Q.31.b.5.5.	
1 " " "	V.1.b.7.7.	
C/307.	V.10.b.6.3.	V.19.d.6.2.
Adv: Sect.	V.12.a.7.7.	
D/307.	V.10.d.6.0.	U.18.b.6.4.
61 D.A.C. HQ.	-	U.29.d.5.3.
No.1 Section.	-	U.29.d.6.4.
No. 2 "	-	U.29.b.central.
61 D.T.M.O.	Billet No.1, AVESNES-lez-AUBERT.	

22.10.18.
1800 hours.

Captain,
A/R.O., 61 Div. Artillery.

AMENDMENT NO. 1

to

61st DIVISIONAL ARTILLERY   ORDER   No. 172.

23rd October, 1918.
----

1.   Left Flank Batteries of Left (24 D.A.) Group will fire 200 yards in advance of barrage shown on Map from ZERO plus 40 minutes to ZERO plus 136 minutes.

2.   ACKNOWLEDGE.

Captain, R.A.,
Bde. Major 61st Div. Arty.

To all recipients of 61st Divl. Arty. Order No. 172.

AMENDMENT NO. 2
to
61st DIVISIONAL ARTILLERY ORDER No. 172.

23rd October, 1918.

Field Artillery - LEFT GROUP
24th October. - ZERO plus 20 to ZERO plus 50 minutes.

1 Battery will fire bursts of Thermite on strong points Q.7.c.2.9., and 1 battery on Q.7.d.0.7.

Acknowledge

J.P. Wye.
Captain, R.A.,
Bde. Major 61st Div. Arty.

To all recipients of 61st Divl. Arty. Order No. 172.

AMENDMENT NO. 2
to
61st DIVISIONAL ARTILLERY ORDER No. 172.

23rd October, 1918.

Field Artillery - LEFT GROUP
24th October. - ZERO plus 20 to ZERO plus 50 minutes.

1 Battery will fire bursts of Thermite on strong points Q.7.c.2.9., and 1 battery on Q.7.d.0.7.

Acknowledge

[signed] F.P. Wye.
Captain, R.A.,
Bde. Major 61st Div. Arty.

To all recipients of 61st Divl. Arty. Order No. 172.

SECRET.

War Diary

AMENDMENT NO: 3
- to -
61st. DIVISIONAL ARTILLERY ORDER NO: 172.

ADJUSTMENT OF BARRAGE START LINE.
1. The 18-pdr. Barrage will come down on the 1st. Protective Barrage Line, shown on the barrage map, at Zero hour, where it will rest for 6 minutes. At Zero plus 6 minutes, the barrage will commence to move forward at the rates shown on the barrage map.

NO SMOKE SHELL IN BARRAGE.
2. Para. 6 (b) of Order No.172 is cancelled.
Right Group will fire 50% A and 50% AX.

CONTINUATION OF BARRAGE.
3. The Protective Barrage for Third Objective is cancelled, and Right Group barrage will continue to lift level with Left Group barrage.
The whole barrage will continue to lift at the rate of 100 yards in 4 minutes to the line Q.2.b.8.8. - Q.4.a.3.8. - Q.5.b.5.5. - Q.6.a.0.0. - R.7.a.0.0., when barrage fire will cease

AMENDMENT NO: 1.
4. Amendment No.1 holds good, but the times will be amended;

For "Zero plus 40 mins. to Zero plus 136 minutes"

read

"Zero plus 6 minutes to Zero plus 102 minutes."

AMENDMENT NO: 2.
5. Amendment No.2 holds good, but the times will be amended;

For "Zero plus 20 to Zero plus 50 minutes"

read

"Zero to Zero plus 20 minutes."

6. The 72nd. Army Brigade, R.F.A. acting in close support to the 182 Infantry Bde. will advance a battery as early as possible to the neighbourhood of LA JUSTICE - Q.10.a.8.9.

ARTILLERY ADVANCE.
7. The times for advance of Field Artillery Brigades will be amended as follows :-
306th. and 72nd. Bdes. R.F.A. will advance at Zero plus 60 minutes.
88th. Bde. and 315 Bdes. R.F.A. at Zero plus 120 minutes.

8. ACKNOWLEDGE. by wire.

Major
Capt. R.A.,
Bde.Maj., 61 Div. Artillery.

23.10.1918.
2030 hours.

To all recipients of 61 D.A. Order No.172.

SECRET.

61st. DIVISIONAL ARTILLERY

LOCATION STATEMENT - 23.10.1918.

War Diary

Unit.	Location.	Wagon Lines.
H.A.R. & 61 Div.	U.24.d.6.7.	
RIGHT GROUP H.Q.		
19th. Div. Art.	V.5.c.5.1.	
87th. Bde.R.F.A. HQ.	V.12.b.1.4.	V.12.a.1.4
A/87.	P.36.d.1.1.	V.14.c.0.1.
B/87.	P.36.d.6.2.	V.16.a.central.
C/87.	P.36.d.9.4.	ST. VAAST.
D/87.	Q.31.c.3.4.	Vicinity ST. VAAST.
306th. Bde.R.F.A. HQ.	V.5.c.8.1.	O.5.a.7.6.
A/306.	V.6.c.2.6.	V.13.a.2.9.
B/306.	V.5.d.6.5.	V.19.b.3.5.
C/306.	V.4.b.3.1.	
D/306.	V.5.c.2.6.	V.13.c.9.1.
307th. Bde.R.F.A. HQ.	P.36.d.1.2.	U.24.d.7.5.
A/307	W.1.a.7.8.	V.19.d.5.5.
B/307		V.19.c.3.3.
C/307	to	V.19.d.6.2.
D/307.	P.36.d.6.8.	U.18.b.6.4.
313th. A.Bde.R.F.A. HQ.	V.4.c.1.1.	N.23.
A/313.	V.5.c.3.4.	
B/313.	V.5.d.6.6.	and
C/313.	V.5.c.1.7.	
D/313.	V.5.c.2.6.	N.18.
LEFT GROUP H.Q.		
24th. Div. Art.	V.5.a.3.2.	
106th. Bde.R.F.A. HQ.	V.11.a.5.5.	
A/106.	P.36.c.6.8.	
B/106.	P.36.c.8.6.	
C/106.	P.36.c.9.1.	
D/106.	V.6.b.0.6.	
107th. Bde.R.F.A. HQ.	P.33.c.7.6.	
A/107.	P.23.c.3.9.	
B/107.	P.23.c.7.6.	
C/107.	P.23.d.7.9.	
D/107.	P.28.c.4.1.	
72nd. Bde.R.F.A. HQ.	P.33.b.3.7.	
A/72.	P.33.b.5.5.	
B/72.	P.33.b.8.6.	
C/72.	P.27.d.5.0.	
D/72.	P.33.b.3.4.	
88th. Bde.R.F.A. HQ.	P.35.c.5.8.	)
A/88.	P.35.b.1.0.	)
B/88.	P.35.b.9.5.	) V.13.a. & c.
C/88.	P.35.b.1.9.	)
D/88.	P.35.d.6.8.	)

- 1 -

LOCATION STATEMENT (Continued)

Unit.	Location.	Waken Lines.
LEFT GROUP (contd.)		
93rd. Bde. R.F.A. Hq.	N.30.b.9.7.	
A/93.	N.30.b.3.2.	
B/93.	N.30.b.7.0.	
C/93.	N.30.a.4.1.	
61st. D.A.C.Hq.	U.24.a.5.7.	
19th. D.A.C.Hq.	M.27.b.8.8.	
61st. D.T.M.O.	Billet No.1 AVESNES.	
19th. D.T.M.O.	AVESNES-les-AUBERT.	
No.1 Coy. 61 Div.Train.	AVESNES.	

Ramsay, Captain,
A/R.O. 61 Div. Artillery.

23.10.1918.

War Diary

S E C R E T.

Copy No: 14

61st. DIVISIONAL ARTILLERY ORDER NO.173.

24.10.1918.

1. The 88th. Brigade, R.F.A. will relieve the 72nd. Army Brigade, R.F.A. as close supporting Artillery Brigade - vide para.10(a) 61 Div. Artillery Order 172 - forthwith, under arrangements to be made by C.R.A. 24th. Division.

2. ACKNOWLEDGE. (24 D.A. only).

[signature]

Captain, R.A.,
Bde. Maj., 61 Div. Artillery.

Issued at 2100 hours.

DISTRIBUTION.

Copy No. 1 - 24th. Div. Art.
2 - 19th. Div. Art.
3 - R.A. XVII Corps.
4 - XVII Corps H.A.
5 - 62nd. Heavy Brigade.
6 - C.B.S.O. 17th. Corps.
7 - 182 Infantry Bde.
8 - 183rd. Infantry Bde.
9 - 184th. Infantry Bde.
10 - 61st. Divn. 'G'
11 - 2nd. Div. Art.
12 - 4th. Div. Art.
13 - 13th. Sqn. R.A.F.
14-15. War Diary.
16. File.

S E C R E T.

Copy No: 31

61st. DIVISIONAL ARTILLERY ORDER NO: 174.

25.10.1918.

1. The Artillery covering the front of the 61st. Division will be re-grouped as follows :-

    (a) FORWARD GROUP, under Brig.-Gen. H.G.LLOYD, CMG, DSO,
    24th. Divisional Artillery - Headquarters with Advanced Infantry Brigade, H.Q.

    106th. Bde. R.F.A. supporting Left Infantry Battalion in the line, in action about Q.10.

    307th. Bde. R.F.A. supporting Right Battalion in the line. To be in action in positions in the neighbourhood of Q.17 and Q.18.

    These two Brigades will be in close support of the Infantry, and will push forward sections for anti-tank defence.

    107th. Bde. R.F.A. and 306th. Bde. R.F.A. will occupy positions East of the ECAILLON River in the neighbourhood of VENDEGIES-sur-ECAILLON and HERMERAIN respectively

    (b) REAR GROUP, under the command of Lt.-Col. A.T.McGRATH, DSO, 88th. Bde. R.F.A. HQ., consisting of :-
    88th. Brigade, R.F.A.
    315th. Army Bde. R.F.A.
    87th. Brigade, R.F.A.
    in action in the neighbourhood of Squares Q.13, Q.20 and Q.27 respectively.

2. In the event of a further forward move of the Artillery becoming necessary, the two leading Brigades will follow in close support within 2,500 yards of the leading Infantry.

    The two back Brigades of the Forward Group about 3,500 yards and the Rear Group at about 4,500 yards from the leading Infantry.

3. Brigades will be moved under orders to be issued by Right and Left Groups respectively into the areas mentioned in para.1, and commands of the Artillery will pass to the Officers therein mentioned at 1800 hours, 26th. inst., when the Headquarters of 19th. Div. Art. will withdraw from action.

4. ACKNOWLEDGE.

Issued at 1500 hours.

Capt. R.A.,
Bde. Maj., 61 Div. Artillery.

DISTRIBUTION.

Copy No. 1 - 5.	19th. Div. Art.	Copy No. 22.	182 Inf. Brigade.
6 -10.	24th. Div. Art.	23.	183 Inf. Brigade.
11.	306th. Bde. RFA.	24.	184 Inf. Brigade.
12.	307th. Bde. RFA.	25.	17 Corps H.A.
13.	315 A. Bde. RFA.	26.	C.B.S.O.
14 -17.	61 D.A.C.	27.	62 Bde. R.G.A.
18.	D.T.M.O.	28.	13 Sqn. R.A.F.
19.	R.A. XVII Corps.	29.	2nd. Div. Art.
20.	61 Divn. 'G'	30.	4th. Div. Art.
21.	61 Divn. 'Q'	31-32.	War Diary.
		33.	File.

War Diary

SECRET.

Copy No: 13

61st. DIVISIONAL ARTILLERY INSTRUCTIONS NO: 26.

26.10.1918.

AMMUNITION.

Cancel 61st. Div. Art. Instructions No. 25 of 17.10.18.

AMMUNITION. 1. (a) Para. 1 (a) of 61 Divisional Artillery Instructions No. 24 is temporarily cancelled.

(b) Until further notice the following amounts of ammunition will be dumped at gun positions :-

18-pr. Batteries. 300 rds. per gun. (45% shrapnel.
(45% H.E.
(10% Smoke.

4.5" How. "   250 " " "   H.E.
30 " " "   GAS (C.G.)

EXPENDITURE. 2. In order to build up a reserve of ammunition for future operations, the normal daily ammunition expenditure by Forward Group batteries, will be limited to an average of :-

20 rds. per gun 18-pr. and 15 rds. per gun 4.5" How.,

except for operations, and will be devoted to targets of opportunity, careful registration, counter-battery work and night harassing fire.

P Wye

Capt. R.A.,
Bde.Maj., 61 Div. Artillery.

DISTRIBUTION.

24th. D.A.	(4 copies)
28th. Bde. R.F.A.	(1)
315 Bde. R.F.A.	(1)
306th. Bde. R.F.A.	(1)
307th. Bde. R.F.A.	(1)
61st. D.A.C.	(1)
61 Divn. 'G'.	(1)
61 Div. 'Q'.	(1)
R.A. XVII Corps.	(1)
War Diary.	(2)
File.	(1)
87th. Bde. R.F.A.	(1)

SECRET.

61st. DIVISIONAL ARTILLERY LOCATION STATEMENT - 26.10.1918.

61st. R.A. Headquarters - Q.14.d.4.9.

Unit.	Location.	Wagon Lines.
FORWARD GROUP.		
24th. D.A. H.Q.	Q.22.a.5.2.	
106 Bde.R.F.A. HQ.	Q.16.a.6.1.	
A/106.	Q.10.b.3.7.	
B/106.	Q.10.b.3.3.	
C/106.	Q.10.a.5.5.	
D/106.	Q.10.a.0.2.	
307 Bde.R.F.A. HQ.	Q.16.a.3.2.	Q.22.d.
A/307.	Q.18.b.5.5.	
B/307.	Q.18.a.5.2.	
C/307.	Q.18.a.0.3.	
D/307.	Q.11.a.2.1.	
306 Bde.R.F.A. HQ.	Q.21.c.8.0.	Q.26.b.1.4.
A/306.	Q.29.a.2.9.	Q.26.d.2.4.
B/306.	Q.28.b.95.95.	
C/306.	Q.22.d.5.0.	Q.26.b.1.4.
D/306.	Q.28.b.4.9.	
107 Bde.R.F.A. HQ.	Q.8.d.5.1.	P.30.a.
A/107.	Q.9.d.9.1.	P.19.d.9.5.
B/107.	Q.16.a.2.9.	Q.19.d.8.5.
C/107.	Q.16.a.2.7.	P.19.b.8.2.
D/107.	Q.9.d.5.0.	
REAR GROUP.		
88th. Bde.R.F.A. HQ.	Q.13.d.6.5.	P.33.d.8.6.
A/88.	Q.13.d.30.95.	P.33.s.3.3.
B/88.	Q.13.b.3.3.	P.33.d.3.7.
C/88.	Q.13.d.8.6.	P.33.d.8.2.
D/88.	Q.13.d.8.8.	P.33.d.8.4.
87th. Bde.R.F.A. HQ.	Q.27.a.9.6.	Q.26.d.2.4.
A/87.	Q.27.b.5.4.	V.12.b.4.3.
B/87.	Q.27.b.7.1.	Q.26.d.
C/87.	Q.21.c.6.0.	V.11.b.1.5.
D/87.	Q.27.b.0.5.	HAUSSY.
315th.A.Bde.R.F.A. HQ.	Q.27.a.85.50.	
A/315.	Q.22.b.2.5.	
B/315.	Q.20.d.2.1.	
C/315.	Q.22.b.2.5.	
D/315.	Q.20.d.3.4.	
61st.Div.T.M.Bs.	MONTRICOURT.	
61st. D.A.C. HQ.	P.33.d.3.2.	
A.R.P.	P.28.d.2.4.	
No.1 Co.61 Div.Train.	ST. AUBERT.	

Captain,
A/R.O., 61 Div. Artillery.

26.10.1918.

SECRET.

Copy No: 19

61st. DIVISIONAL ARTILLERY ORDER NO: 176.

WARNING ORDER.

28th. Oct. 1918.

1. On a date and at an hour to be notified later 182 Infantry Brigade, 61 Division, will attack and capture the spur between MARESCHES and PRESEAU; the final objective will be on the line L.14.d.0.0. - L.20.central - L.26.central - L.32.central.

2. The Field Artillery covering the Operation will be divided into 2 Groups :-

   RIGHT GROUP. Lt.-Col. E.W.S. BROOKE, CMG, DSO, RFA.
   Headquarters, 306 Bde. R.F.A., LARBLIN.

   87th. Brigade, R.F.A.
   306th. Brigade, R.F.A.
   307th. Brigade, R.F.A.
   315th. Army Bde. R.F.A.

   LEFT GROUP. Brig.-General H.G.LLOYD, CMG, DSO, R.A.
   Headquarters, 24th. Div. Arty. - Sunken Road near
   LA JUSTICE.

   88th. Brigade, R.F.A.
   106th. Brigade, R.F.A.
   107th. Brigade, R.F.A.

   Two Trench Mortars, 61 Division, will be in action about SEPMERIS.

3. NATURE OF ATTACK.

   The attack will be in a N.E. and finally E direction; the forming up line for the Infantry being approximately K.30.a.1.0. along road to K.29.a.4.7.

4. GENERAL PLAN OF ARTILLERY SUPPORT.

   (a) The attack will be carried out under a barrage forming on the line K.30.a.5.0. - K.23.d.5.1. and advancing by lifts of 100 yards to the final objective. This barrage will be provided by all Brigades of Left Group and 307 Bde. R.F.A. and 315 Bde. R.F.A. from Right Group. In each case Brigades will be superimposed over the whole zone allotted to the Group to which they belong.

   (b) A secondary barrage will come down on the line K.32.d.5.5. to K.30.c.5.5. and will move forward to the line of the road running E and W through MARESCHES.
   As the creeping barrage mentioned in sub-para.(a) above advances, the secondary barrage (b), pivoting on the right flank, will swing in advance of the creeping barrage and finally form on the protective barrage line.
   This barrage will be provided by 306 Bde. and 2 F.A. Brigades of 6th. Corps.

- 1 -

(c) The 87th./

(c) The 87th. Brigade, R.F.A. will barrage the Southern exits of PRESEAU throughout the Operation, and will establish an O.P. in the neighbourhood of R.7.b. in order to keep the village under observation as far as possible.

(d) 61 Div. Trench Mortars, in action about SEPMERIS, will fire in accordance with Orders to be issued later.

(e) Special tasks for 4.5" Hows. will be notified later.

(f) C.R.A. 24th. Division, will detail an 18-pdr. gun to fire one round THERMITE shell at each lift in the barrage to mark the left flank of the attack.
One salvo THERMITE will be fired by all batteries firing barrage mentioned in para. 4 (a) above at each "halt" in the barrage to show the Infantry that a protective barrage is being formed.

5. **FIELD ARTILLERY ADVANCE.**

(a) At Zero plus 45 minutes, the 107 Brigade R.F.A. will commence to advance by Batteries to the close support of the Infantry.

(b) <u>Trench Mortars.</u> The mobile 6" NEWTON T.Ms. 24th. D.A., will accompany the attacking Infantry.

6. **LIAISON.**

Headquarters Right Group will be established close to 183 Infantry Bde. H.Q. at LARBLIN.
Left Group close to 182 Inf. Bde. in Sunken road about LA JUSTICE.

7. **COUNTER ATTACKS.**

These will most likely develope from the direction of PRESEAU and SAINT HUBERT.
107 Bde. R.F.A. will detail sections to deal with hostile tanks should these appear.

8. Officers patrols will be sent forward in accordance with para. XVII Corps Artillery Instructions No.2 of 25.8.18.

9. ACKNOWLEDGE.

Capt. R.A.,
Bde.Maj., 61 Div. Artillery.

<u>Issued at 1700 hrs.</u>

DISTRIBUTION.

Copy No.1 - 4.	24th. Div. Art.
5.	87th. Bde. R.F.A.
6.	88th. Bde. R.F.A.
7.	315th. Bde. R.F.A.
8.	303th. Bde. R.F.A.
9.	307th. Bde. R.F.A.
10.	61st. D.T.M.O.
11.	61st. Divn. 'G'
12.	R.A. XVII Corps.
13.	3rd. Div. Art.
14.	4th. Div. Art.
15.	182 Inf. Brigade.
16.	183 Inf. Brigade.
17.	184 Inf. Brigade.
18 - 19.	War Diary.
20.	File.

S E C R E T.

61st. DIVISIONAL ARTILLERY

LOCATION STATEMENT - 27.10.1918.

61 R.A. Headquarters - Q.14.d.4.9.

Unit.		Location.	Wagon Lines.
FORWARD GROUP.			
24th. Div. Art. H.Q.		Q.22.a.5.2.	
106 Bde. RFA. HQ.		Q.16.a.4.2.	Q.22.d.4.4.
A/106	(2 guns)	Q.5.a.1.9.	Q.15.d.1.5.
	(4 ")	Q.10.b.7.7.	
B/106.	(2 guns)	K.34.d.4.3.	Q.16.a.8.0.
	(4 ")	Q.10.b.0.7.	
C/106.	(2 ")	K.34.d.8.8.	Q.21.b.7.0.
	(4 ")	Q.10.a.5.8.	
D/106.	(2 Hows.)	K.34.b.9.1.	Q.15.b.7.0.
	(4 ")	Q.10.a.3.4.	
307 Bde. RFA. HQ.		Q.16.a.4.2.	Q.22.d.1.2.
A/307.	(5 guns)	Q.16.d.9.9.	Q.22.a.3.5.
B/307.	(1 gun)	Q.12.b.9.1.	Q.22.d.2.6.
	(5 guns)	Q.18.a.7.0.	
C/307.	(1 gun)	R.7.a.2.9.	Q.22.b.5.9.
	(5 guns)	Q.16.b.2.2.	
D/307.	(1 How.)	Q.6.a. central.	Q.22.a.8.8.
	(5 Hows)	Q.12.b.4.7.	
306 Bde. RFA. HQ.		Q.28.b.2.8.	Q.28.b.1.8.
A/306.	(6 guns)	Q.17.a.2.9.	Q.22.c.9.2.
B/306.	(6 ")	Q.11.c.1.1.	"
C/306.	(6 ")	Q.16.b.7.9.	Q.26.a.8.8.
D/306.	(6 Hows.)	Q.10.d.5.3.	"
107 Bde. RFA. HQ.		Q.9.c.5.0.	P.30.a.
A/107.	(6 guns)	Q.9.d.9.1.	"
B/107.	(6 ")	Q.16.a.2.8.	P.19.d.9.5.
C/107.	(6 ")	Q.16.a.3.5.	Q.19.d.8.5.
D/107.	(6 Hows.)	Q.9.d.5.0.	P.19.b.8.2.
24th.M.T.M.B. 1 6" NEWTON.		K.34.b.95.95.	
61st.M.T.M.Bs. HQ.		P.33.d.5.2.	
2 6" NEWTONS.		Attd: 182 Inf. Bde.	

61 D.A. LOCATION STATEMENT. (contd.)

Unit.	Location.	Wagon Lines.
REAR GROUP.		
88th. Bde. RFA. HQ.	Q.7.d.3.0.	P.33.d.8.6.
A/88. (6 guns)	Q.13.d.30.95.	P.33.a.3.3.
B/88. (6 ")	Q.13.b.3.6.	P.33.a.3.7.
C/88. (6 ")	Q.13.d.2.6.	P.33.d.8.2.
D/88. (6 Hows.)	Q.13.d.8.8.	P.33.d.8.4.
87th. Bde. RFA. HQ.	Q.27.a.9.6.	Q.26.d.2.4.
A/87. (6 guns)	Q.27.c.6.4.	V.12.b.4.3.
B/87. (6 ")	Q.27.b.7.1.	Q.26.d.
C/87. (6 ")	Q.21.c.6.0.	V.11.b.1.5.
D/87. (6 Hows.)	Q.27.b.0.5.	HAUSSY.
315th. A. Bde. RFA. HQ.	Q.27.a.85.50.	W.2.b.5.7.
A/315. (6 guns)	Q.22.b.2.5.	W.2.d.6.5.
B/315. (6 ")	Q.20.d.2.1.	W.2.b.9.9.
C/315. (6 ")	Q.22.b.2.5.	Q.32.d.9.9.
D/315. (6 Hows.)	Q.20.d.3.4.	W.2.b.9.6.
315 B.A.C.	-	W.2.c.9.3.
61st. D.A.C. HQ.		
No.1 Section.	-	P.33.d.3.2.
No.2 "	-	P.33.d.75.20.
		V.4.a.20.15.
A.R.P.	-	P.28.d.2.4.
No.1 Co. 61 Div. Train.	-	Q.32.b.cent.

Murray Capt.
A/R.O., 61 Div. Artillery.

7.10.1918.

SECRET.   COPY NO............

61st DIVISIONAL ARTILLERY ORDER No. 177.

28th October, 1918.

1. The 87th and 88th Brigades R.F.A. and 315 Army Brigade R.F.A. will proceed into action on night 28th/29th in the areas K.34 - Q.5. c and d - Q. 17 and 18 respectively.

   Guns will be left under a guard on night 28th/29th.

   One gun per battery will be accurately registered for line on 29th instant.

   All batteries will be in action with amounts of ammunition shown in para. 4. below by 23.59 hours 29th instant.

2. At 1800 hours on 29th inst the Artillery covering the front of the 61st Division will be grouped as follows:-

   RIGHT GROUP.
   Lieut-Col. E.W.S.BROOKE, C.M.G., D.S.O., R.A.
   87 Bde R.F.A.
   306 Bde R.F.A.
   307 Bde R.F.A.
   315 Army Brigade R.F.A.

   LEFT GROUP
   Brig.General H.G.LLOYD, C.M.G., D.S.O., R.A.
   88th Bde R F A.
   106 Bde. R F.A.
   107 Bde. R.F.A.

3. (a) From 1800 hours 29th instant onwards, dividing line between Groups for S.O.S. purposes will be L.25.c.0.0. - L.15.c.0.0

   (b) Group Commanders will arrange to provide necessary Liaison Officers with the Infantry in the Line.

4. The following amounts of ammunition will be dumped at gun positions by midnight 29/30 inst.

   18 pdr. batteries - 400 rounds per gun.
   87th Bde. R.F.A. }
   306 Bde.   "   }   45% A 45% AX 10% A Smoke.

   88 Bde.R.F.A. }
   106 Bde.   " }
   107 "   " }   60% A 30% AX 10% A Smoke.
   307 Bde.   " }
   315 Army Bde."}

   4.5" Hows. 350 rounds per gun including 50 rounds BCG. except that D/87 Bde. R.F.A. will have per gun:-
   150 rounds BX, 150 rounds B.Smoke, 50 rounds BCG.

5. ACKNOWLEDGE.

Issued at 1700 hours.
                                    Captain, R.A.,
                                    Bde. Major 61st Div. Arty.

                                    P.T.O.

DISTRIBUTION.

Copy	1 -4	24th D.A.
	5	07 Bde. R.F.A.
	6	88th " "
	7	315 Army Brigade R.F.A.
	8	306 Bde. R.F.A.
	9	307 Bde. R.F.A.
	10	61st D.T.M.O.
	11	61st Div. "G"
	12	R.A. XVII Corps.
	13	R.A. 3rd Div.
	14	R.A. 4th Div.
	15	182 Inf. Bde.
	16	183 Inf. Bde.
	17	184 Inf. Bde.
	18-19.	War Diary.
	20	File.

S E C R E T.

R.A.G.10/11.

AMENDMENT NO: 1
to
61st. DIVISIONAL ARTILLERY ORDER NO: 177.

Para.1.

for "The 87th. and 88th. Brigades R.F.A."
read "The 88th. and 87th. Brigades, R.F.A."

F.P.Lys Capt. R.A.,
Bde.Maj., 61 Div. Artillery.

28.10.1918.

To all recipients of 61 D.A.Order No.177.

S E C R E T.

R.A.G.10/12.

AMENDMENT NO: 2
to
61st. DIVISIONAL ARTILLERY ORDER NO: 177.

    61st. Div. Art. Order No.177 of 28.10.18 is postponed for 24 hours, except that the first 3 sub-paras. of para.1 will be complied with as originally laid down.

(signed)
Capt. R.A.,
Bde.Maj., 61 Div. Artillery.

28.10.1918.

To all recipients of 61 D.A. Order No.177.

SECRET.   XVII Corps No. G.(O)427.

XVII CORPS ARTILLERY INSTRUCTIONS No. 1
on
XVII Corps Order No. 173.

1. The Artillery supporting the attack will be grouped as follows :-

FIELD ARTILLERY.   61st DIVISION.   O.R.A., Brig-Genl. R.G. OUSELEY.
                                                     C.B., C.M.G., D.S.O.

   Right Group.   Lt.Col. E.W.S. BROOKE, C.M.G., D.S.O.

        87th Brigade R.F.A.
        315th Army Brigade R.F.A.
        306th Brigade R.F.A.
        307th Brigade R.F.A.

   Left Group.   Brig-Genl. J.H. LLOYD, C.M.G., D.S.O.

        88th Brigade R.F.A.
        106th Brigade R.F.A.
        107th Brigade R.F.A.

   The 42nd and 41st Brigades R.F.A. of VI Corps, will be co-operating in the Right Flank barrage.

HEAVY ARTILLERY.

   Brigade affiliated to 61st Division.
        62nd (Mixed) Brigade R.G.A. (Lt.Col. ILES.).

   Corps Group.
        35th (Mobile) Brigade R.G.A.
        63rd (8") Brigade R.G.A.
        COTTER'S Brigade R.G.A.

2. NATURE OF ATTACK.

   The attack will be carried out by the 182nd Infantry Brigade, 61st Division.
   The jumping off line will be on the road from K.30.a.00. to K.29.a.5.8.
   The advance will start in a north easterly direction, and swinging in conformity with XXII Corps, will advance due East, enveloping MARESCHES and capturing the high ground North and South of ST HUBERT. At the same time, local penetrations will be made by troops from the South over LA RHONELLE River as opportunity offers.
   The objective, boundaries and timings, are shown on the barrage map.

3. ARTILLERY SUPPORT.

   (a) Main Creeping Barrage.   Five Brigades, viz:-
        315th Army Brigade R.F.A.)
        307th Brigade R.F.A.   ) Right Group.
                and
        88th Brigade R.F.A.   )
        106th Brigade R.F.A.   ) Left Group.
        107th Brigade R.F.A.   )
   will form the main 18-pdr creeping barrage, in enfilade. Brigades will be superimposed in the barrage within Group Zones.

/Composition

- 2 -

Composition of barrage - 90% Shrapnel, 10% Smoke, from dawn onwards, during darkness Shrapnel only.

The barrage will be formed at ZERO, on the line K.30.c.80.65. to K.23.d.20.05., and will rest on this line for 15 minutes, when, pivotting on the right, it lifts on the left flank at the rate of 100 yards in 5 minutes for 300 yards, and continues at 100 yards in 4 minutes. It will halt for 10 minutes from ZERO plus 28 minutes to ZERO plus 38 minutes, and continues at same rate. At ZERO plus 50 minutes, the swing will be completed and barrage will lift eastwards at the rate of 100 yards in 5 minutes and come to rest for 10 minutes at ZERO plus 95 minutes, 250 yards east of the road L.19.a.30.25. - L.25.a.32.00. It will lift again at ZERO plus 105 minutes, at same rate up to the protective barrage line over final objective.

(b) Right Flank Barrage.

At ZERO, the 306th Brigade R.F.A. with 41st and 42nd Brigades R.F.A., of VI Corps, will form the right flank barrage, on the line AB. At ZERO plus 15 minutes, the barrage will lift at the rate of 100 yards in 5 minutes, up to the line C D. It will rest on this line, and search 100 yards each side of it. At ZERO plus 50 minutes, the left battery of 306th Brigade R.F.A. will commence to lift up its lane N.E., followed by the remaining batteries of 306th Brigade and 42nd Brigade in conformity with the main creeping barrage, and will come to rest on the line E F G, over the final objective.

The 41st Brigade R.F.A. will continue to search 100 yards North and South of its portion of the line C D, up to ZERO plus 130 minutes, when it will form a protective barrage 250 yards East of the final objective in L.32.

(c) Special tasks and Smoke Screens.

From ZERO to dawn, the 87th Brigade R.F.A. will barrage the northern flank of attack south of PRESEAU with H.E. and Shrapnel. At dawn, it will form a smoke screen to deny observation from PRESEAU, and thereafter be prepared to form further smoke screens under orders of G.O.C., 61st Division.

The fire of the 87th Brigade R.F.A. must be in conformity with the main 18-pdr creeping barrage in order to be kept at safe limits from the attacking troops of XXII Corps.

(d) 4.5" Howitzers.

The 4.5" Howitzers of Right and Left Groups will form a standing barrage on targets to be allotted by 61st Division. It will conform to the 18-pdr main barrage, and at not less than 300 yards from it. If weather is suitable, C.G. Gas shell will be employed in this barrage.

The 4.5" howitzers of 41st Brigade R.F.A. are engaging the trenches and rifle pits from L.33.a.4.8. to L.32.b.9.9. and from L.33.a.3.5. to L.32.b.85.70. from ZERO onwards, and the 4.5" howitzers of 42nd Brigade R.F.A. are engaging the MILL and QUARRY in L.26.c. and shelters along road from L.26.c.55.55. to 55.80., lifting to road L.27.a.70.90. - L.28.c.15.15.

4. RATES OF FIRE.

	18-pdr main barrage batteries.	18-pdr Right flank barrage batteries.	4.5" Hows.
ZERO to ZERO plus 50 minutes.	NORMAL.	NORMAL.	NORMAL.
ZERO plus 50 to plus 55 mins.	RAPID.	NORMAL.	NORMAL.
ZERO plus 55 mins onwards.	* SLOW to RAPID.	*SLOW to RAPID.	*SLOW to RAPID.

* Depending on whether the barrage is on open ground or on sunken roads, villages and trenches.

5. HEAVY ARTILLERY.

Intense neutralisation of hostile batteries from ZERO to ZERO plus 45 minutes, every available gun and howitzer that can reach being utilised. The VI Corps is assisting at this task and the counter-battery programme will be drawn up by the C.B.S.O. in conjunction with C.B.S.Os. of flank Corps.

At ZERO plus 45 minutes, a proportion of guns and howitzers engaged at counter battery work, will be taken off and used to form concentrations on strong points, sweeping approaches, and bombarding sunken roads.

Tasks to be allotted by B.G. Corps Heavy Artillery, after consultation with G.O.C. 61st Division. Bombardments will lift in conformity with main 18-pdr creeping barrage.

If weather favourable, C.G. Gas shell will be employed in these concentrations.

If the hostile artillery again becomes active, counter-battery work will take the place of bombardments.

6. ADVANCE.

At ZERO plus 120 minutes, the 107th Brigade R.F.A. will commence to advance by batteries. Route via left flank of attack. This Brigade will act as the Close Supporting Brigade to the 182nd Infantry Brigade, and will provide two sections for anti-tank defence.

Thereafter, the C.R.A. 61st Division will control the whole of the Field Artillery, and advance Brigades according to the situation.

The VI Corps Brigades will cease fire at ZERO plus 3½ hours, when the C.R.A. 61st Division will re-adjust the protective barrage zones.

7. LIAISON.

Brig-Genl. LLOYD, with 24th D.A., H.Q., will establish his Hd. Qrs. at the 182nd Infantry Brigade Headquarters.

8. TRENCH MORTARS.

The 61st Division will place 4 Medium Trench Mortars in action in SEPMERIES, to co-operate in the barrage on the North bank of LA RHONELLE River.

One Mobile section, 24th Divisional Artillery, will accompany the 182nd Infantry Brigade.

9. ACKNOWLEDGE.

H.Q., XVII Corps.
28th October, 1918.

Brigadier-General.
General Staff.

Distribution Overleaf.

- 4 -

Distribution.	Map Distribution.
Third Army.	—
Third Army R.A.	1
VI Corps.	1
VI Corps R.A.	1
XXII Corps.	1
XXII Corps R.A.	1
61st Division.	60
24th Division.	—
19th Division.	—
G.O.C., R.A. (4).	4
XVII Corps H.A. (2).	10
A.D. Signals.	—
C.E.	—
"Q".	—
13th Squadron R.A.F.	1
16th Kite Balloon Coy.	1
War Diary.	2
File.	2
3rd Divisional Arty. (3) Copies for 41st and 42nd Brigades R.F.A.	12
61st Divisional Arty. (12) Copies for Group H.Qs. and each R.F.A. Bde in the line.	50

S E C R E T.

Copy No: ....

61st. DIVISIONAL ARTILLERY ORDER NO: 178.

To be read in conjunction with XVII Corps
Artillery Instructions No.1 on XVII Corps
Order No.173.

30th. Octr. 1918.

1. On 31st. October 1918, the 61st. Division will attack and capture the high ground East and North of the River RHONELLE, and the Village of MARESCHES. This attack will be carried out in conjunction with an attack by the XXII Corps on the North.

2. **Infantry Dispositions.**
   (a) The attack will be carried out by the 182 Inf. Bde. with two battalions, and with one battalion in Brigade Reserve about K.34.a. & d.
   (b) That portion of the objective South of the river will be made good by 2 Coys. to be detailed by 183 Inf.Bde., and will be held by them until relieved by the 182 Inf.Bde.
   Fighting patrols of the 183 Inf.Bde. will cross the river as the barrage lifts, to establish touch with the right of the 182 Inf.Bde. where the objective line crosses the MARESCHES road, and will cooperate in clearing the right bank of the river South of the road as opportunity offers.
   (c) 184 Inf.Bde. will be in Divisional Reserve, and battalions will stand to ready to move from their present positions.
   (d) The attacking battalions will move across the river on the night 30/31st. October by the bridge at FME. DE L'HOTEL DIEU and the footbridges placed in position in K.29.a. & c., and will form up along the road from the Northern end of FME. DE L'HOTEL DIEU to about K.29.b.8.0. and along the track running between the road and river to about K.29.d.4.5.

3. **Objective and boundaries.**
   The attack will be made in an Easterly direction from behind the Bridge-head now held by 183 Inf.Bde. and troops of 4th. Divn. at FME. DE L'HOTEL DIEU.
   Boundaries and objectives are shewn on barrage map issued to all concerned.

4. **Consolidation.**
   As soon as the objective is captured, it will be consolidated and the defence organised in depth.
   The objective will then become the MAIN LINE OF RESISTANCE.
   Arrangements have been made to fire salvoes of 8" shell with delay action spaced out along the objective line, the craters to be consolidated by the Infantry on reaching the objective.
   These salvoes will be fired as late as safety will permit.
   A proportion of machine guns will be pushed well forward with the attacking infantry to cover the work of consolidation.

5. **Artillery Support.**
   (a) Main Creeping Barrage :
   As this barrage is being fired in enfilade, accuracy for line and careful concentration of lines of fire by Batteries is therefore essential. Protective barrage fire will cease at Z + .
   At each "Halt" in the barrage, 18-pdr. Batteries of Left Group, 307 Brigade, R.F.A. and 315 Army Brigade R.F.A., will fire one Salvo Thermite Shell 200 yards in advance of the barrage line to show the attacking Infantry that a protective barrage is being formed.

- 1 -

C.R.A. Left Group/

C.R.A. Left Group will issue Orders for one gun to fire one round Thermite shell 200 yards in advance of each lift in the barrage along the inter-divisional boundary, to mark the left flank of the attack, and another gun to fire Thermite shell in the same way to mark the inter-battalion boundary along the line, K.29.b.7.5. - L.19.c.50.25. - L.20.c.6.0.

Note: No Thermite shell will be fired into the village of LARESCHES.

(b) Special Tasks and Smoke Screens.
87th. Brigade, R.F.A. will detail an Officer to observe the smoke screen on EX PRESEAU and to report should this screen not be sufficiently dense.

(c) 4.5" Howitzers.
The 4.5-in. Howitzers will conform to the main 18-pdr. barrage and will keep 300 yards in advance of it. As the 4.5" How. barrage encounters the various enemy works shown on the attached tracings, sunken roads or villages, the rate of fire will be increased to rapid.
Gas shell will be used if the wind is blowing between West and S.S.W. but not if North of West.

6. S.O.S. lines to come into force after the operation, will be arranged by Group Commanders in consultation with B.Gs.Comdg. Infantry Brigades concerned and notified to this Office.
The fire of Artillery Brigades will be superimposed over the front of their respective Groups.

7. Bridges for Field Artillery.
One constructed by R.E. 4th. Division will be at K.29.a.2.8.
      "   "   R.E. 61 Division   " " " K.29.a.4.6.
The former will be in position before Zero; the latter about Zero plus 2 hours.

8. Light Signals.
(a) WHITE Very lights will be used by the most advanced troops to denote their positions.
(b) RED flares will be lit by the most advanced troops on or near the objectives.
(c) The S.O.S. Signal is a rifle grenade bursting into RED over GREEN over RED.

9. Cooperation with Aircraft.
(a) Contact aeroplanes will call for flares at :-
    Zero plus 1¼ hours,
    Zero plus 2¼ hours,
    Zero plus 3¼ hours.
(b) A counter-attack aeroplane will be up from daylight onwards.

10. Hostile Artillery Fire.
Reports of Hostile Artillery activity will be forwarded as quickly as possible to 61 Div. Art. Headquarters, giving the following information :-
Time shelling commenced.
Number of guns or Hows. firing.
Calibre.
Nature of shell.
Approximate rate of fire.
Target.
Direction of fire - Grid bearing to flash or of sound.
Position from which bearing was taken.
Time shelling ceased.
The importance of sending this information through as quickly as possible, must be impressed on all Officers and N.C.O.Observers.

11. **Zone Calls.**
Group Commanders will detail batteries to answer Zone Calls in accordance with para.6, XVII Corps Artillery Instructions No.2 of 25.8.18.

12. **Reports.**
61st. Divisional Artillery Headquarters will remain at VENDEGIES.

13. **Liaison.**
Brig.-General H.G.LLOYD, C.M.G, DSO, R.A., 24th. Div. Artillery will establish his H.Q. with H.Q. 182 Inf. Brigade.
Lt.-Col. E.W.S. BROOKE, C.M.G, DSO, R.F.A., with 183 Inf. Bde.

14. **Synchronisation of Watches.**
61st. Divisional Artillery will synchronise watches by telephone with Right and Left Groups at 1830 hours, 30th. inst.

15. **Zero hour.**
Zero hour will be 0515 hours. Any alteration in Zero hour will be notified by code as Minutes plus or minus of 0515 hours, viz :-

    0600 hours will be sent as plus 45.
    0400 " " " " " minus 75.

16. ACKNOWLEDGE.

Capt. R.A.,
Bde.Maj., 61 Div. Artillery.

Issued at 1100

DISTRIBUTION.

Copy No.		Recipient	Copies	
1	- 3.	24th. Div. Art. with 1 extra barrage map.	3	tracings.
4	- 5.	87th. Bde. R.F.A.	2	"
6	- 7.	88th. Bde. R.F.A.	2	"
8	- 9.	106th. Bde. R.F.A.	2	"
10	- 11.	107th. Bde. R.F.A.	2	"
12	- 13.	306th. Bde. R.F.A.	2	"
14	- 15.	307th. Bde. R.F.A.	2	"
16	- 17.	315 A Bde. R.F.A.	2	"
18.		182 Inf. Bde.	3	"
19.		183 Inf. Bde.	3	"
20.		184 Inf. Bde.	1	"
21.		61st. D.T.M.O.	1	"
22.		61st. D.M.G.O.	1	"
23.		61 Divn. 'G'	1	"
24.		61 Divn 'Q'	1	"
25.		61 C.R.E.	1	"
26.		2nd. Div. Art.	1	"
27.		4th. Div. Art.	1	"
28.		R.A. XVII Corps.	1	"
29.		13 Sqn. R.A.F.	1	"
30.		16 Kite Balloon Coy.	1	"
31	- 32.	War Diary.	2	"
33.		File.	1	"

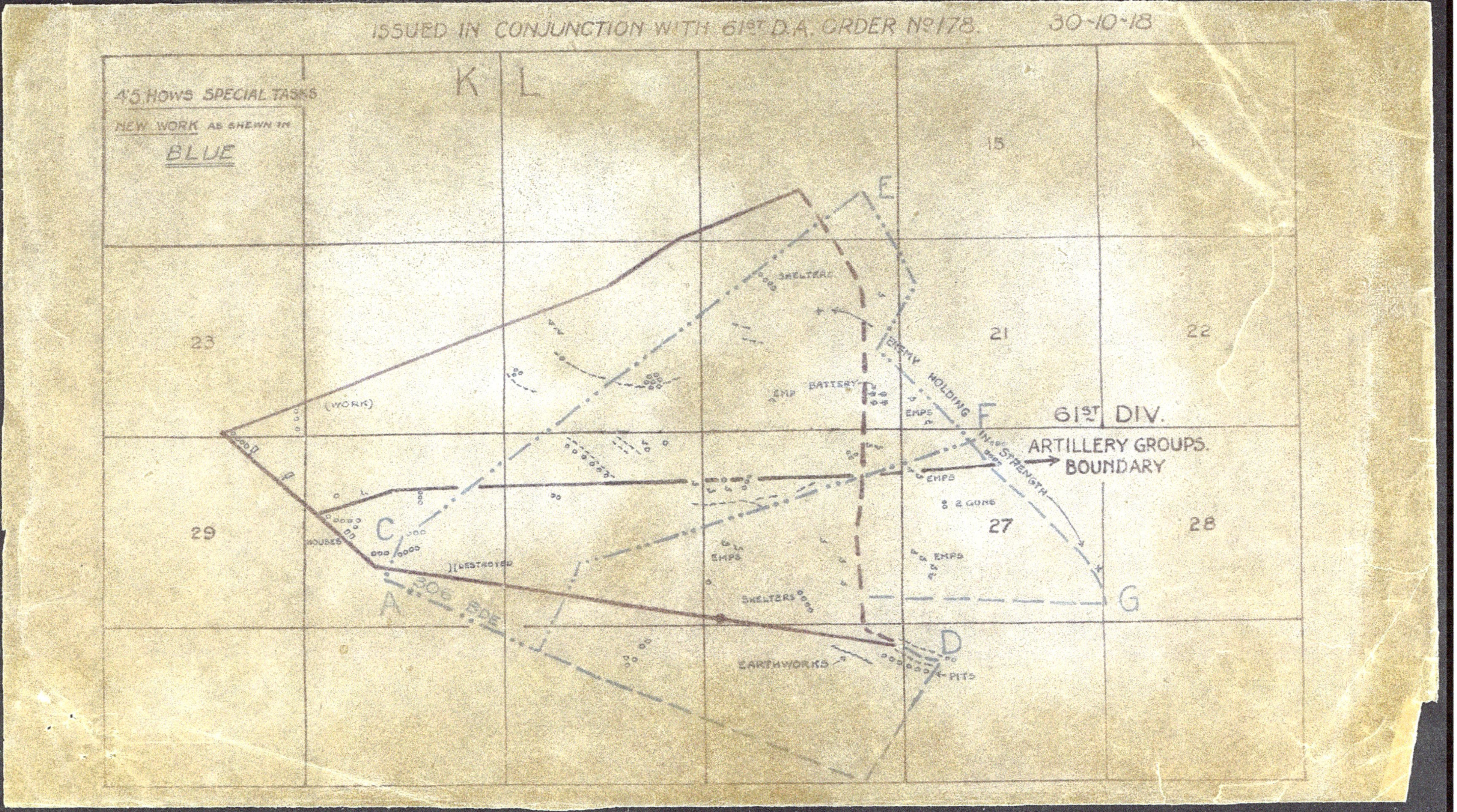
ISSUED IN CONJUNCTION WITH 61ST D.A. ORDER No 178.
30-10-18
4·5 HOWS SPECIAL TASKS
NEW WORK AS SHEWN IN
BLUE
K
L
15
16
23
21
22
29
27
28
E
F
G
C
A
D
SHELTERS
ENEMY HOLDING IN STRENGTH
EMP
BATTERY
EMPS
(WORK)
61ST DIV.
ARTILLERY GROUPS.
BOUNDARY
2 GUNS
HOUSES
DESTROYED
306 BDE
SHELTERS
EARTHWORKS
PITS

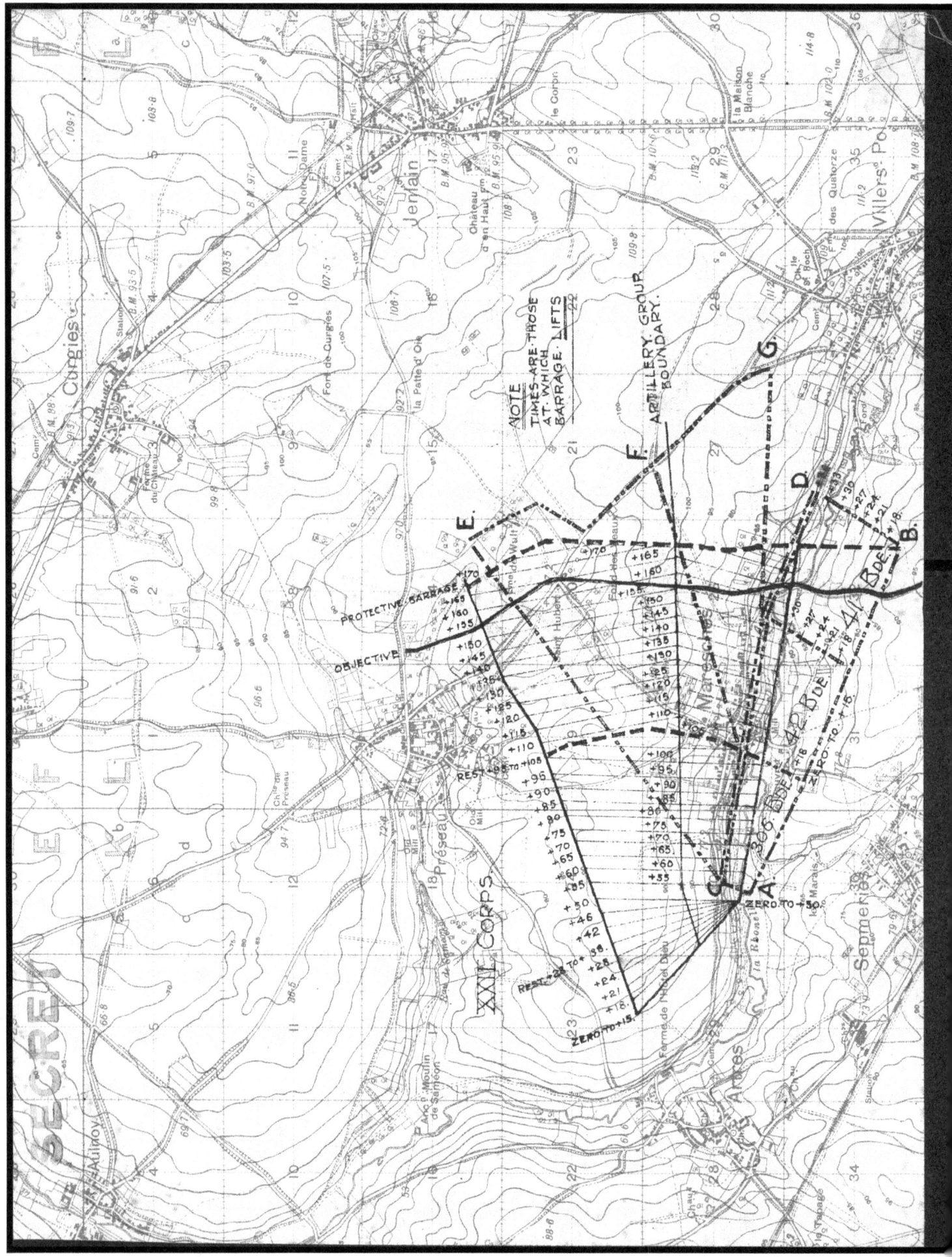

SECRET.

61st. DIVISIONAL ARTILLERY

LOCATION STATEMENT - 30.10.1918.

Unit.		Location.	Wagon Lines.
61st. R.A. Hdqrs.		Q.14.d.4.9.	
FORWARD GROUP.			
24th. R.A. H.Q.		Q.22.a.4.2.	
106th. Bde. R.F.A. H.Q.		Q.16.a.4.2.	
A/106.	(4 guns) (2 ")	Q.10.b.7.7. Q.5.a.1.9.	Q.17.d.1.6.
B/106.	(4 ") (2 ")	Q.10.b.0.7. K.34.d.4.3.	Q.16.a.8.0.
C/106.	(4 ") (2 ")	Q.10.a.5.7. K.34.d.8.6.	Q.21.b.7.0.
D/106.	(4 Hows) (2 ")	Q.10.a.3.4. K.34.b.9.1.	Q.15.b.7.0.
107th. Bde. R.F.A. H.Q.		Q.9.c.5.0.	Q.9.c.3.0.
A/107.	(6 guns)	Q.9.d.9.1.	Q.19.d.5.4.
B/107.	(3 ")	Q.16.a.2.9.	Q.19.d.7.6.
C/107.	(6 ")	Q.15.a.2.7.	Q.19.d.3.6.
D/107.	(5 Hows)	Q.9.d.5.0.	Q.19.b.8.3.
306th. Bde. R.F.A. H.Q.		Q.28.b.20.80.	Q.23.b.1.4.
A/306.	(6 guns)	Q.17.a.2.9.	Q.23.d.2.4.
B/306.	(6 ")	Q.11.c.1.1.	Q.2.d.2.4.
C/306.	(6 ")	Q.15.b.7.9.	Q.2.b.1.4.
D/306.	(")	Q.10.d.5.3.	Q.23.b.1.4.
307th. Bde. R.F.A. H.Q.		Q.23.a.0.5.	Q.22.d.1.2.
A/307.	(6 guns)	Q.18.d.9.8.	Q.28.a.5.1.
B/307.	(5 ") (1 ")	Q.18.a.8.0. Q.12.b.9.1.	Q.22.d.2.8.
C/307.	(5 ") (1 ")	Q.13.a.2.2. R.7.a.2.9.	Q.28.b.5.9.
D/307.	(5 guns) (1 gun)	Q.11.c.4.7. Q.8.c.5.3.	Q.28.a.8.8.

1st. T.M. H.Q.   P.33.d.5.2.
V/61 L.T.M.B. HQ.   Q.13.a.9.9.
2 6" (Mobile) NEWTONS.   K.34.a.5.80.

24th. T.M. H.Q.   VENDEGIES.
1 6" (Mobile) NEWTON.   K.34.b.95.95.

19th T.M. H.Q.   AVESNES-lez-AUBERT.

61st. D.A. LOCATION STATEMENT
(contd.)

Unit.	Location.	Wagon Lines.
REAR GROUP.		
88th. Bde. R.F.A. H.Q.	Q.7.d.3.0.	Q.7.d.3.0.
A/88. (6 guns)	K.33.b.8.0.	Q.13.d.3.9.
B/88. (6 ")	K.33.d.98.42.	Q.13.b.3.0.
C/88. (6 ")	K.34.c.35.05.	Q.13.d.8.8.
D/88. (6 Hows.)	K.33.b.8.2.	Q.13.d.8.8.
87th. Bde. R.F.A. H.Q.	Q.27.a.9.6.	Q.13.a.3.7.
A/87. (6 guns)	Q.18.a.1.2.	Q.31.b.9.9.
B/87. (6 ")	Q.17.b.8.5.	Q.26.d.3.5.
C/87. (6 ")	Q.17.b.2.7.	Q.32.b.5.5.
D/87. (6 Hows.)	Q.17.a.8.9.	Q.26.b.5.4.
315 A. Bde.R.F.A. HQ.	Q.26.b.2.4.	W.2.b.6.8.
A/315. (6 guns)	Q.11.b.45.95.	Q.3.c.4.8.
B/315. (6 ")	Q.5.d.3.2.	Q.26.b.2.4.
C/315. (6 ")	Q.3.c.90.60.	Q.33.c.2.8.
D/315. (6 Hows.)	Q.3.d.6.3.	W.2.b.8.8.
315th. B.A.C.	W.2.c.3.0.	
61st. D.A.C. H.Q.	-	P.33.d.3.2.
No.1 Section.	-	P.33.d.78.20.
No.2 "	-	V.4.a.20.1.
S.A.A. Section.	-	P.33.b.5.9.
24th. D.A.C. H.Q.	-	P.33.b.4.5.
Nos. 1 & 2 Sections.	-	SAULZOIR.
19th. D.A.C. H.Q.	-	AVESNES-les-AUBERT.
No.1 Section.	-	MONTRECOURT.
No.2 "	-	P.33.d.2.3.
A.R.P.	-	P.26.a.2.4.
No.1 Co. 61 Div. Train.	-	Q.32.c.3.

Ramsay
Capt.
A/R.O. 61 Div. Artillery.

30.10.1918.

S E C R E T.

ADDENDUM to
61st. DIVISIONAL ARTILLERY ORDER NO: 178.

Reference 61st. Divisional Artillery Order No.178 of 30.10.1918, para.5,, sub-para (c).

Only B.C.G. gas will be used.

A.P.Nye,
Capt. R.A.,
Bde.Maj., 61 Div. Artillery.

30.10.1918.

To all recipients of 61 D.A.Order No.178.

SECRET.

Copy No: ....

61st. DIVISIONAL ARTILLERY ORDER NO: 179.

31st. Oct. 1918.

1. The 315 Army Brigade, R.F.A. will withdraw from action on 1st. November at an hour to be notified later, and will march to MONTRECOURT Area, where it will be in Corps Reserve.

   Billets from Town Major, MONTRECOURT.

   Batteries will move at one hour interval and will avoid roads where possible.

2. (a) 93rd. Army Brigade, R.F.A. on transfer from Corps Reserve, will march to Wagon Lines, SOMMAING Area, where it will come under Orders of C.R.A. 61 Division.

   (b) Locations of Brigade Headquarters, Batteries and B.A.C. to be reported to R.A. 61 Division, as soon after arrival as possible.

3. ACKNOWLEDGE.

F.P. Wys.

Capt. R.A.,
Bde.Maj., 61 Div. Artillery.

Issued at 1700

DISTRIBUTION.

Copy No: 1 - 2. 315 Army Bde. R.F.A.
3 - 4. 93 Army Bde. R.F.A.
5. 24th. D.A. (Left Group.)
6. 306 Bde. R.F.A. (Right Group)
7. 61st. Divn. 'G'
8. 61st. Divn. 'Q'
9. R.A. XVII Corps.
10. 2nd. Div. Art.
11. 4th. Div. Art.
12. 182 Inf. Bde.
13. 183 Inf. Bde.
14. 184 Inf. Bde.
15 - 16. War Diary.
17. File.

(6392) Wt. W6192/P875 1,500,000 4/18 McA & W Ltd (E 2815) Forms W3091/4.   Army Form W.3091.

Cover for Documents.

Nature of Enclosures.

61st Divisional Artillery

War Diary

for

November 1918.

VOL: 31.

Notes, or Letters written.

WAR DIARY
or
INTELLIGENCE SUMMARY.

(Erase heading not required.)

Army Form C. 2118

Instructions regarding War Diaries and Intelligence Summaries are contained in F. S. Regs., Part II. and the Staff Manual respectively. Title pages will be prepared in manuscript.

Place	Date	Hour	Summary of Events and Information	Remarks and references to Appendices
VENDEGIES	1st		18? Casualties Bn attacked at 0575 hours supported by Artillery barrage. MARBRECHIES captured. Enemy counter attacked with tanks at 1025. hours & successfully dealt with by our Artillery. Division acquired 700 prisoners. R.A.O. 180 inca. Having thrown back to 2.P.S. Fine.	
do.	2nd		Artillery cooperated during morning in support of advance by Brigades & their objectives on high ground E of MARBRECHIES. Total prisoners taken by the Bn were 1650 O.Rs. 2 Pavlov & 2 Peter pom Own Cas. 2 other ranks killed and several Boles wounded. Fine.	
do.	3rd		Bn Division was relieved by 19th & 24th Divisions as per D.R.O. 180. GOC 61st Bde handed over command of artillery covering Divisional front to OCRE 19th & 24th Rds at 0900 hours. R.H.O. & rest of Brigade claimed relief and rejoined Division. Present cast.	
M RUBBRE.	4th		Bdes advanced to E of MARBRECHIES. Infantry held up by M.G. from BRY - Tois joint just and front. GORA ordered 62 D.Bdg withdraw SBaen under ST DB. Fine.	
do.	5th		Bdes advanced during afternoon. Withdrew our harassing fire. Fine.	
do.	6th		Situation as before. Heavy harassing fire. Fine.	

Army Form C. 2118.

WAR DIARY
or
INTELLIGENCE SUMMARY.
(Erase heading not required.)

Instructions regarding War Diaries and Intelligence Summaries are contained in F. S. Regs., Part II. and the Staff Manual respectively. Title pages will be prepared in manuscript.

Place	Date	Hour	Summary of Events and Information	Remarks and references to Appendices
ST ROBERT	7th		R.H.Q. still at ST ROBERT - Bns. still in action. Routine orders DRO 181 issued	
do	8th		During morning moved forward to VENDEGIES - Bns issued NO. without firing. Bns. moved forward to (BRIAN)	
VENDEGIES	9th		Bns moved forward. CRA ordered response at HQ at 1450 hours	
do	10th		Enemy retires to the North. Bns out of action. O.C.trps taken on the present an whole army front. Ration arrived at HQ	
do	11th		Hostilities ceased at 1100 hours in accordance with terms of armistice	
do	12th		Bns. under command of G.O.C. remained in their present area. B. of BAVAI at bayonets. DRO 182 issued.	
do	13th			
do	14th		R.H.Q. moved to RIBOX & opened at 1100 hours. CRA moved back.	

Army Form C. 2118.

WAR DIARY
or
INTELLIGENCE SUMMARY.
(Erase heading not required.)

Instructions regarding War Diaries and Intelligence Summaries are contained in F. S. Regs., Part II. and the Staff Manual respectively. Title pages will be prepared in manuscript.

Place	Date	Hour	Summary of Events and Information	Remarks and references to Appendices
RIEUX	15th	11.00	R.A.H.Q. moved to CAMBRAI opened at RUE de NOYON 11 CROISINE at 11.00 hours. D.R.O. No. 12. issued.	
CAMBRAI	16th		B.A.C. H.Q. moved to WARGNIES and in accordance with D.R.O. No. 12. (S.R.A. returned to Beau H.Q. from 2nd Army Group) D.R.O. No. 2 issued.	
"	17th		B.A.C.+D.A.C. formed unit to BERMERAIN area. D.R.O. No. 2a issued	
"	18th		Base D.A.C. marched to St VAAST area.	
"	19th		R.A.C. + D.A.C. marched to ROISIN – units billeted with Army. D.R.O. No. 183 issued	
"	20th		Been engaged in burying dead & clearing up. – D.R.C. No. 184 issued	
"	21st			
"	22nd		Reconnaissance made for move to BARNEVILLE area. D.R.O. Nos. 184+185 issued Weather observed	

Army Form C. 2118.

WAR DIARY
or
INTELLIGENCE SUMMARY.
(Erase heading not required.)

Instructions regarding War Diaries and Intelligence Summaries are contained in F. S. Regs., Part II. and the Staff Manual respectively. Title pages will be prepared in manuscript.

Place	Date	Hour	Summary of Events and Information	Remarks and references to Appendices
CAMBRAI	23rd		RAHQ remained at CAMBRAI. Bns. OAR commenced march to FOURSUIL area. 315 was heavily bombed being over twice from 806 / 307 Pommier area. Bales continued — remaining night at Pommier area	15
"	24th			
"	25th		RAHQ moved to new area, opened at CHATEAU de BEAUVOIR at BEAUVOIR. WAVANS, on AUXI. Le CHATEAU — DOULLENS road. Bns. RAR occupied the following in new area as follows 307 WAVANS. 306. BEAUCOURT, 115 BEAUVOIR — Building accommodation very bad. 315. NEUVILY	
WAVANS	26th		S/S APA Sec. moved to new area — billets at BEAUVOIR - RIVIERE and R. AIZIECOURT	
	27th		Units engaged in training	
	28th		Localism statement march for	
	29th		CRA went round Brigades, & to Divn. HQ.	
	30th		CRA went to Bvtish HQ & to XVII Corps	

Freddie May
A/Major & A.A.

S E C R E T.

Copy No: 24

61st. DIVISIONAL ARTILLERY ORDER NO: 180.

2/11/1918

1. The 61st. Division (less Artillery, H.Q. and Nos. 1 & 2 Sections D.A.C. and No.1 Coy. 61 Div. Train) is to be relieved on 2nd. and 3rd. instant, by 19th. and 24th. Divisions.

2. Corps Boundaries and Boundaries between Divisions, on completion of relief, are shown on attached tracings.

3. Command of the Artillery covering the front will pass from C.R.A. 61 Division at 1000 hours on 3rd. instant.

4. On passing of command mentioned in para. 3 above, the Artillery covering the front will be arranged as follows :-

24th. Div.	24 Div. Arty. Brig.-Gen. H.G.LLOYD? CMG,DSO,R.A.	Right Group. Lt.-Col.E.W.S. BROOKE, CMG, DSO,R.F.A.	306th. Bde. R.F.A. 307th. Bde. R.F.A. 315 A.Bde. R.F.A. (in wagon lines)
		Left Group. Lt.-Col.B.W.L. SPILLER, DSO, R.F.A.	106th. Bde. R.F.A. 107th. Bde. R.F.A.
19th. Div.	19 Div. Arty. Brig.-Gen. CHRISTIE, CMG, R.A. 20th. Div. Arty.	Right Group.	91st. Bde. R.F.A. 92nd. Bde. R.F.A.
		Left Group. Lt.-Col.A.T. McGRATH,DSO.	87th. Bde. R.F.A. 88th. Bde. R.F.A. 93rd. A. Bde. R.F.A. (in wagon lines)

5. 61 Div. Artillery H.Q. close at VENDEGIES-sur-ECAILLON at 1000 hours 3rd. inst. and re-open at ST.AUBERT at that hour.

6. ACKNOWLEDGE.

F.T. WYE
Capt. R.A.,
Bde.Maj., 61 Div. Artillery.

DISTRIBUTION.

Copy No.1.	306 Bde.R.F.A.		Copy No.13.	61 Div. 'Q'
2	307 Bde.R.F.A.		14.	R.A. XVII Corps.
3	61 D.A.C.		15.	2nd. Div. Art.
4	61 D.T.M.O.		16.	4th. Div. Art.
5	87 Bde. R.F.A. 306		17.	13 Sqn. R.A.F.
6	88 Bde. R.F.A.		18.	16 Balloon Coy.RAF
7	19th. Div. Art.		19.	No.1 Co. 61 Div.Train
8	24th. Div. Art.		20.	XVII Corps H.A.
9	20th. Div. Art.		21.	" " CBSO
10	315 A.Bde.R.F.A.		22	62 Bde. R.G.A.
11	61 Div. Signal Coy.		23-24.	War Diary.
12	61 Div. 'G'		25	File.

SECRET.

Copy No: 12

61st. DIVISIONAL ARTILLERY ORDER NO: 181.

7th. Nov.1918.

1. Headquarters, 61 Div. Artillery, will close at St. AUBERT and open at VENDEGIES at 1130 hours on 8th. instant.

F.P. Wye
Capt. R.A.,
Bde. Maj., 61 Div. Artillery.

DISTRIBUTION.

Copy No: 1. 61 Div. 'G'.
2. 61 Div. 'Q'.
3. R.A. XVII Corps.
4. 19th. Div. Art.
5. 20th. Div. Art.
6. 24th. Div. Art.
7. 306th. Bde. R.F.A.
8. 307th. Bde. R.F.A.
9. 61 D.A.C.
10. 61 D.T.M.O.
11-12. War Diary.
13. File.

S E C R E T.   Copy No: 9

61st. DIVISIONAL ARTILLERY ORDER NO: 182.

                                        13th. Novr. 1918.

1.   61st. Divisional Trench Mortar Batteries will move
as follows :-

    (a) By lorry to AVESNES on the 14th. inst.

    (b) Mobile Trench Mortars and Horse transport by
         march route to AVESNES, staging the night 14th/15th.
         at MARESCHES (Billets from the Town Major).

2.   R.A.H.Q. 61 Division close at VENDEGIES on the
14th. and re-open at RIEUX at an hour to be notified
later.

3.   ACKNOWLEDGE.

                                    Capt. R.A.,
                            Bde.Maj., 61 Div. Artillery.

            Copy No.1 - 61 D.T.M.O.
                    2 - XVII Corps R.A.
                    3 - 61 Div. 'G'
                    4 - 61 Div. 'Q'
                    5 - 306th. Bde. R.F.A.
                    6 - 307th. Bde. R.F.A.
                    7 - 61 D.A.C.
                  8-9   War Diary.
                   10.   File.
                   11.   Staff Captain, R.A.

SECRET.   Copy No: ......8....

61st. DIVISIONAL ARTILLERY ORDER NO: 1.

Ref: Map 51 - 51A.

1.   The 61st. Div. Art. accompanied by No.1 Coy.
        61st. Div. Train, will march to the WARGNIES AREA
        TOMORROW, November 16th. in accordance with the
        movement table on back.

2.   The usual distances will be maintained on the
        line of march, 200 yds. between batteries; 30 yds.
        between every 6 vehicles.
            (Attention is drawn to R.A. 17th. Corps No. R.A.3/94
        if 4.11.18.

3.   S.C.R.A. 61 Div. will march with 61 D.A.C. and all
        reports will be sent to 61 D.A.C. H.Q.

4.   ACKNOWLEDGE.

                                            Major,
Issued at 6pm.   S.C.R.A. 61st. Division.

                        DISTRIBUTION.

                Copy No.1 306th. Bde.
                     2   307th. Bde.
                     3   61 D.A.C.
                     4   No.1 Coy. Train.
                     5   61 Div. Arty
                     6   R.A. 17th. Corps.
                    7-8 War Diary.
                     9   File.

MARCH TABLE.

Series.	Date.	Unit.	From.	To.	Starting Point.	Route.	Remarks.
1	Nov.16.	61 D.A.C.	BAVAI	WARGNIES-le-PETIT.	300 yds. East of Road Junction I.25.b.8.4.	Through BAVAI Main street.	To march at 8.30 a.m.
2	"	No.1 Coy. 61 Div. Train.	I.28.cent.	WARGNIES GRAND.	I.28.central.	"	To march at 9 a.m.
3	"	307 Bde.	Present Lines.	do.	Level crossing at J.30.a.0.3.	J.29.a.3.4. - School at P.4.b.0.1. through BAVAI Main street.	To march at 9 a.m.
4	"	306 Bde.	"	WARGNIES-PETIT.	Cross roads at J.29.a.3.4.	School at P.4.b.0.1. through BAVAI Main street.	To march at 9.45 a.m.

S E C R E T

61st Divisional Artillery Order No. 2A.

Map VALENCIENNES 1/100000 51A 1/40000.

1. The march of the 61st Divisional Artillery to CAMBRAI will be resumed on the 17th inst, and following days in accordance with table overleaf.

2. The usual distances between units will be strictly observed.

3. Billeting parties will report to Area Commandants daily to obtain detailed lists of billets, wagon lines.

4. On November 17th Brigades will detach the necessary number of teams to collect all guns and wagons from the dump at MARESCHES L.25.b.5.6.
   An officer will be detailed from each Brigade to take charge of these teams.

5. R.P. will be notified daily. Supplies will be issued on arrival each day.

6. ACKNOWLEDGE.

17.11.1918.

Captain R.A.
Bde. Major, 61st Div. Artillery.

P.T.O.

SERIAL No.	DATE	UNIT	FROM	TO	STARTING POINT	ROUTE	TIME
1.	17.11.1918.	61 Div. Train	WAGNIES-LE GRAND	BERMERAIN	Cross Roads G.20.a.7.2	VILLERS-POL – CHAISSEE – BRUNEHAUT – LARBUIN.	To start 0815 hrs.
	"	307 Bde.	"	"	"	"	0900 "
	"	306 Bde.	WAGNIES-LE PETIT	"	Cross Roads G.22.d.0.1.	"	0930 "
	"	61 D.A.C.	"	"	"	"	1030 "
2.	18.11.1918.	61 Div. Train	BERMERAIN	ST VAAST	Cross Roads at Church ST MARTIN	ST MARTIN – MAISON BLEUE – HAUSSY	To start 0815 hrs.
	"	306 Bde.	"	"	"	"	0900 hrs.
	"	307 Bde.	"	"	"	"	1000 "
	"	61 D.A.C.	"	"	"	"	1100 "
3.	19.11.1918	61 Div. Train	ST VAAST	CAMBRAI (Main Town)	Road junction E.4.35.32 VALENCIENNES	MAIN ROAD	To start 0815 Hrs.
	"	307 Bde.	"	"	"	"	0915 "
	"	306 Bde.	"	"	"	"	1000 "
	"	61 D.A.C.	"	"	"	"	1045 "

S E C R E T.

Copy No:....7....

61st. DIVISIONAL ARTILLERY ORDER NO: 183.

Ref: Map, VALENCIENNES, 1/100,000.   20th. Nov. 1918.

1. The 315 A. Bde. R.F.A. will move to CAMBRAI on the morning of the 21st. November.

2. The Brigade will march via ST. VAAST at a time to be fixed by O.C. 315 Brigade.

3. The usual distances between Units and every six vehicles will be maintained.

4. Billets will be in the RUE des ROTISSEURS, CAMBRAI.

5. Billeting parties will report to R.A.H.Q. 61 Divn. at RUE NEUVE DES CAPUCINS, CAMBRAI, by 1000 hrs.

6. Supplies will be drawn from R.P. at PLACE FENELON on arrival.
315 Brigade are attached to Headquarters Company, 61st. Div. Train for Supplies and forage.

7. ACKNOWLEDGE.

Issued at 1600 hrs.

Major,
A/Bde.Major, 61 Div. Artillery.

DISTRIBUTION.

Copy No.	
1	315 A. Bde. R.F.A.
2.	61 Divn. 'G'.
3.	61 Divn. 'Q'
4.	17th. Corps R.A.
5.	17th. Corps
6-7.	War Diary.
8.	File.
9.	S.C.R.A.
10.	O.i/c Signals.

SECRET.

Copy No:.........

61st. DIVISIONAL ARTILLERY ORDER NO: 184.

22.11.1918.

Ref: VALENCIENNES Map, 1/100,000.

1. The 315 Army Field Artillery Brigade will march to CAMBRAI on November 23rd. in readiness to march on November 24th. and following days to the BERNAVILLE Divisional Area.

2. The Brigade will march under Orders of O.C. 315 Brigade.

3. The 315 Brigade will occupy billets in CAVALRY BARRACKS, CAMBRAI, now occupied by two Brigades of 61st. Divisional Artillery.

The following billets are available for Officers accommodation :-

No. 6 RUE D'EPEE.
No. 8 "
No. 8 Bis "
No. 12 RUE D'INCHY.
No. 6 "

4. Advance Billeting Parties will report to R.A.H.Q. 61 Div. by 1000 hrs. on 23rd. November.

Major,
A/Bde.Major, 61 Div. Artillery.

Issued at 0700 hrs.

DISTRIBUTION.

Copy No. 1 - 315 Bde. R.F.A.
2 - 306 Bde. R.F.A.
3 - 307 Bde. R.F.A.
4 - 61 Divn. 'G'
5 - 61 Div. 'Q'.
6 - XVII Corps 'G'
7 - XVII Corps R.A.
8 - Area Commandant, CAMBRAI.
9 - S.C.R.A.
10 - O.i/c R.A.Sigs.
11-12. War Diary.
13. File.

SECRET.

War Diary

Copy No: 28

1st. DIVISIONAL ARTILLERY ORDER NO: 185.

Ref: VALENCIENNES - 1/100,000.   22nd. Nov. 1918.
    LENS   1/100,000.

1. The 1st. Divisional Artillery will march to the new area in accordance with March Table overleaf.

2. The usual distances will be maintained between Batteries and every group of vehicles.

3. R.A.H.Q. 1 Div. remain at RUE NEUVE DES CAPUCINS, CAMBRAI.

4. ACKNOWLEDGE.

                                         Major,
                         A/Bde.Major, 1 Div. Artillery.

Issued at 1800 hrs.

DISTRIBUTION.

Copy No.	
1 - 5.	30th. Bde. R.F.A.
6 -10.	307th. Bde. R.F.A.
11 -15.	315 A.Bde. R.F.A.
16 -17.	61 D.T.M.O.
18 -21.	61 D.A.C.
22.	No.1 Coy. 61 Div. Train.
23.	61 Div. 'G'.
23.	61 Div. 'Q'.
24.	R.A. XVII Corps.
25.	XVII Corps 'G'.
26.	Area Commandant, CAMBRAI.
27 -28.	War Diary.
29.	File.
30.	O.i/c R.A. Signals.

MARCH TABLE issued with 61 Div. Artillery Order No.185.

Serial No.	Date.	Unit.	Time	From	To	Starting Point.	Route.	Remarks.
1	23.11.18.	No.1 Coy. 61 Div.Train.	0830	CAMBRAI	BEUGNATRE.	Road Junction. 4.C.55.13.	Via FREMICOURT.	
2	"	307 Bde. R.F.A.	0900	CAMBRAI	FAVREUIL.	"	"	
3	"	306 Bde. R.F.A	0945	CAMBRAI	"	"	"	
4	"	61 D.A.C.	1030	CAMBRAI	BEUGNATRE	"	"	
5	"	315 A.Bde. R.F.A.	–	ST.AUBERT.	CAMBRAI.	Under Orders of O.C. 315 A Bde. R.F.A. Not to enter CAMBRAI before 1200 hours.		
6	24.11.18.	No.1 Co. 61 Div.Train.	0815	BEUGNATRE.	COIGNEUX	Cross roads 5 K 12.45.	SAPIGNIES – BEHUCOURT – ACHIET-le-GRAND ACHIET-le-PETIT. BUCQUOY – HEBUTERNE – SAILLY-au-BOIS.	
7	"	306 Bde. R.F.A.	0915	FAVREUIL.	COIGNEUX	"		
8	"	307 Bde. R.F.A.	1000	FAVREUIL	COIGNEUX	"		
9	"	61 D.A.C.	1045	BEUGNATRE	COIGNEUX	"		
10	"	315 A.Bde. R.F.A.	0900	CAMBRAI	FAVREUIL.	Road Junction 4 C 55.13.	Via FREMICOURT.	
11	25.11.18.	315 Bde.	0900	FAVREUIL.	COIGNEUX.	Cross roads 5 K 12.45	As for Serial 6.	

SECRET.

ADMINISTRATIVE INSTRUCTIONS with reference to
61st Div. Artillery Order No. 185.
----

1. The 61st Div. Art., on the march to an area near DOULLENS will be billeted in staging Camps at BEUGNATRE, FAVREUIL, and at COIGNEUX.

2. An Officer from 306th Brigade, 307th Brigade and 61st D.A.C. will report to R.A.H.Q. at 09-00 hours tomorrow to proceed to the new area.
   Details of accommodation at COIGNEUX will be notified later.
   315th A.F.A. Brigade will occupy the same accommodation in FAVREUIL and COIGNEUX on evacuation by units of 61st Div. Art., under detailed arrangements to be made by O.C., 315th A.F.A. Brigade.

3. Supplies will be delivered each day to units on arrival.
   O.C. No.1 Coy., 61st Div. Train will detail an Officer to be attached to 315th Bde H.Q., for the march, to take charge of supply arrangements.

4. R.A.H.Q. Horse transport, strength, 14 O.R: 24 horses and T.M.Bs, horse transport, strength, 6 O.R: 9 horses will be attached to, and march under the orders of, 61st D.A.C.
   They will carry rations and forage for 2 days.

5. A motor ambulance is attached to 61st Div. Art. and is under the orders of O.C., 61st D.A.C. for the use of all units of 61st Div. Art., and will proceed with the 61st D.A.C. when not in use.

6. There are no facilities for watering between the Canal at CAMBRAI and BEUGNATRE, on the first day's march or at any points on the road during the second day's march.

7. Arrangements for the move of T.M.Bs and R.A.H.Q. will be notified later.

                                                    Major,
                                        B.G.R.A., 61st Division.

22.11.1918.

SECRET.   War Diary

61st. DIVISIONAL ARTILLERY.

LOCATIONS OF UNITS at 0800 hrs. 22.11.1918.

R.A. Headquarters, 61 Divn. — RUE NEUVE DES CAPUCINS, A.10.a.7540

306th. Bde. R.F.A. H.Q. — CAVALRY BARRACKS, A.10.a.

    A Battery. H.Q. — No.5 RUE FEUTRIERS, CAMBRAI.

    B " " — No.32 " "

    C " " — No.14 " "

    D " " — No.17 " "

307th. Bde. R.F.A. H.Q. — No.8 RUE D'EPEE, CAMBRAI.

    A Battery. H.Q. — No.8 GRANDE RUE FENELON.

    B " " — No.6 RUE D'INCHY.

    C " " — No.10b. GRANDE RUE FENELON.

    D " " — A.4.c.4.4. (1/40,000)

61st. D.T.M.O. H.Q. — No.19 RUE de VAUCELETTE.

    X/61 M.T.M.B.   do.

    Y/61. "   do.

61st. D.A.C. H.Q. — ECOLE de FILLES, RUE DE TEMPLE.

    No.1 Section. H.Q.   do.   do.

    No.2 " "   do.   do.

    S.A.A. " " — No.6 RUE D'EPEE.

No.1 Coy. 61 Div. Train. — QUAI ST. LAZARE, CAMBRAI.
(Yard Adjoining Gas Works.)

[signature] Capt.
A/R.O. 61 Div. Artillery.

22.11.1918.

War Diary

SECRET.

AMENDMENT NT: 1,
to
61st. DIVISIONAL ARTILLERY ORDER NO: 185.

MARCH TABLE.

Serial Nos. 6, 7, 8, 9 & 11.

for COIGNEUX read POMMIER.

Route.

Cancel HEBUTERNE - SAILLY au BAC and substitute :

ESSARTS - HANNESCAMPS - BIENVILLERS.

Major,
A/Bde.Major, 61 Div. Artillery.

0600 hrs.
23.11.1918.

To all recipients of 61 D.A. Order No.185.

61st. DIVISIONAL ARTILLERY.

LOCATION OF UNITS as on 28th. Nov. 1918.

Ref: Map LENS 11 - 1/100,000.

R.A. Headquarters, 61 Div.	CHATEAU de BEAUVOIN, BEAUVOIR-WAVANS.
306 BRIGADE R.F.A. H.Q.	BEALCOURT - 4 C 20 46.
A/306.	FROHEN-le-PETIT.
B/306.	BEALCOURT.
C/306.	ST. ACHEUL.
D/306.	BEALCOURT.
307 BRIGADE R.F.A. H.Q.	DRUCAS.
A/307.	WAVANS.
B/307.	"
C/307.	"
D/307.	"
315 A BDE. R.F.A. H.Q.	MAIZICOURT.
A/315.	BEAUVOIR-RIVIERE.
B/315.	"
C/315.	MAIZICOURT.
D/315.	"
315 B.A.C.	BEAUVOIR-RIVIERE.
61 M.T.M.B's.	MONT LOUIS FME. 1½ miles S. of AUXI-le-CHATEAU.
61 D..C. H.Q.	Billet No.3, OQUET.
No.1 Section.	LANNOY.
No.2 Section.	WILLENCOURT.
S....Section.	Billet No.3, OQUET.
No.1 Coy. 61 Div. Train.	FROHEN-le-GRAND.

Murray Capt
for Lieut.
R.A., 61 Div. Artillery.

28.11.18.

(6392) Wt. W6192/P875 1,500,000 4/18 McA & W Ltd (E 2815) Forms W3091/4.   Army Form W.3091.

Cover for Documents.

Nature of Enclosures.

61st Divisional Artillery

War Diary

— for —

December 1918.

VOL: 32.

Notes, or Letters written.

Army Form C. 2118.

WAR DIARY
or
INTELLIGENCE SUMMARY.
(Erase heading not required.)

Place	Date	Hour	Summary of Events and Information	Remarks and references to Appendices
WAYANS	Dec 1st		C.R.A. visits all batteries & Section H.Q. & horse lines (visiting accommodation & horse lines very poor.)	
	2nd			
	3rd			
	4th			
	5th			
AUXI-LE-CHATEAU	6th		RAHQ closed at WAYANS & re-opened at AUXI-LE-CHATEAU at 10 A.M. 306 H.Q. moved to WAYANS CHAU. to BEAUVOIN reached by RAHQ	
	7th		C.R.A. visits 31st Bde A.F.A.	
	8th			
	9th		G.O.C. Division visits all Brigades with C.R.A.	

Army Form C. 2118.

WAR DIARY
or
INTELLIGENCE SUMMARY.
(Erase heading not required.)

Instructions regarding War Diaries and Intelligence Summaries are contained in F. S. Regs., Part II. and the Staff Manual respectively. Title pages will be prepared in manuscript.

Place	Date	Hour	Summary of Events and Information	Remarks and references to Appendices
AUXI-LE-CHATEAU	9th		C.R.A went to Bers: H.Q. SB	
"	10th		A/315 & D/315 moved to MONT LOUIS FM.	
"	11th		G.O.C. R.A 3rd Army inspected 306 Bde, 307 Bde & DAC with C.R.A. Truck Tractors moved to LANNOY SB SB	
	12th - 31st		Divisional Artillery remained in this area under new Command. C.R.A left on leave to England 26th December & in other words assumed by Lt Colonel Baylay D.S.O C.O 307 Bde SB	

[signature]
Brig

CORA 61st Divl Artillery
31st December 1918.

61st. DIVISIONAL ARTILLERY.

LOCATION OF UNITS as on 7th. December, 1918.

Ref: Map LENS 11 - 1/100,000.

R.A. Hdqrs. 61 Div.	No. 62 RUE d'HESDIN, AUXI-le-CHATEAU.
306 Bde. R.F.A. HQ.	CHATEAU de BEAUVOIN, BEAUVOIR-WAVANS.
A/306.	LE MEILLARD.
B/306.	BEALCOURT.
C/306.	ST. ACHEUL.
D/306.	BEALCOURT.
307 Bde. R.F.A. HQ.	WAVANS.
A/307.	WAVANS.
B/307.	NOEUX.
C/307.	WAVANS.
D/307.	WAVANS.
315 Bde. R.F.A. HQ.	MAIZICOURT.
A/315.	BEAUVOIR-RIVIERE.
B/315.	BEAUVOIR-RIVIERE.
C/315.	MAIZICOURT.
D/315.	MAIZICOURT.
315 B.A.C.	BEAUVOIR-RIVIERE.
61 D.A.C. HQ.	LA NEUVILLE.
No. 1 Section.	VILLEROY-SUR-AUTHIE.
No. 2 Section.	WILLENCOURT.
S.A.A. Section.	ACQUET.
61 D.T.M.O. HQ.	⎫ MONT LOUIS FARME, 1½ miles
X/61 Bty.	⎬ due S. of AUXI-le-CHATEAU,
Y/61 Bty.	⎭ on MAIZICOURT Road.
No. 1 Co. 61 Div. Train.	No. 79 RUE d'ABBEVILLE, AUXI-le-CHATEAU.

[signature] Major
for Lieut.
R.O., 61 Div. Artillery.

7.12.1918.

War Diary

61st. DIVISIONAL ARTILLERY.

LOCATION OF UNITS as on 11th. December, 1918.

Ref: Map LENS 11 - 1/100,000.

R.A. Hdqrs. 61 Divn.	No.62 RUE d HESDIN, AUXI-le-CHATEAU.
306 Bde. R.F.A. HQ.	CHATEAU de BEAUVOIR, BEAUVOIR WAVANS.
A/306.	LE EPILLARD.
B/306.	HEUZECOURT.
C/306.	ST. ACHEUL.
D/306.	BEALCOURT.
307 Bde. R.F.A. HQ.	DRUCAS.
A/307.	DRUCAS.
B/307.	NOEUX.
C/307.	WAVANS.
D/307.	WAVANS.
315 A. Bde. R.F.A. HQ.	MAIZICOURT.
A/315.	MONT LOUIS FARME.
B/315.	BEAUVOIR-RIVIERE.
C/315.	MAIZICOURT.
D/315.	MONT LOUIS FERME.
61 D.A.C. HQ.	LA NEUVILLE.
No. 1 Section.	VILLEROY-SUR-AUTHIE.
No. 2 Section.	WILLENCOURT.
S.A.A. Section.	ACQUET.
61 T.M.O. HQ.	LANNOY.
X/61. Bty.	"
Y/61 Bty.	"
No 1 Co. 61 Div. Train.	No.79 RUE d'ABBEVILLE, AUXI-le-CHATEAU.

Lieut.
R.O., 61 Div. Artillery.

11.12.1918.

Army Form W.3091.

Cover for Documents.

Nature of Enclosures.

61st Divisional Artillery

War Diary

for

January 1919.

VOL: 33.

Notes, or Letters written.

Army Form C. 2118.

WAR DIARY
or
INTELLIGENCE SUMMARY.
(Erase heading not required.)

61st Div. Artillery.
January 1919.

Instructions regarding War Diaries and Intelligence Summaries are contained in F. S. Regs., Part II. and the Staff Manual respectively. Title pages will be prepared in manuscript.

Place	Date	Hour	Summary of Events and Information	Remarks and references to Appendices
AUXI-LE-CHATEAU (Ref Map Sheet LENS II 1/100,000)	1st JANY 1919		No change in locations. SB	
	6th	—	One Officer & 85 ORs Demobilized. SB	
	11th	—	One Officer & 30 ORs Demobilized. SB	
	12th	—	30 ORs Demobilized. SB	
	13th	—	49 ORs Demobilized. CRA returned from leave & re-assumed command of 61st Div. Arty. SB	
	14th	—	Also assumed command as BOC Divl. while BGC on leave for 7 days. SB	
	15th	—	56 ORs Demobilized. SB	
	18th	—	1 Officer & 30 ORs Demobilized. SB	
	19th	—	27 ORs Demobilized. SB	
	20th	—	1 Officer & 30 ORs Demobilized. SB	
	21st	—	17 ORs Demobilized. SB	
	22nd	—	2 Officers & 15 ORs Demobilized. SB	
	25th	—	24 ORs Demobilized. SB	
	26th	—	1 Officer & 27 ORs Demobilized. SB	
	27th	—	2 Officers & 30 ORs Demobilized. SB	

Army Form C. 2118.

WAR DIARY
or
INTELLIGENCE SUMMARY.
(Erase heading not required.)

Instructions regarding War Diaries and Intelligence Summaries are contained in F. S. Regs., Part II. and the Staff Manual respectively. Title pages will be prepared in manuscript.

Place	Date	Hour	Summary of Events and Information	Remarks and references to Appendices
AUKI-LE-CHATEAU	28th		1 Officer & 18 ORs demobilized	
	29th		1 Officer & 15 ORs demobilized	
	30th		1 OR demobilized. During the above period horses were steadily demobilized so that by the end of the month the number of animals actually in charge showed only a surplus of 196 over establishment. Great improvements been made to billets during the month & merchandised during has organised with Sn Coy: Brigade & leading countries.	

Spencer Bratten
Lieut
RORA
C107 Divisional Artillery
1st February 1919.

61st. DIVISIONAL ARTILLERY.

LOCATION OF UNITS as on 3rd. January, 1919.

Ref: Map LENS 11 - 1/100,000.

R.A. Hdqrs. 61 Divn.	No.62 RUE d'HESDIN, AUXI-le-CHATEAU.
306 Bde. R.F.A. H.Q.	CHATEAU de BEAUVOIR, BEAUVOIR WAVANS
A/306.	LE MEILLARD.
B/306.	HEUZECOURT.
C/306.	ST. ACHEUL.
D/306.	BEALCOURT.
307 Bde. R.F.A. H.Q.	No.24 RUE d'WAVANS, AUXI-le-CHAU;
A/307.	DRUCAS.
B/307.	WAVANS.
C/307.	WAVANS.
D/307.	WAVANS.
315 A. Bde. R.F.A. HQ.	MAIZICOURT.
A/315.	MONT LOUIS FM.
B/315.	BEAUVOIR RIVIERE.
C/315.	MAIZICOURT.
D/315.	MONT LOUIS FM.
315 B.A.C.	BEAUVOIR RIVIERE.
61 D.A.C. H.Q.	LA NEUVILLE.
No.1 Section.	VILLEROY-sur-AUTHIE.
No.2 Section.	WILLENCOURT.
S.A.A. Section.	LE PONCHEL.
61 D.T.M.O. H.Q.	Billet No.20, LANNOY.
No.1 Coy. 61 Div.Train.	No.79 RUE d'ABBEVILLE, AUXI-le-CHATEAU.

F.P. Wye.
for Lieut. Capt.
R.O., R.A., 61 Division.

3.1.1919.

(6392) Wt. W6192/P875 1,500,000 4/18 McA & W Ltd (E 2815) Forms W3091/4. Army Form

Cover for Documents.

Nature of Enclosures.

61st Divisional Artillery.

War Diary

— for —

February 1919.

VOL: 34

Notes, or Letters written.

Army Form C. 2118.

WAR DIARY
or
INTELLIGENCE SUMMARY.
(Erase heading not required.)

Instructions regarding War Diaries and Intelligence Summaries are contained in F. S. Regs., Part II. and the Staff Manual respectively. Title pages will be prepared in manuscript.

Place	Date	Hour	Summary of Events and Information	Remarks and references to Appendices
AUXI-LE-CHATEAU	3.2.19		32 Ride and 44 L.D. 'Y' Horses despatched for sale at Paris	
	4.2.19		6 Ride and 29 L.D. 'Y' Horses to CANDAS.	
Sheet LENS 11 (1/10000)	6.2.19		4 O.R's despatched for demobilization to CANDAS	
	7.2.19		4 O.R's 2 Officers despatched for Demobilization	
	9.2.19		2 Officers 6 O.R's for demobilization	
	11.2.19		14 O.R's demobilized	
	15.2.19		33 O.R's demobilized	
	17.2.19		1 Ride 10 L.D. 'Y' Horses demobilized.	
	19.2.19		1 C. 7 Ride 43 L.D. Horses 'Y' Category demobilized.	
	20.2.19		76 L.D. 'Z' Horses despatched to No. 5 Veterinary Hospital	
	21.2.19		5 Officers 34 O.R's demobilized	
	22.2.19		12 Ride 24 L.D. 14 Mules 'Z' animals sold at AUXI-le-CHATEAU	
	28.2.19		35 O.R's demobilized.	

Spencer Banks
Lieut
D.A.D. 61st Divisional Artillery
25.2.19.

61st DIVISIONAL ARTILLERY.

LOCATION OF UNITS as on 21st February, 1919.

Ref: Map LENS 11 2/100,000.

R.A.H.Q. 61 Division.　　No. 62 RUE d'HESDIN, AUXI-le-CHATEAU.

306 Bde. R.F.A. H.Q.	CHATEAU de BEAUVOIR, BEAUVOIR WAVANS.
A/306.	LE MEILLARD.
B/306.	HEUZECOURT.
C/306.	ST. ACHEUL.
D/306.	BEALCOURT.
307 Bde. R.F.A. H.Q.	No. 24 RUE d'WAVANS, AUXI-le-CHATEAU.
A/307.	DRUCAS.
B/307.	WAVANS.
C/307.	WAVANS.
D/307.	WAVANS.
315 A. Bde R.F.A. H.Q.	MAIZICOURT.
A/315.	MONT LOUIS FARM.
B/315.	BEAUVOIR RIVIERE.
C/315.	MAIZICOURT.
D/315.	MONT LOUIS FARM.
315 B.A.C.	BEAUVOIR RIVIERE.
61 D.A.C. H.Q.	LA NEUVILLE.
No. 1 Section.	VILLEROY-sur-AUTHIE.
No. 2 Section	WILLENCOURT.
S.A.A. Section.	LE PONCHEL.
61 D.T.M.Q.	No. 62 RUE d'HESDIN, AUXI-le-CHATEAU.
No. 1 Coy. 61 Div. Train.	No. 79 RUE d'ABBEVILLE, AUXI-le-CHATEAU.

　　　　　　　　　　　　　　　　　　　　Lieut.
　　　　　　　　　　　　　　　　B.O.R.A., 61st Division.

R.A.H.Q.
21st February, 1919.

Army Form C. 2118.

61 R.A.H.Q.

WAR DIARY
or
INTELLIGENCE SUMMARY.

(Erase heading not required.)

March 1919

Instructions regarding War Diaries and Intelligence Summaries are contained in F.S. Regs., Part II. and the Staff Manual respectively. Title pages will be prepared in manuscript.

Place	Date	Hour	Summary of Events and Information	Remarks and references to Appendices
AUXI-LE CHATEAU	1-3-19	—	30 L.B. 2 horses 10 Z mules sent to Auxi-le Chateau S.R.	
	2-3-19	—	14 Z Rides 34 Z L.D. and 34 Z mules to Abbeville for demob. S.R.	
LENS II	2-3-19	—	12 Rides 34 Z L.D. 10 Z mules to Beauville for demobilization S.R.	
1/100,000	4-3-19	—	60 L.D. & 77 mules (X animals) to Beauval for demobilization S.R.	
	5-3-19	—	35 Rides 5 L.D. & 7 H.D. (Y animals) to Beauval for demobilization S.R.	
	7-3-19	—	3 L.D. 4/17 mules (Z) to Abbeville for demob. S.R.	
	7-3-19	—	17 O.Rs despatches to London for demobilization S.R.	
	8-3-19	—	3 Rides, 2 L.D., 11 mules (Z) sold at Auxi-le Chateau S.R.	
	10-3-19	—	45 Rides 50 mules to A.C.C.C. Candas for demob S.R.	
	12-3-19	—	20 horses L.D. (X) to Abbeville for demobilization S.R.	
	12-3-19	—	4 Rides 3 L.D. 7 mules to Candas L.A.C.C. for demobilization (Z) S.R.	
	13-3-19	—	20 C horses to Beauval for demob. S.R.	
	14-3-19	—	41 O.Rs & 1 officer despatched to Candas for demobilization S.R.	
	17-3-19	—	30 X Riders to Candas S.R.	
	18-3-19	—	4 S.B.D., 7 L.D. 4 Rides, 1 Ride sent to Beauval for demob. S.R.	
	17-3-19	—	1 officer despatched for demobilization S.R.	
	21-3-19	—	40 O.Rs despatched for demobilization S.R.	
	22-3-19	—	126 X mules to Beauval for demobilization S.R.	
	26-3-19	—	11 X Rides, 2 X L.D., 14 H.B., 2 Y. Ride 15 Candas for demobilization S.R.	
	29-3-19	—	1 Officer 34 O.Rs despatches & CANDAS for demobilization S.R.	

Respectfully
B.G.R.A. 61st Corps Artillery

RA 61 Div

Vol 36

WAR DIARY
or
INTELLIGENCE SUMMARY.
(Erase heading not required.)

Army Form C. 2118.

Instructions regarding War Diaries and Intelligence Summaries are contained in F. S. Regs., Part II. and the Staff Manual respectively. Title pages will be prepared in manuscript.

Place	Date	Hour	Summary of Events and Information	Remarks and references to Appendices
AUXI-LE- CHATEAU.	6.4.19		3 Officers, 12 Other Ranks despatched for demobilization	
1:100,000	11.4.19		1 Officer 20 Other Ranks despatched for demobilization	
LENS 11	18.4.19		1 Officer 12 Other Ranks despatched for demobilization	
	19.4.19		1 O.R. despatched for demobilization	
	22.4.19			
	24.4.19		1 Officer despatched for demobilization	
	25.4.19		2 Officers & O.Rs. despatched for demobilization	
	30.4.19		1 Officer, 30 X & D Ranks despatched to A.O.b.b. bundles for demobilization	

F. Pye
Major RA
for RA 61st Division.

61st DIVISIONAL ARTILLERY.

LOCATION OF UNITS AS on 7th April, 1919.

Reference Map MINS 11, 1/100,000.

R.A.H.Q. 61st Division.   No. 7 Place Hotel de Ville AUXI-le-CHATEAU

306 Brigade R.F.A.H.Q.   No. 7 Place Hotel de Ville AUXI-le-CHATEAU

    A/306.   LE MEILLARD.
    B/306.   HEUZECOURT.
    C/306.   ST. ACHEUL.
    D/306.   BEALCOURT.

307 Brigade R.F.A.H.Q.   No. 24 RUE d'WAVANS, AUXI-le-CHATEAU.

    A/307.   DRUCAS, WAVANS.
    B/307.   WAVANS.
    C/307.   WAVANS.
    D/307.   WAVANS.

315 A.Bde R.F.A.H.Q.   HAIZICOURT.

    A/315.   MONT LOUIS FARM.
    B/315.   BEAUVOIR RIVIERE.
    C/315.   HAIZICOURT.
    D/315.   MONT LOUIS FARM.
    315 B.A.C.   BEAUVOIR RIVIERE.

61st D.A.C.

    H.Q's and Sections.   OUTREBOIS.

No. 1 Co. Train R.A.S.C.   No. 79 RUE d'ABBEVILLE, AUXI-le-CHATEAU.

61st Div. Art. Vehicle Park. - CANDAS.

                                        Capt, R.A.
Staff Captain, R.A. 61st Divisional Artillery.

R.A.H.Q.
7th April, 1919.

61st DIVISIONAL ARTILLERY.

LOCATION OF UNITS AS ON 25th APRIL, 1919.

Reference Map LENS 11, 1/100,000.

R.A.H.Q. 61st Division. No. 7 Place Hotel de Ville AUXI-le-CHATEAU.

306 Brigade R.F.A., HQ. No. 7 Place Hotel de Ville AUXI-le-CHATEAU.

    A/306.   LE MEILLARD.
    B/306.   HEUZECOURT.
    C/306.   ST. ACHEUL.
    D/306.   BEALCOURT.

307 Brigade R.F.A. HQ. No. 9 Rue de Wavans, AUXI-le-CHATEAU.

    A/307.   DROCAS, WAVANS.
    B/307.   WAVANS.
    C/307.   WAVANS.
    D/307.   WAVANS.

315 ARMY BRIGADE RFA HQ MAIZICOURT.

    A/315.   MONT LOUIS FARM.
    B/315.   BEAUVOIR RIVIERE.
    C/315.   MAIZICOURT.
    D/315.   MONT LOUIS FARM.
    315 B.A.C.   BEAUVOIR RIVIERE.

61st D.A.C.

    H.Q's and Sections OUTREBOIS.

No. 1 CO. TRAIN RASC. No. 79 Rue d'Abbeville, AUXI-le-CHATEAU.

61st Div. Arty VEHICLE PARK. - CANDAS.

F.P. Wye.
Brigade Major, R.A. 61st Divisional Artillery.
Major R.A.

R.A.H.Q.
25th April, 1919.

(6392) Wt. W6192/P875 1,500,000 4/18 McA & W Ltd (E 2815) Forms W3091/4.   Army Form W.3091.

Cover for Documents.

Nature of Enclosures.

61st Divisional Artillery
315 Army Brigade F. A.
and No 521 Co R.A.S.C. 61 Divl Train

War Diary
May 1919

VOLUME 37

Notes, or Letters written.

WAR DIARY
or
INTELLIGENCE SUMMARY

Army Form C. 2118.

Place	Date	Hour	Summary of Events and Information	Remarks and references to Appendices
Auxi-le-Château	6 Mar 1919		6 Other Ranks despatched for demobilization	
LENS 11 1/100,000	10 Mar 1919		05 Other Ranks despatched for demobilization	
	14 Mar 1919		91 Other Ranks despatched for demobilization	
	16 Mar 1919		23 Other Ranks deserted to Army of Occupation (15 11th Battalion Leicester Regiment – 22 to II Army RA Reinforcement Camp)	
	16 Mar 1919		7 HD 2 Other horses to A.A.E.E. Tarden	
	17 Mar 1919		22 HD 3 Rule 2 Class horses to A.A.E.E. Tarden	
	29 May 1919		6 Other Ranks despatched to Army of Occupation (to 11th Battalion Leicester Regiment – 5 to II Army RA Reinforcement Camp)	
	29 May 1919		9 Other Ranks despatched for demobilization	
	30 May 1919		1 Officer despatched to U.K. for repatriation to U.S.A	

www.ingramcontent.com/pod-product-compliance
Lightning Source LLC
Chambersburg PA
CBHW080830010526
44112CB00015B/2482